Printers for Macintosh and compatibles

Do you need only moderate print quality and speed, at very low cost?

Dot Matrix

Do you require high quality print, fast output, or quiet operation?

PostScript lasers

Low cost, easy to use. Poor print quality, noisy.

Imagewriter

Is ease of setup and shopping more important than initial cost?

Apple Laserwriter

Do you have the time and energy to shop around in order to realize a cost saving?

Other Appletalk-equipped PostScript lasers

Computer users are not all alike.
Neither are SYBEX books.

We know our customers have a variety of needs. They've told us so. And because we've listened, we've developed several distinct types of books to meet the needs of each of our customers. What are you looking for in computer help?

If you're looking for the basics, try the **ABC's** series. You'll find short, unintimidating tutorials and helpful illustrations. For a more visual approach, select **Teach Yourself**, featuring screen-by-screen illustrations of how to use your latest software purchase.

Mastering and **Understanding** titles offer you a step-by-step introduction, plus an in-depth examination of intermediate-level features, to use as you progress.

Our **Up & Running** series is designed for computer-literate consumers who want a no-nonsense overview of new programs. Just 20 basic lessons, and you're on your way.

We also publish two types of reference books. Our **Instant References** provide quick access to each of a program's commands and functions. SYBEX **Encyclopedias** provide a *comprehensive reference* and explanation of all of the commands, features and functions of the subject software.

Sometimes a subject requires a special treatment that our standard series doesn't provide. So you'll find we have titles like **Advanced Techniques, Handbooks, Tips & Tricks**, and others that are specifically tailored to satisfy a unique need.

We carefully select our authors for their in-depth understanding of the software they're writing about, as well as their ability to write clearly and communicate effectively. Each manuscript is thoroughly reviewed by our technical staff to ensure its complete accuracy. Our production department makes sure it's easy to use. All of this adds up to the highest quality books available, consistently appearing on best-seller charts worldwide.

You'll find SYBEX publishes a variety of books on every popular software package. Looking for computer help? Help Yourself to SYBEX.

For a complete catalog of our publications:

SYBEX Inc.
2021 Challenger Drive, Alameda, CA 94501
Tel: (415) 523-8233/(800) 227-2346 Telex: 336311
SYBEX   Fax: (415) 523-2373

The Home Office Computer Book

The Home Office Computer Book

Steve Rimmer

SYBEX ®

San Francisco — Paris — Düsseldorf — Soest

Acquisitions Editor: Dianne King
Developmental Editor: Christian T. S. Crumlish
Editor: Doug Robert
Technical Editor: Charlie Russel
Word Processors: Ann Dunn, Susan Trybull
Book Designer: Charlotte Carter
Chapter Art: Charlotte Carter
Technical Art: Delia Brown
Screen Graphics: Cuong Le
Desktop Publishing Production: M.D. Barrera
Proofreader/Production Assistant: Rhonda Holmes
Indexer: Julie Kawabata
Cover Designer: Ingalls + Associates
Cover Photographer: Michael Lamotte

SYBEX is a registered trademark of SYBEX, Inc.

TRADEMARKS: SYBEX has attempted throughout this book to distinguish proprietary trademarks from descriptive terms by following the capitalization style used by the manufacturer.

SYBEX is not affiliated with any manufacturer.

Every effort has been made to supply complete and accurate information. However, SYBEX assumes no responsibility for its use, nor for any infringement of the intellectual property rights of third parties which would result from such use.

Library of Congress Card Number: 91-65715
ISBN: 0-89588-797-5

Manufactured in the United States of America

10 9 8 7 6 5 4 3 2 1

For Megan, who has survived the home office

CONTENTS AT A GLANCE

TABLE OF CONTENTS

3   The Operating System — **88**

4   Microsoft Windows — **130**

INTRODUCTION

There is a fundamental difference between a home computer and a computer you use at home. A computer for use in a home office is really a business system that lives in your basement. A home computer, on the other hand, is a very sophisticated video game.

This book deals with two classes of business systems—Apple Macintosh and IBM-PC compatible computers. It doesn't get into the ostensibly "home" computers such as the Apple IIc, the Commodore Amiga, and so on. These are very interesting and oftentimes powerful systems. However, they make half-hearted business computers.

The Catch-22 of microcomputers is that you can't make informed decisions about which computer to buy until you've bought a computer and learned enough about it to become informed. Of course, by then it's too late to change your mind. This book deals with this apparently unavoidable catch by being arbitrary. It will walk you through the decisions you need to make in order to buy and use the computer equipment and software your business requires. It will give you the benefit of the author's many years of experience working at home with a number of machines and programs. It is highly biased in favor of ease of use and affordability. It will not attempt to evaluate *all* the available word processing software, for example, to help you choose the one and only package ideally suited to your needs. The choices it does offer you are usually derived from fewer than half a dozen tried and proven packages.

The hardware and software solutions presented in this book have been chosen specifically with home office applications in mind. It seems fair to mention that in many cases they don't represent the most popular (or the most widely advertised) products. You may well completely ignore some truly wonderful software as a result of reading this book. However, your home office can be up and running two days from now if you're in a hurry, and all the solutions in this book actually work. The sections labeled "Author's Choice" are usually descriptions of solutions the author actually uses.

It seems fair to say that while this book will get you started, you'll probably require some additional books as you go. As a rule, third-party books that discuss specific applications are a lot more useful than the manuals that come with the software. Book authors have the luxury of basing their books on finished software, as well as having the manuals in front of them to improve upon. If you decide after reading this book that your home office should include a copy of Q&A or Microsoft Excel, for example, buy some books on these packages as well.

A Few Words on
Working from a Home Office

The phrase "home office" sounds like a contradiction in terms to many people. Home is where you go when you can't stand the office any longer, and fusing the two seems like a way to defeat the function of both. However, in another sense a home office manages to marry the best of these two disparate universes. Perhaps more to the point, it dissolves that third universe which separates them, the commute from one to the other.

Working at home allows you to use the hour or two you'd normally spend each day travelling— to perform productive work instead. It lets you work when you're most alert and prepared for work, even if that period happens to commence at two in the morning some of the time. It also allows you— or the people who employ you— to dispense with at least some of the overhead of a traditional office. People who don't come to work in the usual sense don't require desks, coffee machines, photocopiers, or telephone lines.

The growing popularity of the home office concept can be attributed to a number of things. As land values increase it becomes less practical to live within easy commuting distance to a city. Commuting, too, costs a great deal more, and has environmental consequences. People who work in home offices frequently get to live in the country and avoid breathing the environmental consequences of the ones who don't.

At the same time, the technology that used to be available only in a central office has become affordable by individuals. That's what this book is about in a sense. You can make your home office work because computers and related technologies will allow you to get real work done by yourself, well removed from the resources of a conventional office. They will also allow you to stay in touch with a central office in meaningful ways if this is part of your job.

Whether you're employed by a larger company or your home office is the head office of your personal business, a computer can multiply the resources you have available. Learning to use one effectively will make the concept of a home office a reality for you.

If you've chosen to work in a home office, it's probably because the most expensive commodity in your life is not gasoline, computer hardware, desk space, or long-distance phone service. It's time. A home office lets you use more of your time more effectively. Applying the right computer and computer applications will improve the effectiveness of your home office, and, in turn, will let you do more with the time you have available.

CHAPTER

1

1

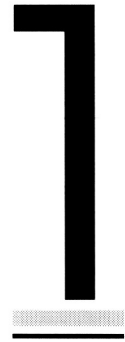

CHOOSING
A COMPUTER

One of the things that most computer owners eventually realize— long after there's no further hope of exchanging their computer for what they *really* wanted— is that you aren't properly equipped to choose a computer until after you've owned one for a while. The way to really get the system you need is to buy four or five and see which one suits you best. If this sounds less than cost-effective, you've probably done well to buy this book.

There is, first of all, no "best" microcomputer system. There is at least one that's best for your needs. The problem is more one of defining your needs than of defining the computer that will suit them. Therefore, before we get into some of the more productive areas of implementing the technology behind a home office, we're going to investigate the details of choosing a computer and, subsequently, the peripherals and other gadgets that will be associated with it.

Selecting a computer does not have to be a shot in the dark or a dreadful, perilous decision wherein the only certain element is that you'll regret it for years to come. You can come to the right decision *for your situation* by examining the choices that are available, working out your own requirements, and, most important, ignoring everything you read, see, or hear from IBM, Apple, and Compaq.

This first chapter will introduce you to the information you'll need to select the right computer for your home office. Read it all, even if you already have an idea as to what sort of computer you need.

THE BASIC SELECTION CRITERIA

Conventional wisdom in buying a computer maintains that you should first identify the functions you want the computer to perform, then locate software that will perform the functions, and then buy a computer that is capable of running the software. This is a really logical, linear approach to selecting hardware. However, it tends to fall apart when applied to actual computer systems, because there are very few functions available on one computer system that aren't immediately copied by all the other major systems. The point is, all of the major applications that we'll discuss in this book can be had for pretty well any computer you wind up owning. The main question is, which computer performs the functions you want in the *manner* you want them performed?

Clearly, we must refine our selection criteria. There are, in fact, a number of fairly concrete factors you can juggle while you're considering which computer to buy:

— Cost effectiveness

— Ease of installation

— Ease of use

— Availability of cost-effective software

— Availability of cost-effective hardware

— Expansion capabilities

— Speed

While you are considering these factors, you will be focusing on two main types of machines. As you no doubt have heard, there are two principal contenders in the personal and home-office computer market: Apple and IBM. Apple makes the various Macintosh systems. IBM makes the PC— a name that most people use to refer to any non-Apple personal computer— and its descendants, which have spawned a vast universe of "IBM compatible" systems, many of which have more of just about everything on the above list than real IBM systems.

PC

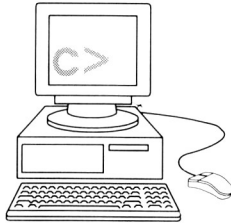

Do you want a computer that is cost-effective and flexible, but not intuitively easy to use?

Do you require the fastest system available and have lots of money?

80486

Do you require a computer capable of running large applications and maximizing the use of your time?

80386

Do you plan to use larger applications but don't have a large budget?

80386SX

Do you only plan to run modest applications, and require an inexpensive system?

80286-based PC/AT

Very slow, unsuitable for most present applications.

8088-based PC/XT

MAC

Do you want a computer that is easy to set up and use but relatively expensive?

Do you want the fastest, most powerful Macintosh (and have a fair bit of cash to spend)?

Macintosh II

Do you want a very fast, powerful system, and can live with a monochrome screen?

Macintosh SE

Do you want a color Macintosh at a moderate cost?

Macintosh LC

Underpowered for most business applications.

Macintosh Classic

APPLE MACINTOSH

We'll begin with the Macintosh because A comes before I, rather than because of some laboratory rating system. The Macintosh is a very good computer for some applications, but it's nowhere near as universal a solution as Apple's advertising agency would have you believe.

Depending on how you try to work it out, about one in ten users of personal computers for business turns on a Macintosh in the morning, with almost the entire remainder being seated before IBM PC-compatibles of some sort. This might lead you to suspect that all is not as it appears in the ads.

In its traditional sense, the Macintosh is what is called an "appliance" computer. It comes in a box with all the parts needed to make it work, and in theory only needs to be plugged in to get it running. There are no cards to install, no drives to format and very few cables to connect. In fact, this is only provisionally true. Some Macintosh systems are really this simple to boot up, but Macintosh users long ago began to demand the flexibility and power that comes with the sort of options that serve to make computers a bit more complicated. High-end Macintosh systems are only a bit less complicated than high-end PCs.

The important thing about the Mac is that it only comes from Apple. For practical purposes there is no such thing as a Macintosh-compatible. Several far Eastern companies have tried to make Macintosh-compatibles, or "clones," but have been effectively suppressed by Apple's legal actions.

Having at least the computer itself come from a single source has made the Macintosh relatively uncomplicated to buy and set up. The range of available machines is small, and to Apple's credit the computers they build all work properly.

On the other hand, the lack of direct competition has allowed Apple to price its Macintosh systems rather heavily weighted in favor of its own bottom line, rather than yours. You can definitely get more computer for your dollar if you don't buy a Macintosh, but for reasons that will become clearer as you read through this chapter, buying the least expensive business computer simply because it's the least expensive is not a very good strategy.

Both Macintosh and IBM have recently begun to address the issue of price with low-end systems that look to be considerably more cost-effective than either manufacturer's hardware has traditionally been. We'll discuss the Apple version of this, the Macintosh Classic, presently.

The positive features of the Macintosh may well outweigh its price for your needs. It has many strengths, not all of which will be apparent if you merely read Apple's advertising copy.

The Macintosh Operating System

One of the computer terms you'll hear bandied about a lot is "operating system." An operating system is a program that mediates between you and your computer. It performs several functions. When your computer is idle, awaiting the next thing you want to do with it, the operating system provides you with a convenient way to tell the computer "be a word processor," "delete all last month's data," or "go away and let me think." When a program is running, the operating system provides the program with help that relates specifically to the hardware of the computer. Your program can tell the operating system things like "go get a character from the keyboard," "make the speaker beep," or "go away and let me think."

The basis of the Macintosh is a very sophisticated operating system that is generically called a "graphical user interface." Apple's Macintosh operating system itself doesn't really have a name per se, although it's usually referred to as the "Finder."

Figure 1.1 illustrates the main screen of the Finder.

A graphical user interface allows you to deal with most computer related functions as analogs of more conventional real world functions,

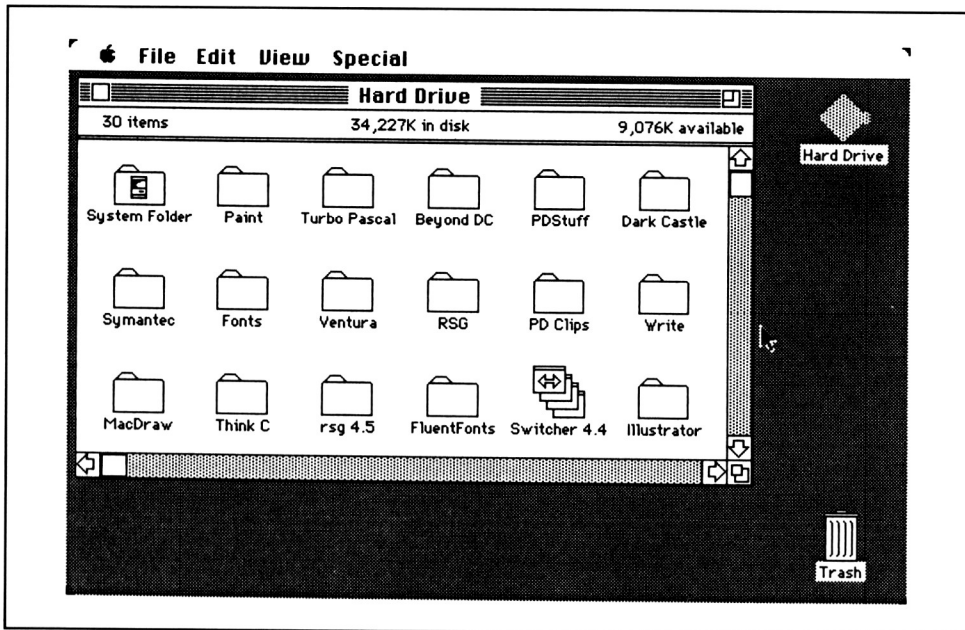

Figure 1.1: The Macintosh Finder

rather than by typing in oftentimes cryptic commands. It's based on a device called a "mouse." A mouse is a box with a plastic ball protruding from its underside. As you roll the mouse across the surface of your desk, a graphic arrow, called a "cursor," moves across your screen. The mouse allows you to point at things on your screen. You might think of the light pointers often employed with slide presentations.

In an effort to further associate the computer-generated analogy of the Mac's Finder with the real world, the Mac refers to the Finder's display as its "desktop."

A button on the mouse allows you to tell the computer to do something with what you point at. Pushing the button is called "clicking" the mouse.

The Macintosh uses pictures to represent objects and functions in the Finder. These pictures are called "icons." Apple likes to talk about these icons and the things they relate to as a "metaphor." Thus, it calls the Finder a "desktop metaphor."

The Macintosh Finder has a number of elements that behave a lot like what you might do in real life to perform common business functions. For example, to dispose of something on the Mac, you would grab it (click on it with the mouse) and take it across to the trash can, which you can see in the lower right corner of the screen. To write a letter, you would point to the MacWrite program— a word processor— and click on it to turn it on.

Most people can operate a mouse easily with very little practice. It's worth noting that there is a small minority of people for whom the mouse is not a natural extension of their arms, and for whom a graphical user interface such as the Mac's Finder will never be particularly "user friendly." However, assuming that you aren't one of them, you really will be able to get productive work out of a Macintosh after an hour or so.

The Consistent User Interface

All of the graphical elements that are used in the various applications you might run on a Macintosh are generated by the computer itself, not by the programs you run on it. This is very important, as it means that your word processor will open a document in exactly the same way that a spreadsheet program would open a worksheet file. The consistent user interface of the Macintosh is one of its most effective elements. Once you know how to run one application on the Mac you'll be well along with any other ones you choose to add to the system.

Figure 1.2 illustrates screens from three unrelated Macintosh applications. Note that there are recognizable common elements in all of them.

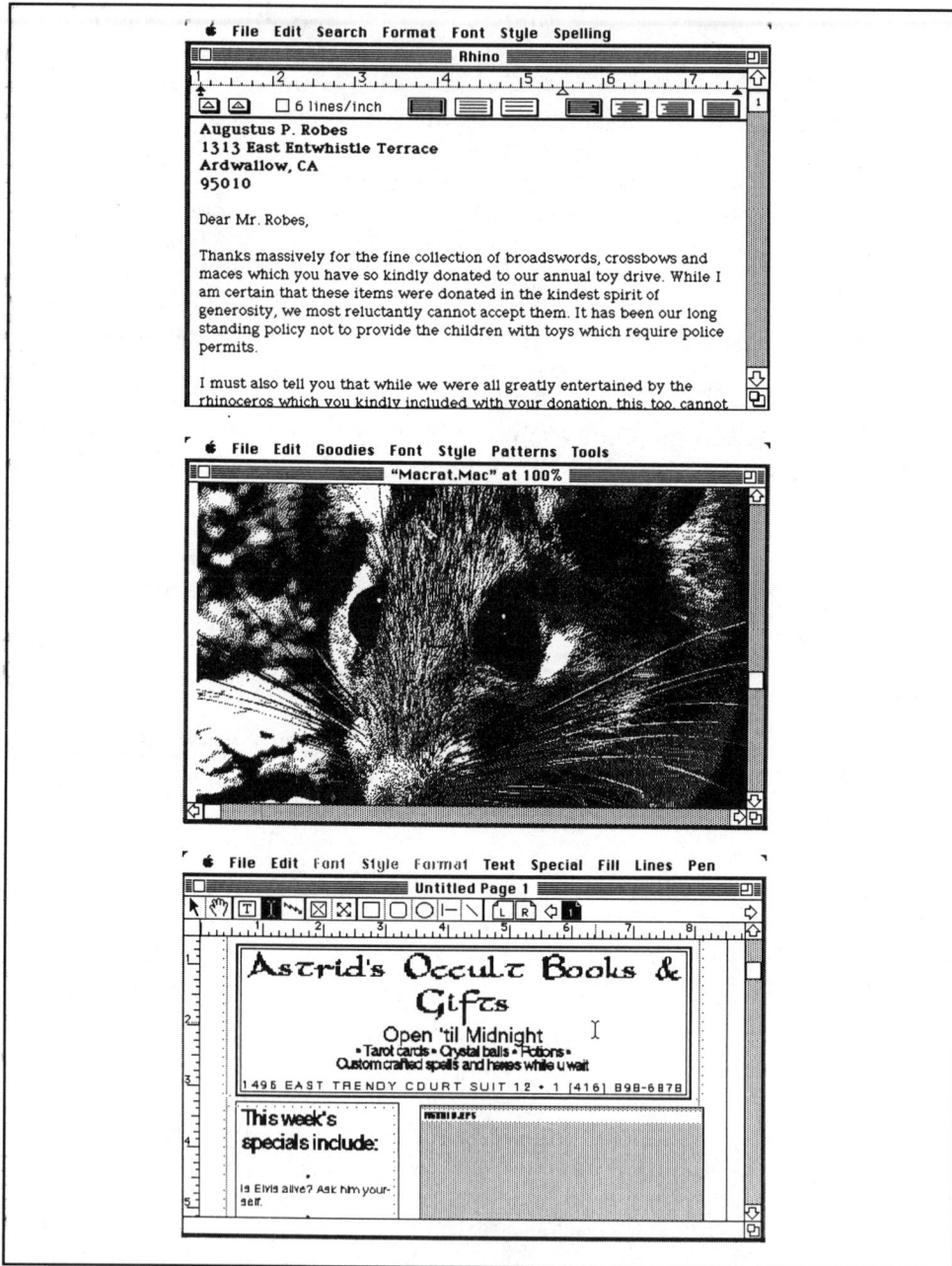

 File Edit Search Format Font Style Spelling

Rhino

☐ 6 lines/inch

Augustus P. Robes
1313 East Entwhistle Terrace
Ardwallow, CA
95010

Dear Mr. Robes,

Thanks massively for the fine collection of broadswords, crossbows and maces which you have so kindly donated to our annual toy drive. While I am certain that these items were donated in the kindest spirit of generosity, we most reluctantly cannot accept them. It has been our long standing policy not to provide the children with toys which require police permits.

I must also tell you that while we were all greatly entertained by the rhinoceros which you kindly included with your donation, this, too, cannot

 File Edit Goodies Font Style Patterns Tools

"Macrat.Mac" at 100%

 File Edit Font Style Format Text Special Fill Lines Pen

Untitled Page 1

Astrid's Occult Books & Gifts
Open 'til Midnight
• Tarot cards • Crystal balls • Potions •
Custom crafted spells and hexes while u wait
1495 EAST TRENDY COURT SUIT 12 • 1 [416] 898-6878

This week's specials include:

Is Elvis alive? Ask him your-self.

Figure 1.2: Screens from MacWrite (a word processor), MacPaint (a drawing program), and Ready-Set-Go (a publishing package)

All of this user friendliness does not come without its price. Managing all those graphics— essentially a very elaborate "shell" that mediates between you and the computer— takes a lot of work on the part of the system. The Finder and all the associated elements of the operating system use a certain amount of the system's resources, and part of the time the computer would otherwise have to run programs is occupied by running the user interface.

An important axiom of operating systems is that the more they do for you, the more of your computer's resources they need for themselves. The Finder is a very sophisticated, and hence a very hungry operating system.

One of the factors that adds to the cost of a Macintosh is its need for memory. A PC-compatible computer can perform relatively sophisticated tasks with about half the memory of a low-end Macintosh. A low-end Macintosh can't actually do very much. There is something disheartening in buying a lot of memory for your computer and then having the operating system eat half of it.

Figure 1.3 illustrates a box in the Macintosh's finder that illustrates the total memory in the computer and the amount that's free for use by programs. The remainder is what's used by the Finder and the other

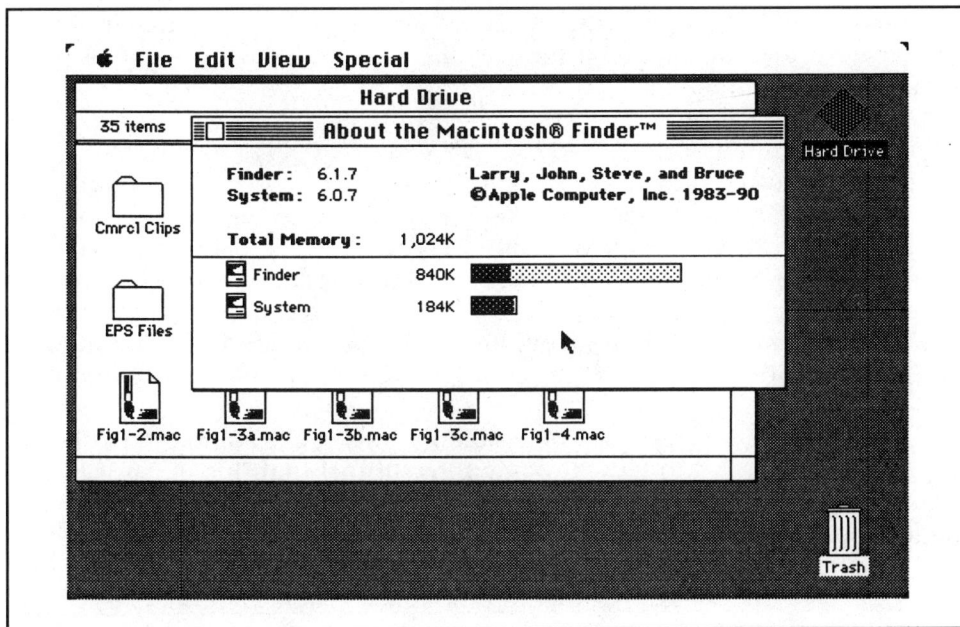

Figure 1.3: The free memory in a typical Macintosh

bits of the Macintosh operating system. You might want to compare this to a similar display on a PC-compatible computer, to be discussed shortly.

You can look at the issue of system memory in several ways, depending upon your own needs and resources. To use the analogy of buying a car, you might go out to buy the most cost-effective car or, if performance is more important than economy, you might shop for the fastest car. If your criterion for the ideal car is that it should be faster than a Jaguar or a BMW— and if all thoughts of cost-effectiveness are distant— you might buy a restored 1969 Delta 88 Oldsmobile, or one of several species of Ferrari. My '69 Olds can bury Jags and BMW's by virtue of its 455 cubic inch engine and a four-barrel Holley carb nestled atop it. However, it drinks gas like a demon. Ferraris can do the same thing with much less voracious appetites, but they cost about as much as a house. If you really like what Ferraris do, however, one of these cars may be worth the price to you.

Likewise, if your criteria for a computer happen to coincide with the benefits of a Macintosh— extreme user friendliness, ease of setup, and so on— you should probably accept the cost of lots of memory and a generally pricy computer.

We'll discuss the phrase "lots of memory" in more concrete terms when we deal with the applications that will be running with that memory.

For all its overt sophistication, there are a lot of things that the Macintosh's Finder lacks. Many of them are things that you may not fully appreciate until you've used it for a while. The most troublesome of these is its lack of multitasking.

Multitasking is the ability of an operating system to run more than one program at a time, and to allow you to quickly move from one application to another. For example, you might have a program— a database manager— that keeps track of names and addresses of people you correspond with, and a word processing program. Under a multitasking environment, you could pause in the middle of a letter and enter the database manager to find the correct spelling for someone's name, for example, or leap into your word processor from another program to look at a letter you wrote last month because its recipient has just called you to talk about its contents.

In order to give the Macintosh some multitasking capabilities, Apple created "MultiFinder"— literally, a multitasking Finder. MultiFinder requires several times the memory of the basic Finder and it has been plagued with problems. For one thing, it slows down the applications running under it noticeably.

As a final note, you should probably consider that one of the ways that the Macintosh makes choosing a computer and its peripherals easy is by giving you relatively few choices. As we'll discuss in more detail later in this book, the types of laser printers that are supported by the Macintosh are among the most expensive. Macintosh hard drives have a "smart" interface that makes them easier to add to your computer but also adds about fifty percent to the price of a drive of similar capacity for a PC. Maintenance for a Macintosh tends to be more expensive than it is for most PC-compatibles.

Macintosh Processors

The heart of any microcomputer is its microprocessor, the chip that does the thinking. The Macintosh computers are based on the 68000 series of microprocessors.

It's beyond the scope of this book to get into a detailed discussion of the various strata of 68000-based processors. Most of the differences would only impress engineers. There are a few things worth mentioning, though, to help you make sense of the various types of Macintosh computers available.

The 68000 chip was the basis of the early Macintosh systems. It's called a "first generation" chip. By contemporary standards it's cheap, but very slow.

The 68020 is somewhat faster than the 68000. The 68030, the current generation of these processors, is faster still— and quite a bit more expensive. The 68030 offers several other technical benefits too, but they're not relevant to this discussion.

The effective speed of a microprocessor is determined by how fast its internal architecture lets it think and by how fast the chip itself runs. The speed at which a microcomputer runs is measured in megahertz, abbreviated MHz. The current generation Macintosh system that is based on the old 68000 processors— the Macintosh Classic— gets a bit more performance out of it than the original Macintosh systems did by running it a higher speed.

How Much Macintosh Do I Need?

When I bought the Macintosh I have now— or at least, when I bought the beginnings of it— buying a Mac really was easy. There was only one, the "Fat" Macintosh. Since I first bought it my Mac has had several memory infusions, brain transplants and internal surgery. Not a lot of its original self remains. It's now equivalent to what's called a "Macintosh Plus."

The original Macintosh systems had a number of things about them that people didn't like. Like Model-T Fords, Macintosh graphics came in any color you liked, provided it was black. The small nine inch black and white screen was a permanent fixture of the system. Perhaps worst of all for experienced computer users, the original Macintosh didn't have slots.

In computer terms, a slot is a place to plug in something that the original designer of the computer didn't envision existing but allowed for anyway. In computers with slots, such as PC-compatible systems and, paradoxically, in the computers that Apple got rich making before it developed the Mac, you could add cards for different sorts of printers, displays, modems, mice and other gadgets by plugging extra circuit boards into the available slots.

Initially Apple resisted having slots in their Macintosh computers because it involved people opening their machines, setting jumpers and switches and generally getting bytes under their fingernails. Apple envisioned the Macintosh as being the computer for business people and well-heeled professionals, all of whom were supposed to be above such things.

In fact, without slots the original Macintosh had only very limited ways to communicate with things outside its own case, and no possibility for expansion if you didn't like, for example, the small black and white screen.

Meanwhile, IBM PC-compatible computers were growing in popularity because one could have a new color display or more memory or a bigger hard drive by simply plugging something into a slot, rather than having to buy a whole new computer. It's not that Apple minded people having to buy new Macs every couple of years— they just didn't foresee themselves getting away with it for much longer.

The result was the Mac II, something that looked superficially like an IBM PC with a flat case and a separate monitor on top. The Mac II was everything the Mac Plus was not. It was big, could support a color display and had the long sought-after slots. Of course, it also cost a lot.

The Macintosh II has recently spawned the Macintosh IIsi, which is a somewhat lower priced version of the original. It has slots for extra peripheral cards and a very high performance 68030 processor.

Following the Mac II was the Mac SE. This looks like a traditional Macintosh, but it has provision for slots and a current generation processor.

There's also the Macintosh LC. This system features a 68020 processor— not quite the state of the art but a decided improvement over the 68000 in the Mac Classic, discussed below. It does not have slots, but it does use an external monitor, which gives you some flexibility in the type of display you choose. As such, it will support color.

Recently, Apple created yet another Macintosh system called the Macintosh Classic. The Mac Classic is in many respects my old Macintosh

Plus in a newer case—that is, my old Mac Plus before it was upgraded. The basic Macintosh Classic sells for less than a thousand dollars. However, it lacks enough memory to do much more than run the simplest of Macintosh applications. It lacks a hard drive, which is well nigh essential for anything more involved than playing computer games, and exceedingly useful even for that. It's based on the same processor that was in my Mac Plus, the 68000, which is none too fast by contemporary standards. By the time you add enough hardware to the Macintosh Classic to make it useful, it's no longer inexpensive.

If you plan to use a Macintosh as a serious business computer, you should plan on having a minimum of two megabytes of memory in it, with four being decidedly preferable. If you have designs on running Multi-Finder so you can pop between multiple applications quickly, eight megabytes will not go to waste.

A hard drive on any business system is not a luxury—it's essential. Macintosh files tend toward obesity. A forty megabyte hard drive is probably the smallest you should consider, with more space still if you plan to run several large programs, or programs that traditionally generate large files. Database management, desktop publishing and most graphics related applications such as drawing and design software can be expected to eat hard drive space pretty quickly. You'll get a feel for this in greater detail later in this book.

You will also need a printer. We'll be discussing these in Chapter 2.

Even with all these options worked into a Macintosh Classic system, the computer itself is still based on an old and relatively slow processor. You might want to consider talking yourself up to a somewhat more capable Macintosh if you envision making moderate to heavy demands on your computer.

Unpacking a Macintosh

A great deal of the value of a Macintosh will be apparent when you first unpack it. A Macintosh is agreeably painless to set up.

While the physical location of the various ports and connectors on a Mac may vary a bit from model to model, everything is labelled with standardized icons and everything is easy to find. Unless there's been a problem at the factory or your dealer, all the parts you need to get it up and running will be included.

Plug it in and you'll be ready to go.

IBM PC COMPATIBLE SYSTEMS

The IBM PC was introduced at roughly the same time as the Apple Macintosh. Unlike Apple, however, IBM was not successful in preventing other manufacturers from creating computers that would run IBM PC software— nor, in fact, did it try particularly hard. The result has been that there are a lot more IBM PC-compatibles than there are Macs on the planet, and overall a lot more useful applications available for them.

Choosing an IBM PC-compatible is markedly more difficult than buying a Macintosh. The very thing that makes PC-compatibles powerful— their flexibility— also offers one a bewildering array of choices.

This is further complicated by the number of companies making PC-compatible systems. No one knows exactly what this number is, save for its being very large. In addition, like the Mac, PC-compatible systems have evolved over the years and there are several strata to choose from.

A brief family tree of the PC may offer you an initial path into the wilderness. There will be a few things in this discussion that might not make immediate sense— for example, knowing that a computer will hold up to 655,360 bytes of memory is of little use if you don't know how big the average program is. You might just want to skim over these things for the moment. We'll go over them in detail a little later on.

The original IBM PC was introduced in 1981. Although available in several configurations, all IBM PCs of the day were driven by a microprocessor called an 8088 and had anywhere from 64 kilobytes of memory on up. The serious version had two floppy drives. This is much the same configuration that the original Macintosh offered, as it happens.

Shortly after the PC was released, IBM introduced the IBM PC/XT, which featured a hard drive.

At this time in history, there were numerous companies who had made their fortunes building Apple II+ compatible computers. The Apple II+ was the first viable commercial computer from Apple, the distant precursor to the Macintosh. Apple felt that it was badly abused by the compatible manufacturers, and introduced its Macintosh amidst ominous warnings that anyone attempting the same thing with its new machine would be dealt the blunt end of a lawyer. As IBM was issuing no similar threats, the compatible computer industry seized on the PC as its next offering.

The original IBM PC was very conservatively designed, and it was not long before compatible machines were available for a fraction of its price with twice its performance. The original PC/XT ran its processor at 4.77 megahertz, a rough indication of how long it would take the processor to perform a particular task. So-called "turbo" XT-compatibles usually ran at 8 megahertz, just under twice the speed.

The real meaning of computer speed is hard to express in meaningful terms until you've used a computer for a while. The speed of the original IBM PC was such that almost no present-day software will run on one without unbearable waiting. Recalculating a large financial spreadsheet that would take a minute on a state-of-the-art system today would take half an hour on a first-generation PC.

The original PC imposed several standards upon all of its successors, some of which were not very well thought out on reflection. Because software written for PC-compatibles must be "backwards-compatible"— it must run on older machines to a reasonable extent— designers of later machines have been stuck with these limitations.

The most infamous of these is the memory "barrier" of the PC. The computers that predated the first PC could hold a maximum of 64 kilobytes of memory, which was considered to be a lot back then. A kilobyte is 1024 bytes, or about half the memory required to store a page of single spaced, typewritten text. The designers of the PC felt that while no one could say how much memory might be needed five or ten years hence, a tenfold increase would certainly be more than enough.

The 640 kilobyte memory limit became a permanent element of PC architecture because the original PC was designed with several immovable elements immediately beyond the top of program memory. For various technical reasons, once the locations of fundamental parts of a computer are finalized and software starts to appear assuming that they'll stay put, it's largely impossible to move them even if their initial locations turn out to have been a bad idea.

There was subsequently a considerable amount of juggling in various attempts to sneak around this restriction.

The next generation of microcomputers from IBM was the IBM PC/AT. This system was based on a much more advanced microprocessor, the 80286. It ran at 8 megahertz, but an 80286 running at 8 megahertz can do a lot more work than an 8088 running at the same speed.

The PC/AT (one is shown in Figure 1.4) could also work with as much as sixteen megabytes of memory. However, because of the memory structure that was held over from the earlier PC and PC/XT systems, only the first 640 kilobytes could be used to run programs in. The rest of it, called "extended" memory, could only be used to hold data.

This is not as awkward as it sounds. For programs such as spreadsheets— at the time the most memory hungry applications commonly in use— data storage represented most of the real estate the programs wanted to occupy.

We'll discuss memory in greater detail presently.

Figure 1.4: An IBM PC/AT. (Photo courtesy of IBM)

Just as with the original 8088-based systems, PC/AT-compatible computers appeared that were both less expensive and more powerful than the real IBM PC/AT. For example, a recent AT-compatible system, the Dell 210, runs at 20 megahertz. In fact, other aspects of its internal architecture make it well over three times as fast as a real PC/AT.

A lot more remains to be said about compatible systems.

The next generation of microprocessors were the 80386 chips. Every bit as revolutionary as the 80286 chips were, they spawned another new generation of systems. However, IBM did not create a next-generation descendant of its original PC to use this chip. PC evolution gets a bit more convoluted at this point.

Deciding that it had lost more of the growing personal computer market to compatible system manufacturers than it cared to, IBM's 80386-based systems represented a marked departure from the architecture of the PC/XT and PC/AT systems. The IBM PS/2 range of computers (except for the PS/2 30, which uses an 8086 chip) encompasses both 80286 and 80386-based machines with varying capabilities. However, while they will run all the software of earlier machines, they have substantially different internal hardware. Called the MicroChannel Architecture, it allows peripheral devices such as printers, display cards and disk drives to work a lot faster because each one can be "smart." This means, for example, that when the computer asks for a file from a disk drive, the disk drive can get the file under its own intelligence rather than having to put the computer on hold until the file is retrieved.

Along with its new hardware standard, IBM also brought in some legal talent and began to erect barriers between the PS/2 and anyone who wanted to make other systems using the MicroChannel Architecture.

By the time of the release of the PS/2, the compatible manufacturers had grown pretty sophisticated. A number of them banded together to create their own "smart" architecture, one with performance comparable to MicroChannel but without infringing on any of IBM's landmines and patents. Called EISA— Enhanced Industry Standard Architecture— it's available in several high-end systems by Compaq, Tandy and others.

While all this was happening, most of the rest of the personal computer industry merely took the 80386 chip and built it into AT style systems. These computers lack an authentic IBM two-letter designation, and are usually referred to as "386 machines." The conventional AT architecture has acquired a name of its own— ISA, for Industry Standard Architecture— to distinguish it from the newcomers.

High-end 386 machines are available running at 25, 33, and even 40 megahertz. In conservative tests, a 25 megahertz 386 system can run simple programs at about thirty times the speed of the original PC/XT. A 386 system can address 4 gigabytes of memory. A gigabyte is a thousand megabytes. There are few people on earth who can begin to imagine a use for 4 gigabytes of memory, and fewer still who can afford them.

The 80386 can do a lot of other clever things, which we'll discuss in a moment. As an aside, this book was written and illustrated on an 80386-based Dell 325 computer.

Shortly after the 80386 appeared, Intel, its creator, released the 80386SX. This is a version of the basic 80386 processor that has been described alternately as "economical" and "limited," depending upon whom you talk to. Intended to run at a maximum of 16 megahertz, "386SX machines," as they're called, typically offer most of the performance of a high-end true 386 system, but at a greatly reduced price. The things that the SX version of the chip gives up— it can only address 16 megabytes of memory, rather than 4 gigabytes, for example— are features that few computer users will ever miss.

The next generation of microprocessors was the 80486. In fact, the 80486 was little more than a slightly faster, slightly refined 80386 with a built-in ancillary chip to do complex number crunching, something the 80386 had formerly required a second, outboard chip (a math coprocessor) to do. The 80486 was specifically designed for high-end computer aided drafting and networking systems, and will not be relevant to anything in this book.

Of Compatibles and Clones

When the first PC-compatible systems appeared in the early eighties, building compatible systems was very much a cottage industry. It was not uncommon to find that your computer had been assembled in someone's garage, or by an assembly line in the Far East that had been previously making toasters until computers had started looking more profitable. The reliability of such systems was questionable— it was not uncommon to have them explode, crash repeatedly or refuse to run certain software for no easily explained reason. On the other hand, some of them were very dependable, and are running to this day— albeit rather slowly.

Very low-end IBM PC-compatible systems were usually referred to as "clones." As the name suggests, they were merely copies of the original, with little attempt at innovation save for a possible increase of the original 4.77 megahertz clock rate to eight. Many of these early clones even cloned part of the operating system, the only copyrighted feature of the PC. This was the instance of IBM's only real interest in legal action over the early PC-compatible industry.

Quite a few very much better PC-compatible systems emerged from this jungle— although, regrettably, a lot of questionable machines are still manufactured and sold. Among the more reputable compatible manufacturers at present are Compaq, Dell, Tandy/Radio Shack, Arc, Zeos and Northgate. These are all pretty substantial companies, and their systems and support are on par with what you'd get if you bought authentic IBM equipment.

As will become apparent if you start looking for a computer, many of these companies charge almost as much for their systems as does IBM. These better compatibles cost a lot more than the generic clones that purport to do much the same work.

As a rule, the higher priced compatible systems are generally faster, more intelligently designed, and usually at least a bit less expensive than comparable equipment from IBM. This should not be regarded as a slight on the engineering skills of IBM per se. One of the many axioms surrounding microcomputers is that you can always spot the pioneers, as they're the ones with the arrows in their backs. The compatible manufacturers usually have a nice stable target to shoot at.

Buying real IBM equipment offers certain intangible commodities, including a reputation for reliability and service and, perhaps most important for corporate users who buy twenty or thirty machines at a time, the axiom "Nobody ever got fired for buying IBMs." As you will probably be spending your own money for a computer and are unlikely to fire yourself, much of this will probably not apply to you.

The IBM PS/1

There has long seemed to be a faction at IBM that felt that somewhere there was a market for a "home" computer, if only someone could come up with a suitable machine. This appears to have been much of the impetus behind the original PC, one manifestation of which was provided with a cassette recorder to store data on, rather than expensive floppy disks— they were expensive back then— as well as a 40-column screen mode that could be displayed on a television set in lieu of a monitor. Perhaps it was the same group of grey suits who later came up with the IBM PC junior.

People who deal with computers a lot laugh about the original PC and the PC junior.

The IBM PS/1 is perhaps the latest chapter in the quest for a home computer. It's certainly more sophisticated than any of its predecessors. One suspects it has been driven by much the same collection of forces that produced the Macintosh Classic. IBM has produced a computer that is intended to capture part of the market that has typically been the province of very low priced clones.

Like the Mac Classic, the PS/1 has been designed not to upstage IBM's more costly systems. It's not powerful when you buy it and it has been engineered to make sure it remains that way.

The PS/1 points up the difference between a home computer and a computer that you might want to use at home. It's based on the 80286 processor running at 10 megahertz, which is the low end of things for business systems. It has a single floppy disk— we'll have a look at disks and disk drives later in this chapter. It has a VGA card and monitor— also to be discussed— but these are integral to the system and can't be changed.

The most powerful configuration of the PS/1 comes with a 30-megabyte hard drive, which is not really all that big when it's confronted with several large business applications.

Other features of the PS/1 are a MIDI music port, a mouse port and a built-in modem. With the exception of the mouse, you probably will not find these features of much use in a business environment. The MIDI music port is of no use unless you'll actually be composing music as part of your work and the modem is too slow for most real world applications. Modems will be dealt with in greater detail in Chapter 7.

The PS/1 is tiny. Its "footprint"—the amount of space it will occupy on your desk—is smaller than the base of its monitor.

The best feature of the PS/1 is that it's very, very easy to set up and get into. It comes with its operating system and a lot of software all pre-installed on its hard drive. This includes a shell program that mediates between users of the computer and the operating system, in much the same way the Macintosh Finder does. If you have problems with the system, you can actually call a dedicated PS/1 support division of IBM.

The biggest failing of the PS/1 after its rather conservative choice of processors is its lack of expandability. On a conventional PC you can plug in additional cards to add more memory, a better display, better communications, and so on. The PS/1 has no slots, and hence will accept no cards. You can buy an optional expansion chassis to allow it to accept three conventional peripheral cards, but at this point the PS/1 ceases to be attractive, compact, economical, or easy to deal with.

The PS/1 might be a contender as a home computer at such time as people start *needing* computers in their homes—but most of the functions that are touted as features of home computers are really best done in the traditional, manual ways. Computerized Christmas card lists are too corporate for most people, most cooks don't want to have to turn on a computer to find a recipe for the evening meal, and few families regard gathering around the monitor a suitable substitute for an evening spent talking or watching that other tube, the television.

If you're looking for a system to run a home office with, the PS/1 will delight you when you first unpack it and frustrate you a week later and forever after. Once you no longer need it to be user friendly, its lack of power and flexibility will prove a severe limitation.

The PS/1 is a very well made computer, but for another group of users.

Is It Compatible?

There are a lot of people who have bought very cheap clone computers and, aside from the rather bad injection molding in their cases and their unfamiliar names, have found them admirable machines. Such computers are cheap, reliable workhorses.

There are many more people who have bought ostensibly identical clone machines and have never seen them do a useful day's work. Usually after six or eight months of being run around by the store that sold it to you— or trying to *find* the store that sold it to you if you bought it from one of the more mobile ones— you'll probably give up and either buy a better computer or abandon the whole idea entirely.

If I could write a book that would enable someone to tell the difference between a good clone and a bad clone I would immediately break the contract for this one and go on to become very rich.

Buying very inexpensive clone computers is a gamble, and one in which you can't be said to have a lot riding in your favor. It's rare indeed that you'll be able to buy such a computer and actually return it if it turns out to be a lemon. Most often its dealer will offer to fix it, and in many cases not even that. This assumes, of course, that its dealer is still there.

Allowing that you can't afford to spend a lot of your time dealing with a machine that crashes or mangles your data or otherwise misbehaves, you should probably consider avoiding these very low-end computers. You'll experience a significantly lower level of frustration if you buy, at the same price, a name-brand machine with less performance.

Aside from failing in catastrophic ways, some clone systems have more subtle problems. Not being completely compatible with a "real" PC system, they may refuse to run certain programs, or run them irregularly. Semi-compatible compatibles usually handle popular programs adequately but get into trouble when confronted with software that makes use of more exotic areas of the system. These are the sorts of things you won't find out about for six months.

The most crucial element in ensuring the compatibility of a PC is its "BIOS." BIOS is an acronym for "basic input output system." In a PC, the BIOS is a chip with part of the operating system on it.

The BIOS not only has to work— it has to work with the particular hardware it's running on. There is BIOS source code in the public domain that is free for the taking, and worth almost as much as it costs. Such BIOS designs don't produce terribly compatible computers.

Early clone manufacturers thought to get around the BIOS problem by simply lifting the BIOS from a real IBM PC— BIOS chips, like most forms of software, are easy to copy. This stirred up a nest of lawyers without actually resulting in very many working computers. IBM's BIOS worked well in the computer it was designed for, but usually poorly in one in which it was transplanted.

There are several companies that will custom-design BIOS software for a particular computer, most notably Phoenix and AMI. A Phoenix or AMI BIOS pretty well ensures you that the computer running them will be free from BIOS-level software incompatibility. Fortunately, unlike other issues of PC compatibility, you can tell who wrote the BIOS of a particular machine. When the system first boots up, a copyright notice by the BIOS manufacturer will appear in the upper left corner of the screen. Avoid systems with a mystery BIOS.

Figure 1.5 illustrates the BIOS copyright notice of a computer with a Phoenix BIOS in it.

```
Phoenix 80386 ROM BIOS PLUS Version 1.10 A03
Copyright (C) 1985-1988 Phoenix Technologies Ltd.
All Rights Reserved

Dell System 325
```

Figure 1.5: A Phoenix BIOS copyright notice

The Processor

Before you can start refining the actual PC-compatible system configuration you want, you should probably decide on the basic level of machine you need. Here are a few quick guidelines. Some of them will not be completely understandable until you've had a chance to read a bit further in this book.

To begin with, don't buy an 8088 or 8086-based computer, that is, a PC, XT or Turbo XT-compatible system. These are very inexpensive, but very slow. After a while, whatever computer you buy will probably prove slower than you'd like it to be. These first-generation machines will take about a day to begin to get frustrating.

The realistic low end for business microcomputers are the faster 80286-based machines, that is, AT-compatibles. Ten megahertz is reasonable, sixteen is better, and twenty really clips along. Most undemanding business applications will get along reasonably well with a 286 system, and because these machines aren't regarded as being really state of the art anymore, they're not all that expensive.

While computer designers talk about 486 systems, the real state of the art is the 386. The fast ones are still quite expensive. However, if you will be running demanding applications such as Microsoft Windows, a 386 system may well be worth the investment. Remember that no matter how fast it looks in the store it will eventually seem slow on your desk.

You can almost buy a 386 at 286 prices if you get a 386SX machine. You will give up the speed of a high-end 386 system, but you'll pay a lot less for your computer.

Don't consider a 486-based machine unless you need blinding speed, do a lot of very high-end computer-aided drafting, or just have a great deal of money to spend.

Math Coprocessors

Each of the types of PC processors we've just discussed has available for it a very expensive ancillary chip called a "math coprocessor." Math coprocessors are designated by numbers that end in seven. If you have a machine-based on an 80286, its math coprocessor is an 80287. Because math coprocessors can be expensive, and 80387's exceedingly so (about $500 at the time of this writing), some 386 machines come with the facility for using either an 80387 or an 80287 with somewhat reduced performance.

There is no such thing as an 80487— the 80486 processor has its math coprocessor as an integral part of its chip.

Microprocessors regard mathematics involving integer numbers and mathematics involving real, or "floating point," numbers differently. Integers are whole numbers, while floating point numbers have decimal points and any number of places to the right thereof. Integer mathematics can be handled quickly by the processor itself. The processor does not know how to do floating point math.

Under normal circumstances if a program wishes to do floating point math, it must include routines to emulate floating point operations in software, which is very slow. Programs that do a lot of floating point math— computer-aided drafting packages such as AutoCAD are most notable for this— can forgo floating point emulation if the machine they're running on has a math coprocessor. The coprocessor allows the computer itself to do floating point math, which is many times faster than doing it in software.

Most programs that use floating point math to some extent are smart enough to figure out whether a math coprocessor is installed and to use it if it is. Otherwise they default to the slower floating point emulation in software. A few, such as the release 10 and later versions of AutoCAD, are so dependent on floating point calculations that they will refuse to run unless a math coprocessor is available.

Relatively few programs actually use floating point math. Most business software will ignore a math coprocessor entirely, and derive no benefit at all from the presence of one. Unless you will be using software that can actually take advantage of this chip, don't buy one. Math coprocessors can cost several hundred dollars, depending on the level of machine you want to install one in.

Specifically, the sorts of software that will benefit from a math coprocessor are CAD programs, spreadsheets in some exotic applications, and certain specialized statistical and scientific applications.

Memory

It's hard to imagine a larger can with more worms in it than the one that accompanies the PC memory issue. You will probably want to read this section more than once to fully understand all the nuances of the memory situation. PC memory is a model of bad planning and afterthoughts. While you will ultimately be able to get it sorted out— the available solutions do work and are quite easy to implement once you know what you want— working your way through the decision process can be a little daunting.

For reasons we've already seen, there's a barrier to adding main program memory to a PC beyond 640 kilobytes. Because this really isn't enough memory for many of the things people want to do with microcomputers, a variety of other sorts of memory have been devised for the PC.

Historically, the first application to feel the memory crunch was Lotus 1-2-3, the spreadsheet package. The developers of Lotus in conjunction with Intel (the creators of the processors upon which PCs are based) and Microsoft (the authors of the PC's operating system) developed what came to be called LIM *expanded* memory. LIM stands for "Lotus Intel Microsoft." Expanded memory is also referred to as EMS memory. EMS stands for *expanded memory specification.*

Expanded memory is very tricky, or very funky depending upon how you look at it. High in the address space of a PC equipped with expanded memory there's a memory window, or "page frame." You can think of this as working like a conventional glass window, that is, as a small opening that can look out onto a much larger area. The page frame is relatively small, originally 16, and now typically 64 kilobytes. Somewhere invisible to the computer there's a lot of memory— perhaps several megabytes.

When a program that knows how to access expanded memory, such as Lotus 1-2-3, wants to get at the first 64 kilobytes of the invisible extra memory, it tells the expanded memory driver to make it visible in the page frame window. It can then be read and written to normally. If it wants to get at the next 64 kilobytes it so instructs the driver. The first 64 kilobyte chunk vanishes and the next one appears in the window. In this way, all the expanded memory can be addressed, no matter how much of it there actually is.

This is a good arrangement for storing data and, in fact, for storing parts of programs. However, it doesn't really remove the 640 kilobyte barrier. It only sneaks around it for programs that are smart enough to use the expanded memory.

The 80286, 80386 and 80486 processors were designed to address much more memory than the original 8088 processor. However, because the barrier still exists at 640 kilobytes, the extra memory added to a computer based on one of these processors isn't available as conventional memory either. It's called *extended* memory. One of the principal areas of confusion in dealing with PC memory is that the words "extended" and "expanded" sound very much alike.

Extended memory lives in the space beyond the range of memory that an original 8088 could deal with. It, too, is useful only as data-storage memory rather than memory to run programs in. At least, we'll allow that this is true for the moment.

The extended memory specification is often called XMS.

Extended memory is faster to access than expanded memory, and is more flexible. As a rule, expanded is more widely used because it was developed earlier and is applicable to old 8088-based computers, and extended memory is not.

On computers using an 80286 or better processor, special "drivers" are available for using extended memory as expanded memory for programs that require expanded memory. (Drivers are little additions to a PC's operating system that manage the extra memory for any programs that wish to use it.)

Some programs make use of extended memory by placing parts of themselves in extended memory and freeing up some main memory. This is not practical with expanded memory.

Many newer 80286-based systems have a very odd memory arrangement. These machines claim to come with 1 megabyte of memory, even though a full house is only 640 kilobytes. This is primarily because the most economical way to buy memory is in 1-megabyte chunks. The remaining 384 kilobytes of memory can be one of two things, depending on how clever the designer of the computer was.

The simplest application for the extra memory is also the least useful. The chips in which a computer's BIOS live are relatively slow. Every time something happens that involves the BIOS— a frequent occurrence under most programs— the computer slows down for a fraction of a second. As such, some 1-megabyte AT-compatibles can "phantom" the BIOS. This means that they copy the contents of the BIOS into some of the unused 384 kilobytes of memory and then make the BIOS itself appear to vanish. This speeds up the contents of the BIOS, and hence the computer.

A more useful application for the extra memory is to make it appear as extended memory, which can then be used as expanded memory with a suitable driver if you like. If you buy a 1-megabyte AT system, you should make sure that it offers you the option of using the extra 384 kilobytes of memory in either capacity.

One of the advancements that makes the 80386 chip more powerful than its predecessors is its ability to manage its own memory. As far as the 80386 chip itself is concerned, there is no main memory, expanded memory, or extended memory. All memory is alike to it. The operating system can tell it where to put the available memory to make it most useful. As such, an 80386, 80386SX and 80486 system can use any memory above 640 kilobytes for whatever you want. One of the things this entails is that it can pretend to be multiple 640 kilobyte machines, that is, it can run several programs at once.

As a final note, you might hear the term *virtual memory* bandied about. The term might suggest that there is a way to use memory that isn't really there. In fact, it involves nothing quite so magical. One typical example of virtual memory is an expanded memory emulator, of which there are several. The emulator allows computers with no expanded memory to run programs that insist on having some. It allows you to pretend that a big disk file is really extra main memory.

Just as with real expanded memory, when you ask for the first 64 kilobytes of expanded memory, the expanded memory emulator reads the first 64 kilobytes from its file on the disk. When you ask for the next 64 kilobytes, it writes the first 64 kilobytes back to the disk and gets the next 64 kilobytes, and so on.

The drawback to this is that a disk file is many times slower than real memory. Using virtual memory rather than real memory will usually leave you with applications that are too slow to really use.

How Much Memory Do I Need?

There are a few very simple guidelines to deciding on what sort of memory you need and how much of it to buy.

You should not even consider a system with less than 640 kilobytes of main memory. Contemporary machines with 80286 or better processors usually have at least a megabyte, that is, about one million bytes or 1024 kilobytes.

You will not need any memory beyond this to run most small applications. We'll discuss the details of the memory used by particular software packages throughout this book. You will need some extra memory of some sort to run large spreadsheets. Extra memory is also required for some larger desktop-publishing packages.

You can speed up the performance of your computer dramatically by using some of your extra memory as a disk "cache." We'll discuss what this does in Chapter 11. The performance improvement in having a cache is so dramatic for many types of programs that it's all but essential.

Finally, if you will be running Microsoft Windows, as discussed in Chapter 4, you should have at least two megabytes of extended memory. Four is better, and eight will improve the performance of larger Windows applications further still. However, you probably won't know whether you want to use Windows until you read a little further.

Most contemporary middle and high-end PC-compatible systems will allow you to have between eight and sixteen megabytes of memory in the system without having to buy additional memory cards. This is called "on-board memory," as slots or sockets are provided for it on the main "motherboard" of the computer.

If you buy a machine with room for lots of extra memory on the motherboard you can add more memory without having to buy expensive memory cards.

Display Adapters and Monitors

Because PC-compatible systems have slots, you can install whatever sort of display card and monitor combination best suits your needs. The choice of displays is pretty easily understood.

To begin with, there are two largely obsolete display adapters that you will probably not want to consider. The first is the CGA adapter or "color card." It can display limited color text and graphics, but with very bad resolution. Too crude for use with much of the currently available software, it's also really hard on your eyes.

The other obsolete display card is the MDA or "monochrome display adapter." It does very good text—and that's it. It has no graphics facilities at all. These cards are still used in many dedicated PC applications, such as PC-based cash registers and terminals.

The least expensive practical display adapter is a Hercules card, also called an HGC card or a monochrome graphics card. This card can display crisp text and monochrome graphics. Originally developed by the Hercules company, it has been "cloned" by many other manufacturers. Hercules has since moved on to better things.

A typical Hercules-compatible card costs less than fifty dollars. Hercules cards drive what are called "TTL" monitors, which start at around a hundred dollars. If you're struggling with a tight budget this will get you a workable, if unexciting display.

While color isn't essential for most business applications, a good color display can make your software a lot easier to use and more readily understood. If you can afford it, you will do well to spring for something beyond a completely monochrome Hercules card.

The next generation of display adapters are EGA cards. These can support up to 43 lines of text on your screen at once, although the conventional 25-line mode is a lot easier to read. They can also do graphics in up to sixteen colors.

The current generation of display cards are the VGA adapters. A VGA card and monitor doesn't cost all that much more than an EGA card, and the slight increase in price is more than worth it. A VGA card can do higher-resolution business graphics and more lines of text and it can handle full color. Full color graphics— in reality, graphics with 256 unique colors— can look essentially photographic. While of limited usefulness for many business applications now, 256-color modes offer an area that software will likely grow into over the next few years.

The business graphics mode of a VGA card can display sixteen-color images in 640 by 480 dot resolution, which seems natural for most programs that use graphics.

In reality, you will probably not buy a real IBM VGA card. It is, like real IBM computers, quite expensive and lacking many features that later VGA-compatible cards offer. What most people think of when they discuss VGA cards are actually "super" VGA adapters— cards that support the standard modes of a VGA card and then some.

A typical super-VGA card will offer you at least one sixteen-color business graphics mode in addition to the stock 640 by 480 mode, typically 800 by 600. It will also offer better 256-color graphics.

The relevance of super-VGA card modes will become a bit more apparent when we discuss the software that will use them, most notably Microsoft Windows.

If you can afford it, a super-VGA card and an "analog" multisync color monitor will provide you with the best display options for a wide variety of software. The word "multisync" indicates a monitor that will handle all the various graphics modes of a super-VGA card.

As with computers themselves, there are some less than ideal super-VGA cards available. Among the better manufacturers of super-VGA cards are Paradise, Headland Technologies, ATI and Trident.

Rock-Bottom VGA

Having become the standard in display adapters, very low-price VGA systems have been turning up costing little more than a Hercules card and a TTL monitor. These systems consist of a stripped down VGA card and a grey-scale "page white" monitor. This latter device is a VGA-compatible monitor that will display colors as levels of grey.

While these systems don't provide much of an upgrade path— getting real high-end super-VGA performance out of one requires replacing both the monitor and the card— they're a good, solid way to arrive at a workable display for your computer if your budget is tight.

The most widely available of the low-end standard VGA cards is the ATI Basic 16, which costs less than a hundred dollars.

Disk Drives

The original PC systems came with 5¼" single-density floppy disk drives. Each disk could hold 180 kilobytes of data. This isn't very much. Double-density disks could hold 360 kilobytes, on 48 "tracks."

The IBM PC/AT introduced "high-density" 5¼" floppy disk drives. A high-density disk, also called a 96-track disk, can hold four times what a double-density disk can, thus, about 1.2 megabytes. Both disks look the same, but the surface of a high-density disk can hold more data. High-density drives are "backwards-compatible"— they will also read and write double-density disks.

As an aside, most floppy disk manufacturers only make high-density disks by design. Each batch of disks are sorted. If they'll hold data on 96 tracks they become high-density (HD) diskettes. If they won't, they're tested to see if they'll work as double-density (DD). For this reason, attempting to use less expensive DDs as HDs never works. On average a double-density disk pretending to be a high-density will have so much unusable area that only about 350 kilobytes will be available— that is, what would have been available had you used it as a double-density disk in the first place.

The origin of the phrase "floppy disk" may strike you as fairly obvious. They're not very rugged, and the magnetic media inside is exposed and easily damaged by dust, fingerprints, paperclips or spilled Classic Coke. This is why the Macintosh systems were built around 3½" "microfloppies," which have rigid plastic cases and mechanical shutters to protect their magnetic innards when the disk isn't in the computer. More recently, PC-compatible systems and IBM's PS/2 systems have had microfloppy drives available for them.

It seems paradoxical that you can get more data on something that is physically smaller, but the limit to how tightly you can pack the tracks of a floppy disk is actually inherent in the accuracy to which the mechanism that reads the tracks can be positioned. A double-density microfloppy can hold 720 kilobytes. A high-density microfloppy can hold 1.44 megabytes. Microfloppy drives are smart enough not to allow a double-density disk to be used as a high-density. The only drawback to microfloppies is that they're more expensive than conventional 5¼" floppies.

Figure 1.6 illustrates 5¼" and 3½" floppy disks.

Laptop computers use microfloppies almost exclusively. Desktop machines are available with either type of drive, and many come with one of each.

Hard drives, which are essentially permanent internal drives, are available in capacities ranging from 20 megabytes—approximately 20 million bytes—on up. It's very hard to know in advance how big a hard drive you'll need, but you will unquestionably manage to fill whatever you get. As you work through this book you'll be able to work out how much hard drive space is required by each of the applications you plan to use.

Figure 1.6: The two formats of floppy disks commonly used with PC-compatibles

You can't really run any useful business applications without a hard drive.

PC Operating Systems

Thus far we've not talked at all about the PC equivalent to the Macintosh's Finder—its operating system. Regrettably, this subject is no less involved than that of PC hardware.

The PC's principal operating system is called DOS— that's *disk operating system*. The main DOS that is available, MS-DOS, is a product of Microsoft, the largest producer of microcomputer software on Earth.

DOS provides a user environment that is in many respects the antithesis of that found on the Mac. It's decidedly user-unfriendly, but it's small, fast, and ultimately more functional once you understand it. In place of the mouse, icons, menus, dialogs, and graphics of the Mac, DOS provides a prompt called a "command line." In order to make DOS do something you type a command and DOS responds by performing a function— or by displaying "Bad command or file name" if you've typed a command it doesn't recognize.

Before you can use DOS, you must learn at least some of its commands. Their names are often cryptic, their syntax awkward.

The advantage of DOS over a graphical user interface like the Finder is that DOS takes up less than 100 kilobytes of memory, far less than the Macintosh's operating system. It ties up almost none of the computer's power with its own functions— all the system resources can be available to the programs that you run under DOS. For example, all other things being equal you could run a bigger spreadsheet on a PC than on a Macintosh because DOS would leave you with more free memory than the Finder would.

One of the best features of DOS is that you don't have to use its commands if you don't want to. You can run a "shell" from DOS that will provide you with a more user-friendly environment. In practical terms, you can have your computer set up to run such a shell as soon as it boots, such that you never have to go near DOS.

The most comprehensive and powerful shell program is Microsoft Windows 3, which you may have heard of. Windows makes DOS look like the Macintosh's Finder. However, in addition to what the Finder does, Windows can handle *multitasking*. This means that you can have several programs running at once and move between them as your work requires. It also means that the programs you're not using at the moment can keep working while they're in the background, rather than just sitting there waiting to be activated.

The true value of multitasking may not be apparent right now, but it's something you will appreciate as you grow into your computer system. It means, for example, that you can write one letter while another is printing, manage your database while your spreadsheet is recalculating, and so on.

The other thing to consider about Windows is that you can get back to the DOS command line whenever you need it. You can have the user-friendly environment of a graphical interface when you need it and the power of a small, fast operating system when you have to do something that needs all your computer's power.

Windows is a very complex subject, which is why it has a chapter in this book all to itself, Chapter 4.

Revisions of DOS

As with any complex piece of software, DOS has gone through numerous revision levels. For practical purposes, the earliest version of DOS was 2.0– there was a DOS 1.0, but it's not compatible with very much contemporary DOS-based software.

As DOS advanced through the eighties, it came to be equipped with more features and had the odd bug fixed. This continued into version 3.3. The next release was DOS 4.0, which represented a major change in the structure of DOS. For one thing, it had its own shell interface. Many DOS users felt that version 4.0 was a victim of the Peter Principle– DOS had been promoted until it was no longer capable of being what it had started out to be: a small, fast operating system. With DOS 5, Microsoft has improved the shell interface and the means by which DOS deals with large programs and files, while offering DOS 3.3 users even more powerful versions of the commands they have grown familiar with.

Many PC-compatibles still come with DOS 3.3. It's bug free as far as anyone knows, and it works well. Virtually all DOS software will run under DOS 3.3– version 4.01 offers some additional features but no facilities that DOS 3.3 does not. The only significant advantage of DOS 4.01 is in the way it handles large hard drives, which is more elegant than the DOS 3.3 approach. DOS 5 is even more elegant, but it is still somewhat larger than DOS 3.3.

There is at least one DOS "alternative," an operating system that does everything DOS does and a bit more. Called DR DOS, it's a product of Digital Research, a company that actually wrote the operating system upon which DOS is founded but subsequently fell on hard times.

DR DOS is an interesting package with several advanced features, but it shows its rough edges in some cases. There are programs that, as of this writing, it will not run. One such program is AutoCAD release 10 (and 11), which is a large but fairly standard application.

You can achieve DOS compatibility most reliably by using "real" DOS; that is, MS-DOS (from Microsoft) or PC-DOS (if you buy a real IBM system).

Unpacking a PC Compatible

The amount of work you have to do to unpack a PC-compatible and get it working will vary a lot with the system you buy. As a rule, the higher-end systems come with most of the work done, and many will power up as easily as a Macintosh. Lower priced systems usually leave you with at least some of the arduous tasks.

If your system comes with its system software already installed, you can plug it in and get ready to do some work. If it doesn't you will have to install DOS, possibly preceded by doing a hard drive format. While neither of these tasks is particularly difficult if you know what you're doing, they're a bit mysterious if you don't. It's an extremely good idea to make sure that the computer you buy either has DOS installed or comes with a very precise set of instructions for formatting the hard drive and loading DOS onto it.

You should start setting up your system by clearing off some desk space and opening the cartons. Save all the packing material— it's handy if things have to get sent back to your dealer for service. If you have room, set the monitor on your desk beside the computer for a moment, rather than on top of it.

Most systems come with all their cards in place— if this is true of yours you won't have to open the case. If not, read the instructions that come with your computer to work out how to get the case open. Many computer cases are designed by extraterrestrials with very small fingers.

The only peripheral card that most contemporary PC-compatibles may want you to install yourself is the display adapter card. Figure 1.7 illustrates a typical VGA display adapter and a Hercules card— in this case, a real one.

The Hercules card is what's called an "eight-bit" card. The VGA card is a "sixteen-bit" card. The difference is in the number of gold edge connectors at the bottoms of the cards. Sixteen-bit cards have two sets of them while eight-bit cards have only one.

Note that some 80386 and 80386SX-based systems may have a third kind of slot, called a "proprietary memory expansion slot." These slots are designed to hold memory cards that are unique to your computer. They vary from machine to machine. You can ignore this type of slot for the moment.

Figure 1.7: VGA and Hercules display adapters

Inside your computer you'll find some unused long plastic connectors called "slots." The location of a machine's slots varies a bit from system to system. Very compact PCs often have the slots running sideways.

Most AT and 386-compatible systems will have a few eight-bit slots and the rest sixteen-bit slots. You can plug an eight-bit card into either type of slot, but sixteen-bit cards can only go into sixteen-bit slots. As a rule, you should put eight-bit cards in eight-bit slots if you have no good reason for doing otherwise, as this will leave your sixteen-bit slots free for any sixteen-bit cards that come along. As far as the computer's concerned, all the slots are the same.

In many PC cases, one end of the row of slots will find itself beside the power supply of the computer, usually a large silver box with a fan on top and a sticker that says "No user serviceable parts inside" in eleven languages. If you have the choice, locate your display card in a slot as far from the power supply as you can. Power supplies emit at least a bit of electromagnetic radiation that could confuse your display card. While it's an unlikely possibility, it's one that can usually be avoided by selecting a slot on the other side of the machine.

To install a VGA card, remove the screw that holds the backplate behind the slot you intend to occupy. Put the backplate somewhere safe so you'll never see it again. Place the screw somewhere else— you'll be wanting it shortly. Press the card into the slot, rocking it gently until it seats itself. Try to avoid impaling your fingers on the points of solder protruding from the back of the card.

Once you've installed your display card you should fasten it in place with the screw that previously held the slot backplate.

Next, run the appropriate cable from the monitor to the computer. If you have a Hercules-compatible display card and monitor, the monitor connector will be a nine-pin D shell. If you have a VGA card and monitor, the connector will be a D shell having fifteen pins. In many VGA monitor connectors there will be three or four pins missing, which is normal.

If you have a VGA monitor, carefully read the instructions that discuss setting up the monitor before you plug in the power cord and turn anything on. Most contemporary monitors are pretty good at protecting themselves from mistakes, but it's theoretically possible to damage a VGA monitor by sending it data it's not set up to expect.

Powering Up

When you first turn on your computer you should see a BIOS copyright notice in the upper left-hand corner of the screen. These notices vary a lot. If nothing appears, turn everything off and check your system. Here are a few common problems:

— The monitor isn't plugged in.

— The monitor isn't turned on.

— The cable from the monitor has come loose.

— The display card has popped out of its slot.

— The display card wasn't seated in its slot to begin with.

— The display card is in a bad slot. This happens. Try a different one before you resort to despair or harsh language.

Assuming that your system gets as far as the BIOS message, you should see some diagnostics as the system checks itself out and, ultimately, some activity from the disks.

When a PC boots up, it tries to load DOS from the A floppy drive. If this fails— which it will do if the A floppy drive is open— it goes and tries the C hard drive. You should hear a groan from the floppy and then a whir from the hard drive. Almost all systems have a front panel light to indicate hard drive activity. This will flash when the system attempts to boot from the hard drive.

If your computer responds with a prompt that looks like one of these, DOS is installed and ready to run:

C>
C\>
C:\>

These are usually referred to as C prompts.

If you encounter an error message rather than a C prompt you will have to prepare your hard drive and install DOS. This procedure varies considerably from system to system, and with the various versions of DOS. It should be outlined in the documentation that came with your computer.

Once DOS is up and running and your computer comes up with a C prompt when you boot it, you're ready to install some applications on your hard drive. From this point, what you do with your drive will be determined by the applications you want to use, something that will be dealt with throughout the rest of this book.

LAPTOP AND OTHER PORTABLE COMPUTERS

One of the areas of growth in microcomputer technology over the past few years has been in portable systems, or "laptops." Depending upon the nature of your application for a computer, a portable machine might be more productive than a desktop one, or at least a useful adjunct to one.

To begin with, everything in this chapter that deals with desktop PC systems is equally applicable to laptops. (At this writing, Apple laptops had been introduced too recently to have gained any reputation and to have reduced their initial prices to a more affordable range.) You can get laptop implementations of everything from a stock PC right on up to a high-end 386 machine. Laptops are available with several megabytes of memory, impressive hard drive capabilities, and VGA display adapters all built in.

Figure 1.8 illustrates several laptop machines.

Laptops offer several immediate advantages to someone considering a home office. If you will be working at home part of the time and in a conventional office for the rest of your schedule, taking your computer with you is a great deal more convenient than merely carrying

Figure 1.8: Several laptop computers. (Photos courtesy of Toshiba, Mitsubishi, and Dell computers)

a box of floppy disks around. You can't forget the file you need at home if you have the whole computer in your briefcase.

Secondly, computer security— the prospect that someone might read or tamper with the files on your machine in your absence— really ceases to be a concern if you take the computer with you when you go. Of course, the flip side of this is that if someone decides to actually steal your computer, portable machines can be made to get up and walk a lot more readily than a desktop computer that weighs almost as much as a desk.

It used to be the case that laptops were severely limited systems, but this has largely been overcome by better laptop technology. A laptop machine can do everything a desktop computer of the same class can.

While there are a number of unconventional portable computers available, the large majority of laptop systems fall into a standard design. The case usually consists of something the size of a large book in which the top flips open to reveal a keyboard and a display panel. This case design is usually referred to as a "clamshell."

The two areas in which laptops tend to compromise a bit is in the layout of their keyboards and the facilities of their displays. In order to keep the size of a laptop down, the keyboard is usually only about half as wide as that of a conventional desktop PC. While contemporary laptops usually offer full size keys, you'll probably find that they're laid out a bit oddly and will take some getting used to, especially if you touch type. The numeric keypad of a proper PC keyboard is usually absent in a laptop.

Figure 1.9 illustrates a laptop keyboard and that of a desktop PC.

The other thing that characterizes laptop machines is the display technology they use. Obviously a portable computer that relied on a fragile, heavy glass picture tube would cease to be portable. Laptops use one of two types of displays. The most common are liquid crystal panels. These use the same display technology that is found in digital watches, usually with a backlight to enhance their contrast. The alternative are "plasma" panels, which are the orange display panels that some bank machines feature.

Plasma panels are heavier and consume more power than do liquid crystal displays but they're easier to read under most light conditions. As a rule, plasma panels can be read more easily in subdued light, while liquid crystal panels become more readable as the light level increases. Liquid crystal displays overcome a tendency to be hard to read in poor light by providing internal light of their own.

Neither liquid crystal nor plasma displays are as easy on your eyes as a good glass monitor.

Laptops feature the same display adapters that desktop PCs do, although in most cases the adapter consists of a few chips on the machine's motherboard, not a separate card. Consequently, you can't upgrade a

Figure 1.9: Laptop and conventional keyboards

laptop's display later on. Laptops can be found with CGA, EGA, and VGA display adapters. CGA displays should be avoided for most business applications. As laptops are usually pretty expensive anyway, you should probably spring for one with a VGA display adapter.

Laptop computers have another important distinction, this being their power sources. Traditionally, laptop machines have run on batteries, such that you could use your computer in the absence of an electrical outlet. As laptops have grown more sophisticated, adding hard drives, better displays and more memory, they've gotten more power hungry. This meant either adding more batteries to a system—the batteries are very, very heavy—or giving it a shorter useful life between recharges. Of course, to avoid the hassle of dealing with batteries, you should make sure you carry the AC power cord so you can just plug the computer into a wall outlet.

There are many laptops available that are described as "transportable," rather than "portable." This means that they don't have batteries. While small and light, they can only be used where there's electrical power. Fortunately, there aren't really that many places that don't allow for plugging in your computer. Such machines, while restricted to being within extension-cord range of a plug, are typically much lighter than true portables would be, as they don't require any batteries.

Notebook Portable Computers

The most recent innovations in laptops are the "notebook" machines, such as the NEC UltraLight and the Texas Instruments TravelMate.

Notebook computers are smaller and lighter than laptops. The TravelMate, for example, weighs about four pounds and is about an inch larger in each direction than the size of this book.

As it turns out, a floppy drive is the most awkward thing to fit into a small computer because it requires somewhere to emerge from the case. Notebook machines often omit one altogether. There's an internal hard drive to store files on. For example, the NEC UltraLight has neither floppy nor hard drives. Instead, it has memory that is permanently powered and that looks to DOS like a disk drive. If you want to move a file from your laptop to a desktop machine, you must do so over a serial cable. There's a program called LapLink that makes "porting" files between laptop and desktop computers like this pretty painless.

Unless you find one with a lot of memory and a hard drive—such machines are increasingly available—you will probably not want to use a notebook computer as your principal system. However, if you need a modest amount of portable computer power to take with you, you might find that a small notebook system and a desktop computer back home make a powerful combination.

Using a Laptop as Your Main Computer

The two principal drawbacks to using a laptop machine—its small keyboard and its display panel—can both be easily overcome if you're using it at home. Most contemporary laptops have ports that allow you to plug in a normal PC keyboard and a regular glass monitor. This is a highly desirable feature, because when your portable has come home it can have all the attributes of a desktop machine.

While many laptops offer a bit of expansion capability—you can plug a single expansion card into some higher-end laptops, and most middle and high-end machines allow for some on-board memory expansion—they are nowhere near as flexible as desktop systems with slots and lots of space inside for cards. If you buy a powerful portable computer that will handle all your requirements for the foreseeable future this probably won't be a drawback. However, you should bear it in mind if you're thinking about using a portable system as your principal machine.

As a final note, if you're planning to use a portable system with mouse-based software, consider whether you'll be taking it to places where there's some space to work the mouse. Few things look sillier than someone in an airport departure lounge with a laptop on his or her knees trying to run a mouse on the armrest of a chair.

AUTHOR'S CHOICE

Author's Choice for Macintosh

The Macintosh SE series of machines are not the least expensive Macs, but they are probably the best suited for business applications. They offer slots to plug in expansion cards and all the ports you'll need to set up your system with a useful assortment of peripherals.

If I were buying a Macintosh this week I would avoid the Macintosh Classic, as it's underpowered. I would also avoid the Mac II, which is very nice but very expensive.

Author's Choice for PC Compatibles

My personal favorite for the most cost-effective, trouble-free PC-compatible systems are the ones made by Dell. Priced midway between the very low-end clones and real IBM machines, they offer generous warranties, good engineering and manufacturing, and a toll-free number to call for help.

Of the half dozen or so Dell systems that my friends and I have, none has ever done anything other than run programs and play games. That is, they haven't detonated, caught fire, or refused to boot up in the morning.

My choice of display cards are the ones made by Paradise— which, as it turns out, are what get plugged into Dell machines if you order a VGA card and monitor.

Finally, the nicest monitors I've encountered have been the NEC 3D tubes. They're a bit expensive, however. If you want an inexpensive monitor, the Tatung CM-1495 is surprisingly good for what it costs.

Author's Choice for Laptops

For a long time I thought that the NEC MultiSpeed laptop I carried on several trips around Britain had permanently dislocated my shoulder. The bruises did eventually heal, though, and after a while my arm worked almost normally. However, I can't walk the concourse at Manchester airport without recalling what it was like making the journey with an anvil dangling from my arm.

Laptops seem deceptively light when you buy them. Most potential users who would never consider carrying a fifteen pound briefcase with them will cheerfully hoist a computer weighing at least this much. If you travel, a heavy portable computer is something of an albatross. You have to keep your eye on it, protect it from injury and carry it with you everywhere you go.

You also have to find power for it— either to run it if it's a transportable or to charge its batteries. If this entails a separate power supply, plan on another box to lug about.

The power issue is one to consider carefully. The NEC MultiSpeed that so distorted my posture was a good example of a computer really designed to travel. While its weight seemed a bit excessive, its power supply claimed to be able to digest anything that could travel along a wire. I "adapted" it to European 220 volt power by cutting the North American plug from its power cord and replacing it with a British one. The wires within even turned out to have European color codes for just such an eventuality. The NEC survived the experience nicely, automatically switching to 220 volts, and lived to be lugged through several other airports.

When I finish this book we're going back to Britain for a while. I'll be taking a TravelMate notebook computer that weighs four pounds and will fit into a large coat pocket. It's a bit slower and harder to use than a full-size laptop. Its keyboard is smaller. It has no floppy drives and its screen looks like a glow-in-the-dark postage stamp. None of these things matter: Laptops are meant to be carried, and after you have carried one for a while, all that matters is weight.

A WORD ABOUT THE GREY MARKET

One of the unusual things to have popped up in the marketing of computers of late has been the "grey" market. The implication in this is that it's a lot like the black market, but not quite as nasty.

The grey market applies to computer equipment in varying degrees depending upon the individual circumstances. In most cases it does not represent anything that is actually illegal, but not all of its true features may be visible to someone buying grey market hardware.

If you buy a computer from an authorized dealer of its manufacturer— for example, a Macintosh from an authorized Apple dealer— you can be certain that your system came directly from the manufacturer and will be supported by the manufacturer if something goes amiss. There's a cost to this support that is built into the price of the computer.

In many cases, name-brand computers become available to unauthorized dealers from sources usually unmentioned. These are not necessarily "hot" or illegal. They've just been imported or purchased through channels other than those that are normally used by authorized dealers.

And then again, in some cases they're wholly illegal clones with forged labels.

Grey market hardware is usually a lot less expensive than what you'd buy from an authorized dealer. The catch is that there's usually no support for it should you have problems with it. Grey market dealers may or may not be able to fix what they sell, and many manufacturers will not repair equipment that has been bought on the grey market, or at the very least will not honor its warranty.

Buying equipment on the grey market is just as uncertain as buying no-name clones with bad injection molding.

A WORD ABOUT BUNDLING

If you go looking for computers, you'll probably encounter what are called "bundled" systems. This refers to computers that have some software included with them. In most cases, you may find that your system has DOS bundled with it. Some machines come with a lot of additional software as well.

Bundling arrangements can save you a lot of money. Typically, system manufacturers that bundle software with their machines get it at a great deal less than you would if you went out to buy it. As such, even allowing that the cost of the software is worked into the price of the system as a whole, you'll still save a considerable amount over the cost of buying the computer and all the software separately.

This assumes that you want all the software, of course. Very often bundling arrangements supply you with more software than you need, or with packages other than the ones that you might have chosen. It's usually the case that software companies that are willing to offer manufacturers the most attractive bundling deals are ones that are struggling to sell their software in the usual way, and wish to gain "market share." Some bundles read like a buyer's guide to unheard-of programs.

There's one Korean computer manufacturer that offers a software bundle including a DOS clone, a Windows clone, a dBASE clone, a Word-Perfect clone, and so on. Upon close inspection very little of the bundled software works as well as the popular packages it's cloned from and in time you'd most likely replace the parts you use.

Consider heavily bundled computers carefully—very often they offer you a first class deal on a lot of software you'll never really use.

SUMMARY

Having made it to the end of this chapter you probably could buy a computer and a have a pretty good chance of getting what you need. However, both to fine tune your shopping list a bit and to save yourself additional trips to the computer store, you should read a bit further before you lay down your Visa card.

One of the things that people who know about computers can do very impressively is to assemble a disparate collection of hardware and software and come up with a box that's ideally suited to do exactly what they want. This doesn't really result from years of night school courses or an innate rapport with silicon. Rather, it's something that comes fairly easily once you really know what you want to do—and have an idea what's available to do it.

The next few chapters of this book will help you get a better handle on what you want to do, or rather, on what you want your computer to help you with while you're doing it.

CHAPTER

2

2

PRINTERS

Of all the devices you may eventually connect to your computer, printers are likely to cause you the greatest initial confusion. Although usually pretty simple to set up and use, printers are almost as difficult to choose as your computer itself. There are a lot of them.

As with choosing a computer, a large part of choosing the right printer is defining exactly what you want to do with it. You might want to define as well what you might want to do with it in the future. Computers lend themselves to a certain degree of upgrading and fine tuning if you find you haven't bought quite enough memory or the right sort of display. With a few exceptions, the only way you can upgrade a printer is to buy another printer.

The printer you ultimately choose will be at least partially determined by the software you will be using to generate whatever you plan to print. If you aren't sure what applications you'll be running, you might want to forgo a final decision about printers until you've had a chance to read the chapters that deal with the software you're interested in.

TYPES OF PRINTERS

Before we get into the details of specific printers for Macintosh and PC systems, let's take a look at the general types of printers available.

The model numbers and interfacing details will probably change, depending on the system you plan to associate your printer with, but the concepts will remain the same.

The most rudimentary sort of printer that most people encounter prior to being beset with a microcomputer is an electric typewriter. A typewriter is really a printer in which the computer interface has been dispossessed by a keyboard. In fact, in the early days of personal computers there were typewriters that would ostensibly serve as printers as well, albeit not terribly good ones.

The problem with using a typewriter as a printer is that the mechanical elements of a traditional electric typewriter are not designed to type at the sort of speed a computer would like to print at. In its simplest sense, a computer transmits characters to a printer by sending down one character, waiting until it has been printed, and then sending down another. A printer that can print no faster than an electric typewriter will keep your computer waiting a lot.

In reality, the situation need not be quite as inflexible as this, even if your computer is dealing with an unusually slow printer. We'll discuss this in greater detail later in this book when we look at print caches and spoolers.

An Introduction to Dot Matrix

The first popular computer printers were called "dot matrix." You have unquestionably seen the output of dot matrix printers— they're used for everything from personalized junk mail to bank machine printouts. Dot matrix print is unmistakable.

A dot matrix printer generates print in something like the way that a typewriter does, that is, by hammering the impressions of characters through an inked ribbon. However, unlike a typewriter, which uses fixed metal dies, a dot matrix printer forms each character on the fly from a matrix of pins. This means that rather than having to move a metal key up from its resting place, the printer need only move a small number of very small metal pins a few hundredths of an inch.

Mechanical movement is always a limiting factor in the speed at which a printer can print. Dot matrix printers can print quickly because they have few moving parts, and those only move short distances.

Simple dot matrix print is readable but ugly, as it's formed from relatively few dots. The lowest-cost dot matrix printers print with an eight-by-eight or eight-by-nine pin matrix, which is pretty coarse.

You can improve the quality of dot matrix output by adding more pins to the print matrix. The current generation of high-end dot matrix printers can manage very tight, attractive characters by virtue of having 24-pin print heads, that is, a matrix with 24 pins on a side, rather than eight.

Another factor that limits the speed at which a dot matrix printer can print is the temperature of its print head. The movement of the pins in the print head generates heat, and more pins will heat the print head faster. Print heads usually have heat-dissipating fins for this reason, but all other things being equal, a 24-pin print head will usually be able to print at about a third of the speed of an eight or nine pin print head.

Most 24-pin printers cheat on this by offering multiple resolution modes. If you want to print quickly and don't mind ugly print, you can put such a printer in "draft" mode, which will make it behave like a low-end, eight or nine pin printer. If you want the printer to produce really attractive text— what's called "near letter quality" print— you can enable all 24 pins.

Near letter quality print is pretty well what it claims to be. It's attractive and reasonably easy to read, but it won't fool anyone into thinking it has come from a printing press or even from a real typewriter.

In addition to printing text, most dot matrix printers can print some monochrome graphics. This can be useful for things like charts and drawings, and most software that handles graphics will drive dot matrix printers if you insist. The results are not exactly electrifying.

While there are some exceptions to this rule, most dot matrix printers want to be fed with either single sheets of paper— by hand— or with tractor-feed computer paper. Depending on your application for a printer, this might be of little consequence. However, letters and reports with the remains of torn-off tractor-feed tabs look a bit funky.

The expense of running a printer is something that many people overlook when they figure out what one costs. This will become more significant when we discuss some of the other, more state-of-the-art printing technologies.

Dot matrix printers have fairly few parts, but they do wear out frequently. They consume ribbons, and some printer ribbons are quite elaborate and expensive to replace. They also require that their print heads be replaced from time to time. Both tasks can be performed without the need of a trip to the shop.

Dot Matrix Advantages and Disadvantages

There are several good reasons for choosing a dot matrix printer:

— They're the least expensive way to get reasonably fast, moderately attractive printing.

— They use very low cost supplies.

— They're easy to maintain.

— They're small.

— Most software will drive a dot matrix printer.

— You can use multiple-part carbon forms on a dot matrix printer.

There are also several good reasons for not choosing a dot matrix printer:

— They produce dot matrix print, which isn't as attractive as your readers have certainly seen elsewhere.

— They're noisy. More to the point, they produce a particularly irritating noise.

— Most of them require tractor-feed paper, which is cumbersome to work with.

Most computer stores will try to sell you a dot matrix printer as a general, all-around workhorse printer. Before you decide to buy one, however, you should become familiar with the alternatives. A few years ago, all the alternatives were too expensive to think about, but this situation is rapidly changing.

An Introduction to Daisywheel Printers

This section probably also contains a farewell to daisywheel printers.

A daisywheel printer is an electric typewriter which has been fine tuned for use with a computer. Rather than a type ball or a bed of keys, it has a wheel that resembles a flower— hence its name— wherein each petal holds a character.

Like an electric typewriter, a daisywheel printer produces perfect, fully formed characters. A daisywheel printer can print somewhat faster than an electric typewriter mechanism because the wheel spins, rather than constantly changing direction as a Selectric type ball does.

The principal drawback to daisywheel printers is that they've long since fallen out of fashion, and few are made anymore. By contemporary standards, daisywheel printers are very slow, pretty noisy, and can generally be gotten around by technology that is less troublesome to work with.

They're still handy for doing the occasional letter, however.

Advantages
and Disadvantages of Daisywheel Printers

The advantages of daisywheel printers are fairly obvious:

— They produce print that looks like it has come from a typewriter.

— They can produce single-page documents quickly.

The disadvantages are probably also fairly obvious:

— It's all but impossible to find one.

— They're noisy.

— They're slow.

— They're big and heavy.

— They don't do graphics.

An Introduction to Inkjets

Inkjet printer technology is quite new and very exotic. They have all the advantages of a daisywheel printer and none of the drawbacks. On top of this, they're fairly inexpensive.

You will recall from the discussion of dot matrix printers that one of the limiting factors to print speed was the heat generated by the dot matrix pins moving in the print head. To look at this another way, the same factor limits the ultimate *resolution* of dot matrix print. A print head that printed with enough pins to create the appearance of typewriter print would have to print so slowly as to make it useless, lest it melt itself.

Inkjet printers are very dense dot matrix printers without any moving parts in their print heads.

There are relatively few inkjet printers available at the moment— the two most common ones are the Hewlett-Packard DeskJet and the Canon BubbleJet. These two printers work slightly differently, although their output is about the same.

An inkjet printer works with a print head having a matrix of tiny tubes, rather than pins. Microscopic drops of liquid ink are propelled through the tubes onto the surface of a sheet of paper, producing characters. The printer's electronics define which tubes will fire ink drops.

True inkjet printers expel the ink from the print head tubes using electromagnetic fields. BubbleJet printers heat the ink, causing it to expand rapidly and discharge itself from the tubes, very much in the way gunpowder discharges a bullet from a rifle. In practice, both variations produce the same sorts of results.

Because nothing moves or gets particularly hot in an inkjet print head, the head can be small and there can be a very dense matrix of jets in it. The latest generation of inkjet printers can manage resolution of 300-dots-per-inch, which is sufficient to create type that appears to have been laid down with a printing press or a typewriter.

Inkjet printers are all but silent—the only sound you'll hear emanating from one is the whisper of paper feeding through the printer. They're also quite small. Hewlett-Packard DeskJets are about the size of a dot matrix printer. The Canon BubbleJet is a tiny thing not much larger than this book.

Figure 2.1 illustrates two popular inkjet printers.

Both printers have sheet-feeders, rather than tractor-feed mechanisms. This means that they accept standard photocopier paper, and produce output that doesn't require that its tractor-feed tabs be torn off and its sheets separated.

It's worth noting that sheet-fed printers such as inkjets usually have finite amounts of paper they'll hold at a time. By comparison, you can have as big a pile of tractor-feed paper hanging around behind a dot matrix printer as you like. The DeskJet can hold 250 sheets. The BubbleJet can only hold 30.

There are a few drawbacks to inkjet printers. The most notable is that they're not all that fast. A DeskJet, for example, prints two pages per minute on average, which is the bottom of the range for contemporary printers. This is suitable for a few letters, but you wouldn't want to print a long report this way.

The second drawback—and a rather messy one—is that the liquid ink used by inkjet printers is still liquid when it hits the paper, and it stays that way for several minutes thereafter. The drying time varies with things like ambient temperature and humidity, the type of paper you use and the relative density of the ink. However, the output of an inkjet printer will smear if you don't leave it alone to dry for a few minutes after it emerges from the printer.

This becomes more of a problem if you try to print large graphics—as opposed to text—with an inkjet printer. You can wind up with pretty soggy pages.

Finally, inkjet printers use fairly expensive supplies. Their ink cartridges cost a lot and they don't last all that long.

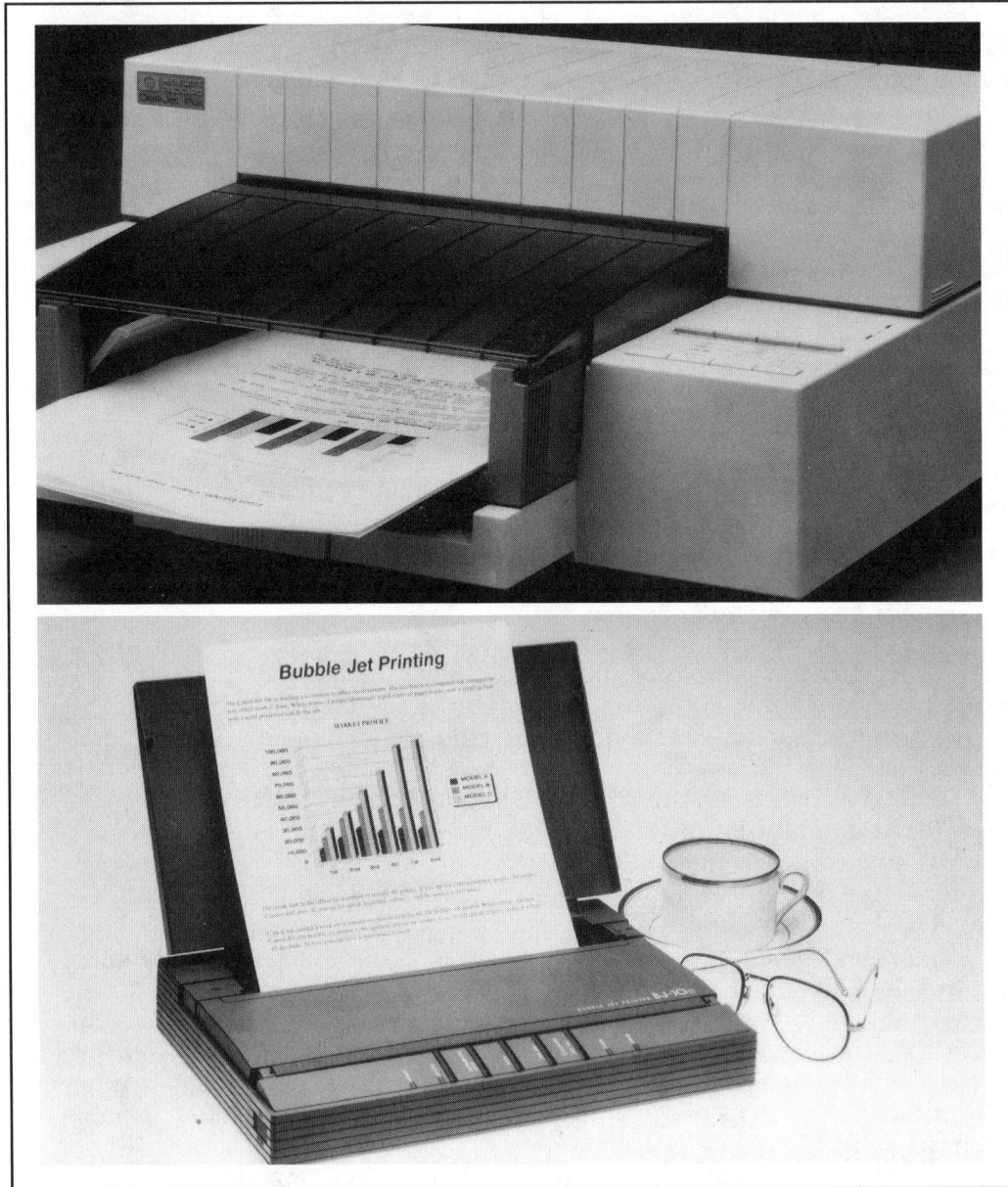

Figure 2.1: The Hewlett-Packard DeskJet and the Canon BubbleJet printers. (Photos courtesy of Hewlett-Packard and Canon USA)

Inkjet printers are probably the optimum choice for applications in which you want to produce relatively few pages of print and you want the results to look typewritten.

Advantages and Disadvantages of Inkjet Printers

The advantages of inkjet printers are as follows:

— They produce true typewriter quality print.

— They're silent.

— They're small.

— They're easy to use.

— They use sheet-fed paper.

These are the disadvantages of inkjet printers:

— They're slow.

— They're moderately expensive to maintain.

— Their ink can smear if you don't let it dry.

An Introduction to Laser Printers

A few years ago when laser printers first became available, they were huge, vastly expensive machines that required almost constant maintenance and ate expensive supplies as if they were candy. The first laser I bought required extensive cleaning at least once a week and monthly infusions of two hundred dollar toner cartridges. The cleaning was a delicate, tedious procedure that could take hours if the beast had seen fit to spray its internals with toner.

Laser printer owners could always be spotted in a crowd back then. They looked like chimney sweeps.

A lot of the unspoken dread of lasers has survived to this day. Fortunately, few of the real drawbacks to lasers have survived with it. Contemporary laser printers are no longer expensive, are pretty easy to maintain, and don't cost a lot to keep fed. My current laser printer gets cleaned monthly if I feel like it, and consumes twenty-dollar toner cartridges, or bulk photocopier toner if there's a lot of printing to do.

Laser printers produce fast, impeccable results and are well worth considering when you start thinking about printers.

Laser printers work through *xerography,* the same principal that drives photocopiers. In fact, a laser printer *is* a photocopier, save that its scanning plate is replaced with a laser. Xerography is based on a rather peculiar characteristic of a synthetic material called mylar. Mylar is a metallic green plastic that comes in sheets, or in cylinders—called "drums"— for use in laser printers. If you apply a static electric charge to mylar and then shine a light on it, the areas where the light is will lose their charge while the areas that are still dark will retain it.

Fine carbon particles scattered across the mylar will tend to be attracted to the charged areas. If you lay a sheet of paper over the mylar, the carbon can be induced to stick to the paper, where it can be baked into the surface to form a permanent impression.

In the case of a photocopier, the light pattern that shines on the charged mylar comes from a reflection of an original sheet of paper. In a laser printer, a laser scans across the mylar, turning on and off under computer control to form a matrix of tiny dots. Lasers are used because they can generate very precise points of light.

Contemporary laser printers can produce type generated at 300-dots-per-inch, as can inkjet printers. However, because laser printer dots are more precisely formed and because laser printer toner doesn't run and bleed like liquid ink does, the output of a laser printer will usually look a lot crisper than that of an inkjet.

Figure 2.2 illustrates some laser printer output.

Laser printers are fast—or, at least, they can be. Higher-end lasers can print twelve pages per minute or more depending on the content of the pages. Lower cost "personal" lasers print less rapidly, sometimes as slowly as four pages per minute. It's worth noting that all other things being equal, slower lasers usually produce slightly better print.

Laser printers use standard photocopier paper. You can also get laser-printer-compatible acetate, which will allow you to print overhead transparencies. Alternative printing materials will be touched on at the end of this chapter.

Laser printers are relatively quiet, but, because they use quite a bit of power, they require fans. High-end, high-speed lasers can require a lot of power and, as a result, pretty muscular fans. My laser printer draws one and a half kilowatts when it actually prints, requiring a special electrical service all to itself. Most lower-priced lasers have more modest power requirements.

Personal lasers, though surprisingly small considering what they do, still require some fairly significant table space. Aside from the "footprint"

Choosing a Computer

y car is the sort of car one owns if one works at home. A restored 1969 Oldsmobile Delta 88, it gets single digit gas mileage and is of a class of vehicles that can only be supported by the very rich or by people who don't drive to work. The very rich drive restored 1969 Cadillacs if they drive old cars at all.

Just as you might not walk into a car dealer and ask for a car with no further specifications—lest you wind up with something equally unsuitable to your needs as a 1969 Oldsmobile—so too should you have a bit more of a detailed shopping list when you go to buy the computer hardware and software for your home office. All in all, it's probably a lot easier to buy a car.

One of the things that most computer owners eventually realize—long after there's no further hope of exchanging their computer for what they *really* wanted—is that you aren't properly equipped to choose a computer until after you've owned one for a while. The way to really get the system you need is to buy four or five and see which one suits you best. If this sounds less than cost effective you've probably done well to buy this book.

The home office this book was written from has five computers in it. In its defense, they were not all bought to see which one suited it best. Rather, they form the ongoing tools for writing books like this one.

Before we get into some of the more productive areas of implementing the technology behind a home office, we're going to investigate the details of choosing a computer and, subsequently, the peripherals and other gadgets which will be associated with it. As much as is possible though the medium of paper and ink, you'll have the opportunity to sit before each of the aforementioned five computers—as well as the one upstairs

and the laptop in the back seat of the Oldsmobile—and try them out with the work you'll be doing and the level of computer expertise you have.

As with choosing a car, selecting a computer need be neither a shot in the dark or an dreadful, perilous decision wherein the only certain element is that you'll regret it for years to come. You can come to the right decision for you by proceeding through the choices logically, working out your own requirements and, most important, by ignoring everything you read, see or hear from IBM, Apple and Compaq.

The first part of this book will introduce you to the information you'll need to select the right computer for your home office. Read it all, even if you already have an idea as to what sort of computer you need.

Choosing Functions

Conventional wisdom in buying a computer maintains that you should select the functions you want the computer to perform, locate software which will perform the functions and then buy a computer which is capable of running the software. This is a really logical, linear approach to selecting hardware. However, just as it wouldn't help much in the real world of buying a car, it tends to fall apart when applied to computer systems, too.

There are very few functions available on one computer system which aren't immediately copied by someone for all the other major systems. All of the major applications which we'll discuss in this book can be had for pretty well any computer you wind up owning.

Clearly, the criteria for selecting a computer must get a bit more refined.

There are, in fact, a number of fairly concrete factors you can juggle while you're considering which computer to buy. They are:

- Cost effectiveness
- Ease of installation
- Ease of use
- Availability of cost effective software

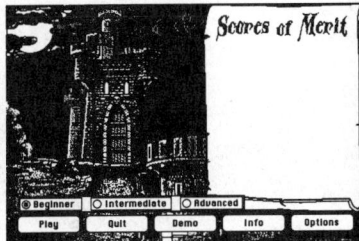

Figure 2.2: Output from a laser printer

of the printer itself (the amount of space it takes on a horizontal surface), you'll have to allow room for a paper tray and, in some laser printers, an output bin as well.

Figure 2.3 illustrates several laser printers.

Figure 2.3: The Apple LaserWriter II and the Fujitsu RX7400 personal laser printers. (Photos courtesy of Apple and Fujitsu)

One of the most important considerations in laser printers is how they're communicated with. This is called a "printer control language." There are two of these commonly in use. They'll be dealt with shortly when we discuss printer software compatibility.

Alternative Laser Printer Technologies

The most restrictive element of a laser printer is its laser. Lasers— even the small ones used in printers— require a lot of power. They're fragile, and include moving parts that can get out of alignment in time. It's difficult and expensive to design a mechanism that will scan a laser across the eight inches of mylar needed to print a normal letter-size sheet of paper while keeping the dot size and shape constant across the entire transit.

For this reason, quite a few laser printer manufacturers have come up with alternatives to using actual lasers. The most common laser substitute is called a light emitting diode array. You will have no doubt encountered light emitting diodes (or LED's)— they're used to form the red numerals on digital alarm clocks, and they serve as power indicators on stereos and activity lights on disk drives. A laserless laser printer based on light emitting diodes uses a strip of about 2500 very tiny diodes, which turn on and off just as the beam of a laser would.

Each diode is about 1/300th of an inch across.

Printers based on light emitting diode arrays usually cost about as much as traditional lasers. However, they are much less prone to misalignment, and hence require fewer trips to the shop. They usually produce nominally better print, but this will only become really noticeable if you print a lot of graphics.

My "laser" printer, a NEC LC-890, is actually based on a diode array.

A second alternative to lasers is what's called "liquid crystal shutters." Liquid crystals are found as the grey numeric readouts of digital watches. A liquid crystal panel has the ability to make parts of itself dark or transparent under computer control.

A liquid crystal shutter printer works by having a long, thin liquid crystal panel with a bright light behind it. As with a light emitting diode array printer, the panel is divided into about 2500 tiny sections, each one about 1/300th of an inch across. The printer's electronics can generate dots by "opening" some of the shutters, allowing light to pass through and strike the printer's mylar sheet.

The drawback to liquid crystals in any application is that they can't be switched on and off as quickly as a laser or a light emitting diode can be. As such, liquid crystal shutter technology finds itself used in lower-end, low-speed printers. However, those printers that employ it are generally small, require relatively little power, and are arguably more reliable than comparable lasers, as they have fewer moving parts.

How the Environment Affects Lasers

The performance you achieve with a laser printer can be affected by where you put it. This can be important in applications that involve having a laser printer at home.

To begin with, laser printers and their derivatives are pretty fragile as computer technology goes. Even the printers that don't have actual scanning lasers have elaborate paper-feeding mechanisms that must remain perfectly aligned if the printer is to produce good output.

Laser printers dislike being moved. At the very least, you have to remove the toner cartridge from a laser before it's transported. You'll probably have to clean it once it has been set up at its new location, too. Moving a laser printer risks disturbing its internals, and should be avoided.

For the same reason, laser printers should be placed on solid furniture that isn't likely to transmit vibrations to them.

The electrical considerations for lasers vary with the voracity of the printer in question. Lower-end personal lasers can usually be plugged into a wall outlet without undue consideration of the fuses. However, you should bear in mind that they draw a lot of power. They're also sensitive to noisy power, and a power-line filter is usually essential if you share your home with a furnace motor, air conditioner, coffee machine, or a few hair driers, all of which can introduce noise into your electric wiring.

Finally, the quality of print a laser printer produces can be affected considerably by the air around it. Lasers don't work very well if the atmosphere is hot or, worse still, damp. Dust and smoke upset them. All of these conditions can shorten the life of a laser printer as well as affect the quality of its output.

Laser Maintenance— What's Really Involved

The amount of routine maintenance you'll have to perform and the supplies you'll have to buy for a laser printer will be affected considerably by how you use the printer. To consider the extreme, a printer that lives in a clean, dry room and is used to print relatively few text pages will require a lot less maintenance than one that is situated in a hot, dusty attic and grinds out graphics all day.

Most laser printers require periodic cleaning, because toner frequently escapes from the xerographic drum of the printer and gets on its paper-feed mechanism or its light source. Most contemporary printers have been designed to make cleaning pretty simple— it can usually be performed with a soft cloth and a cotton swab in a couple of minutes.

The sort of things you print will determine how often you will want to clean your printer. I print pages that have a lot of graphics on them, and the print aberrations caused by a bit of spilled toner are quite noticeable on these. I clean the printer relatively frequently because of this—far more frequently than the printer manual says I should have to.

By comparison, the old first-generation laser I mentioned earlier has been relegated to printing letters. Letters consist mostly of white space with some very low density text. This printer required almost constant cleaning when it used to be used for graphics, but it can be left for months at a time now. Text- only printing vastly reduces the requirement for laser printer maintenance.

When you're shopping for a laser printer, you might want to have a peek inside the one you're thinking about with an eye to cleaning it. There's one very important consideration. The mylar drum of a laser printer is mildly light sensitive. If you shine a bright enough light on one for a long enough time—a 100 watt desk lamp at close range for several minutes will do— you'll permanently fog it and it will require replacement. Laser printer drums are quite expensive, running to a few hundred dollars in most cases.

Most lasers are designed to allow them to be opened for cleaning without placing the drum in direct light. There are exceptions. One notorious exception is the Fujitsu RX7100 series of printers, which places the drum directly under the pop-up top of the printer. It's notorious at one of the publishing companies I work with, in any case. They seem to feed it drums at about the same rate as most people feed their printers toner, and have taken to cleaning the printer under a blanket.

Laser printers have several parts that require periodic replacement. The most frequently replaced item is usually the toner cartridge. Toner will be used more rapidly if you print fairly dense pages. Toner cartridges vary widely in price among the various printers that use them, and each printer design has its own type of toner cartridge. One of the reasons I chose the laser printer I did was because its toner cartridges are very simple and very cheap—they consist of little more than a plastic box with a trap door to let the toner out.

Although you *can* refill a laser printer's toner cartridge, you'll invalidate the printer's warranty by doing so. The procedure requires an adventurous spirit: it might take a bit of experimenting to find a type of photocopier toner that suits your laser. It's also possible that some types of photocopier toner may violently disagree with your laser, necessitating a trip to the shop.

My older laser printer uses photocopier toner these days, both because its proper cartridges are expensive and because the only place that sells them is about seventy-five miles away.

The next most frequently replaced item in a laser printer is the mylar drum, or "photoconductor." Contemporary lasers usually house the drum in a plastic case, such that the whole works can be snapped in and out quickly with a minimal exposure to light. A few lasers still use discrete mylar drums—the drum consists of nothing more than a loop of mylar, which you must install on rollers inside the printer. These things are usually a bit cheaper, but they're easy to mangle while they're being installed.

Some printers use a combination toner cartridge and mylar drum, such that when the toner is exhausted both items must be replaced. This is a two-edged sword. It's expensive, because in most cases there will be some life left in the drum. However, it does ensure that you'll achieve more consistent print quality, as you'll never wind up printing on the last gasps of a drum. Partially deceased xerographic drums produce dreadful print.

Finally, there are several smaller items that usually need to be replaced from time to time. The most common of these is a cleaning pad, a felt strip that wipes each page as it passes across the hot fuser roller of the printer. Cleaning pads usually snap in and out with little trouble. However, the area they snap in and out of is exceedingly hot. Change the cleaning pad before you turn the printer on.

When you're pricing laser printers, make sure you figure out how much the supplies for the printers you're considering will cost. If there are several things to be changed in the printer, make sure you can buy them separately as you need them. Avoid elaborate toner cartridges that are easy to use but expensive. A printer designed around inexpensive supplies will live on long after the appeal of one that is quick and expensive has paled.

The Advantages
and Disadvantages of Laser Printers

As you might have realized by now, laser printers are a complex issue, and one that is beyond the scope of this book to cover fully. We have yet to deal with laser printer software and language, too. However, you might want to consider the following general characteristics of lasers and laser-type printers.

The advantages of laser printers include:

— They produce superb print.

— They're fast.

— They're fairly quiet.

— They use sheet-fed paper.

— Virtually all contemporary software supports laser printers.

The disadvantages of lasers include:

— They're expensive to buy.

— They're expensive to maintain.

— They're sensitive to their environment.

— They're big.

— They may require special electrical considerations.

— They can't be moved easily.

Laser printers are probably not the ideal choice for applications in which you want to print a few letters now and again. Likewise, they're not suited to doing thousands of mailing labels economically—a fast dot matrix printer would be preferable. However, if you anticipate printing reports or numerous letters—or if you just want fast, attractive, easy to read print all the time—a laser is a good choice.

PRINTER SOFTWARE STANDARDS

The simplest sort of printer is one that is described as a "dumb teletype." A dumb teletype printer simply accepts characters sent to it and prints them. It can respond to very few special commands—a carriage return will bring the print head back to the left side of the page, a line feed will move it down one line, and a tab will move it to the right by up to eight spaces.

Dumb teletype printers can be "driven," or printed to, by virtually any application that prints straight text. Unfortunately, a printer this simple can't do much except very simple text. It can't print in boldface or italic type, change fonts, handle graphics, do subscripts and superscripts—in short, it's incapable of many of the things that people traditionally have wanted printers to do rather than typewriters.

Many of the printers to be discussed in detail in this chapter default to behaving like dumb teletypes. However, in order to implement the extra features that make contemporary printers so powerful—and so confusing—they have built-in printer control languages. These take several forms, depending upon the printer in question.

Dot matrix printers have a very simple printer control language that is based on "escape sequences." An escape sequence is a string of special characters that begins with the Esc character, as created by the Esc key found on a PC keyboard, and then has some predefined additional characters to tell the printer to do something special. For example, the escape sequence *Esc G*— the Esc character followed by the letter G— will make most dot matrix printers begin to print in double-strike mode, that is, with bold text. The escape sequence *Esc H* will turn off the double-strike mode.

The first popular dot matrix printers to have a standardized set of escape sequences were the Epson FX-80 series of printers. While these printers have long been superseded, their escape sequences live on. Almost all contemporary dot matrix printers are capable of responding properly to FX-80 escape sequences. However, because contemporary dot matrix printers have more features than the old FX-80 printers had— beginning with more pins in their print heads— they usually in fact support supersets of the FX-80 sequences.

Having touched on the lore of dot matrix escape sequences, it's important to note that you will probably never have to deal with them directly. Unless you buy a particularly weird dot matrix printer, you will find that most popular applications will know how to set themselves up with all the right escape sequences. Thus, for example, if you have a Panasonic KX-P1124 dot matrix printer— a popular 24-pin printer at the moment— and you wish to use it with WordPerfect— a popular word processor— you would simply tell WordPerfect to install itself for this particular printer. The WordPerfect "printer driver"— the part of the WordPerfect program that deals with various printers— knows what all the pertinent escape sequences are. Thereafter, if you tell WordPerfect to print a particular bit of text in bold or italic or in double underlined expanded superscripts, it will automatically send down the proper escape sequence for your printer.

Drivers will be discussed later in this chapter.

The sets of escape sequences for dot matrix printers are a rather contentious issue at present. While most new dot matrix printer designs have begun with the Epson FX-80 sequences, they've added to the basic set in their own ways. As such, if you want to use only the more rudimentary features of a high-end dot matrix printer, your software need only know how to install itself for a common FX-80. However, if you want your near-letter-quality printer to actually print in near letter quality, the applications that will print to it must know the specific escape sequences for your specific printer.

For this reason, it's a great deal safer to buy a commonly used, popular dot matrix printer than it is to save a few dollars on one that claims to be just as good. The aforementioned Panasonic KX-P1124 and the Epson

LQ series of printers are good examples of state-of-the-art dot matrix printers that are widely supported— that is, recognized by most programs' print drivers.

There are great tottering heaps of printers that are less expensive than these machines and that claim to be just as capable. In many cases they are. However, just because a printer will print in near letter quality mode, for example, does not necessarily mean that your word processor or spreadsheet program will know the escape sequences to put it into near letter quality mode. Much of the frustration that people experience with setting up dot matrix printers stems from escape-sequence incompatibility problems.

Laser Printer Control Languages

Laser printers, while available from dozens of diverse manufacturers, do not exhibit the variations on their control languages that dot matrix printers do. There are only two laser printer control languages in common use, and understanding the distinction between them is pretty easy.

The two languages are PCL and PostScript. We'll deal with PCL first, as it's the simplest and the most commonly used language for lower-end printers. PCL stands for Printer Control Language.

The LaserJet Control Language: PCL

The PCL language was developed by Hewlett-Packard for their LaserJet laser printers. It has subsequently been duplicated by countless other laser printer manufacturers. It's somewhat similar to the escape-sequence structure of dot matrix printers, save that it does not exhibit the variations found in dot matrix printers.

To begin with, it's probably worth noting that true LaserJet printers— the ones actually made by Hewlett-Packard— come in a variety of flavors. The original LaserJet had fairly limited memory, and was really suitable only for printing text. It was followed by the LaserJet Plus, which had enough memory to print both text and graphics. Recently, these machines were superseded by the LaserJet II and then the LaserJet III, of which more will be said later. Most LaserJet-compatible printers actually emulate the LaserJet Plus.

When it first wakes up, a LaserJet behaves like a dumb teletype, just as a dot matrix printer does. If you send it text it will output your words in very crisp, 12-point Courier type.

The great thing about LaserJet printers is that you can print things in 12-point Courier even if your software doesn't know how to drive a LaserJet.

LaserJet printers support additional typefaces and type sizes by means of "downloadable" fonts and font cartridges that plug directly into the printer. Font cartridges would seem to be the simplest way to go, but very few of the applications discussed in this book will use the fonts in font cartridges. This makes for a good reason to read the following paragraphs on downloadable fonts.

If you wanted to print something in 12-point Times Roman type on a LaserJet, you would have to send it a file that tells it what 12-point Times looks like. This file is called a downloadable font, as it gets loaded from your computer— where it lives— to your printer each time you want to print using this particular typeface. In most cases, if a particular application wants to drive a LaserJet and print in a font other than 12-point Courier, it will actually handle the downloading for you when you go to print.

The drawback to downloadable fonts is that they must initially reside on the hard drive of your computer, and downloadable fonts are distressingly large. Furthermore, in situations that call for several different typefaces in a variety of sizes, you will require a lot of these distressingly large files. This gets compounded when you wish to have various type effects available, too. For example, in order to have Times Roman available in the normal weight, in italic, in bold, and in bold italic, you would need four files for every point size you wished to be able to use.

Downloading font files is also time consuming.

Finally, once downloaded, the font files you wish to print with must reside in the memory of your printer, which is finite. You can only use a limited number of different fonts in a LaserJet before you'll exhaust the available memory in the printer.

Having discoursed on all these limitations to LaserJet printers, it should be noted that they tend to become nettlesome only when a LaserJet finds itself being used in fairly extreme circumstances. If you plan to print documents in a reasonable number of fonts and at modest point sizes, the amount of hard drive space your fonts occupy and the time required to download the fonts to your printer will both be pretty manageable.

Unlike the PostScript language, which we'll discuss in a moment, PCL is not really a licensed entity. Laser printer manufacturers who wish to have their printers emulate the LaserJet Plus by duplicating PCL can do so without even asking Hewlett-Packard for permission. In addition, it's relatively easy to write a PCL "interpreter," the intelligence that drives a laser printer. All of these things mean that LaserJet Plus compatible laser printers are the least expensive lasers you can buy. They are also the most widely used lasers— perhaps for this reason— and there is little commercial software that prints that will not drive a LaserJet.

Advantages and Disadvantages
of PCL (LaserJet Plus Compatible) Printers

If your requirements of a laser printer are modest, you will probably find that LaserJet Plus compatible printers represent the most cost-effective way to get laser quality output. The slower ones cost less than a thousand dollars as of this writing, which compares favorably to many high-end dot matrix printers.

The advantages of LaserJet Plus compatible printers include:

— They're inexpensive.

— They're widely supported by most applications.

— They can behave like dumb teletypes for those few applications that don't support them.

The disadvantages of LaserJet Plus compatible printers are:

— They require font cartridges or downloadable fonts for every-thing beyond 12-point Courier.

— They have very limited graphic and text manipulation capabilities.

— They allow for only a finite number of different fonts on a page.

Some of the disadvantages might not make immediate sense just yet— the graphic potentials of lasers will become more apparent when we discuss PostScript printers in a moment.

As an aside, many LaserJet users will tell you that the limitation on the number of different fonts a LaserJet Plus will allow on a page is not a limitation at all, but rather a positive feature. Any page that includes enough different fonts as to exhaust the memory of a typical LaserJet Plus will probably be too busy looking to look good.

PostScript Printers

The PostScript language was developed by a company called Adobe. The first PostScript laser was the Apple LaserWriter, which was intended to be driven by Apple's Macintosh computers. For this reason, PostScript is often associated with Macintosh systems, although PostScript printers are available for both Macs and PCs. In fact, most of the PostScript printers—including Apple's own—come equipped with interfaces for both systems.

PostScript is a very sophisticated language. It can do things that a LaserJet could not even dream of. This includes printing halftone graphics, manipulating text, scaling text and graphics, and printing elaborate drawings.

Unlike fonts for LaserJet printers, PostScript fonts are not stored as actual images of characters. When you send a LaserJet a 24-point Times Roman font, you are actually sending it a series of images of the characters, such that it can simply copy each image onto the appropriate location of the paper when it's time to print something in that font. This is why a LaserJet needs a different font—a different set of images—for every typeface and size.

PostScript fonts are stored as outlines, or "vectors." Every character consists of a series of instructions regarding the drawing of the outline of the character and its subsequent filling. In order to produce 24-point Times Roman, the printer scales its outline for Times Roman to 24 points and generates an image from it.

This means that you can specify any size of any font available to a PostScript printer and have it print at the best resolution the printer can produce. This also means that the actual fonts take up much less space. Contemporary PostScript printers come with at least 35 fonts, all of which are available in any size you like. Figure 2.4 illustrates the usual font allotment of a PostScript printer.

In addition, you can download more fonts if you like. Downloadable PostScript fonts require a fraction of the disk space of LaserJet fonts, and download very quickly. Figure 2.5 illustrates a selection of downloadable PostScript fonts.

The fonts in Figure 2.5 came from the Adobe typeface library. This is a CD-ROM manufactured by NEC. If your application for a laser printer involves the need for lots of typefaces, you might be interested in this service. It gives you access to several hundred different faces at a cost of under a hundred dollars a font.

Not all software will take advantage of all the font and text manipulation capabilities of a PostScript printer. Word processors typically do not give you the option of printing all your text at a thirty degree angle, although a PostScript printer would be able to reproduce it if they did. If you get into desktop publishing you'll find that a PostScript printer will allow you to do a great deal more than a LaserJet can. This is also true for applications involving drawing programs.

Courier
Courier Bold
Courier Bold Oblique
Courier Oblique
Helvetica
Helvetica Bold
Helvetica Bold Oblique
Helvetica Narrow
Helvetica Narrow Bold
Helvetica Narrow Bold Oblique
Helvetica Narrow Oblique
Helvetica Oblique
ITC Avante Garde Gothic Book
ITC Avante Garde Gothic Book Oblique
ITC Avante Garde Gothic Demi
ITC Avante Garde Gothic Demi Oblique
ITC Bookman Demi
ITC Bookman Demi Italic
ITC Bookman Light
ITC Bookman Light Italic
ITC Zapf Chancery Medium Italic
✤✻■✳❂✪▼▲ (ITC Zapf Dingbats)
New Century Schoolbook Bold
New Century Schoolbook Bold Italic
New Century Schoolbook Italic
New Century Schoolbook Roman
Palatino Bold
Palatino Bold Italic
Palatino Italic
Palatino Roman
Σψμβολσ Σετ (Symbols Set)
Times Bold
Times Bold Italic
Times Italic
Times Roman

Figure 2.4: The standard 35 fonts of a PostScript printer

Akzidenz Grotesk Light
Americana Extrabold
Arnold Böcklin
Bauer Bodoni
ITC Bauhaus
Belwe Condensed
Caslon Open Face
COPPERPLATE GOTHIC 29BC
ITC Benguiat
ITC Berkeley Oldstyle
Candida
Eurostyle
ITC Eras Book
Fette Fraktur
Friz Quadrata
ITC Garamond
Glypha
Goudy Heavyface
Italia
Letter Gothic
OCR-A
Memphis Extrabold
Optima
PEIGNOT Demi
Post Antiqua
Present Script
Prestige Elite
ITC Tiffany Heavy
Trump Mediaeval
University Roman
VAG Rounded Thin

Figure 2.5: Some of the more exotic downloadable PostScript fonts

A lot more will be said about the advanced characteristics of Post-Script printers as they relate to the specific software packages to be discussed later in this book.

At present there are dozens of laser printers that will handle PostScript. This includes conventional 300-dot-per-inch lasers, but it also includes numerous very much more sophisticated—and expensive—output devices. PostScript is available for everything up to 2450-dot-per-inch laser phototypesetters. While it's unlikely that you will want to own a laser phototypesetter—they start at several hundred thousand dollars—the fact that they do exist and will handle the same PostScript as a laser printer can be quite useful. If your applications call for extremely good output, you can use a PostScript laser printer for proofs and take the PostScript output of your word processor, desktop publishing package, or drawing program down to a typesetting company on a floppy disk and have them generate final output for you.

With all the power of PostScript, you might well ask why anyone would consider buying a LaserJet-compatible printer. There are several reasons, but the predominant one has to do with the price of PostScript printers. The PostScript printer control language is a very complex thing, and not something that can be easily knocked off, as is the case for the LaserJet's PCL. In order to be able to produce a printer that handles Post-Script, the printer's manufacturer must pay a license fee to Adobe, the owners of PostScript, for every printer manufactured. This license fee is built into the price of a PostScript printer.

In addition to the cost of the PostScript license fee, PostScript itself requires more printer memory to run than PCL does. A typical Post-Script printer comes with two or three times as much memory as a Laserjet Plus printer does. Three megabytes is a useful minimum, and four and a half is not uncommon for printers that will be handling very complex pages.

As a very rough guide to the cost of PostScript, at the time of this writing the going price of low-end LaserJet Plus compatible printers was well under a thousand dollars. The lowest priced PostScript printers were hovering just below three thousand.

While PostScript printers are certainly not very cost-effective if you'll only be printing a few letters or straight, text-only reports, they begin to look very attractive indeed if you have designs on more elaborate output. The availability of numerous display fonts coupled with the relatively small size of downloadable PostScript fonts makes having lots of variety in the typefaces you use a practical consideration. Furthermore, if you envision including graphics in your output, a PostScript printer is eminently more useful than a PCL printer.

A DIGRESSION ON TYPEFACE NAMES

We have spoken thus far about typefaces such as Times Roman and Helvetica. These names are, in fact, trademark entities owned by a company called ITC. The typefaces themselves are ostensibly trademarked as well, although as of this writing a recent ruling by the United States patent office has stated that typefaces—the actual appearance of characters—cannot be protected by copyright.

Part of the cost of a PostScript printer's license pays for the right to use real Times Roman, real Helvetica, and all the other real fonts that are included with the printer. Adobe licensed the fonts from ITC.

LaserJet-compatible printers don't include licenses for the real ITC fonts. For this reason, they cannot legally call a font Times Roman, although they are allowed to print with a font that looks exactly like it. For this reason, software that prints to Laser-Jet-compatible printers usually does so with fonts having pseudonyms. The usual pseudonym for Times Roman is "Dutch." The usual pseudonym for Helvetica is "Swiss." (While the origin of "Dutch" is unclear, the derivation of "Swiss" is only mildly convoluted: The Helvetii were an ancient Celtic tribe that resided in what is now Switzerland.)

A single line of type set in real Times Roman and a Times Roman look-alike called Dutch would probably look pretty well identical. However, if you set several pages of identical copy in the two fonts, you'll probably find that they occupy significantly different amounts of space. The tiny differences in the widths of the characters tend to add up over several pages.

The printing industry largely uses real ITC fonts to do its typesetting, and the real ITC fonts in a PostScript printer will match the ITC fonts in a conventional phototypesetter perfectly. As as result, your laser printer output will match conventional typesetting if it's done with a PostScript printer. It probably won't if it's output by a LaserJet.

This may be important if your use of a laser printer involves printing addendums or inserts to existing typeset documents.

The Advantages
and Disadvantages of PostScript Printers

PostScript printers are very useful tools, but they are not the best choice for every application that involves lasers. You should consider what you might want to do with one before you start figuring out how to pay for it.

The advantages of PostScript printers include:

— A generous assortment of built-in fonts are all instantly available.

— Downloadable fonts are widely available.

— Downloadable fonts download more quickly and take up less hard-drive space than those for PCL printers.

— All fonts are available in any size you like.

— You can use real ITC fonts.

— PostScript graphics are very attractive.

— PostScript output can be sent to high-resolution PostScript phototypesetters.

The disadvantages of a PostScript printer are largely financial:

— PostScript printers are expensive compared to PCL (LaserJet Plus) compatibles.

PostScript and PostScript Clones

The PostScript language, while a very involved work and as such very difficult to emulate, is by no means impossible to rewrite. In fact, several printer manufacturers have chosen to duplicate PostScript rather than pay the license fees to Adobe for the use of real PostScript.

Printers that use synthetic PostScript, usually called PostScript "clones," are a contentious issue. They don't typically cost all that much less than real PostScript printers. They are not allowed to use real ITC fonts, but they usually provide you with font clones for at least the 35 standard resident faces of a real PostScript printer.

None of the PostScript clones to date have been perfect replacements for real PostScript. Their fonts don't look quite as good, and they seem to deteriorate more in applications that entail their being rotated or otherwise manipulated. PostScript clones behave oddly at times, and they frequently operate slower than real PostScript, which is none too fast to begin with.

Using a PostScript clone printer rather than a real PostScript device adds another element of complexity to your applications, with very little actual cost saving. If something refuses to print, you will have the printer itself to suspect, along with the usual cables and such. Unless you have a very good reason for wanting a PostScript clone, it's worth paying a bit extra for a real PostScript printer.

The Best of All Worlds

Thus far, we've discussed LaserJet Plus and PostScript printers separately. In fact, the two meet in many areas, and you may find that if you're unsure which sort of printer you really need, you can have it all ways.

To begin with, almost all contemporary PostScript printers have what are called LaserJet emulation modes. Very simply, on a printer so equipped, you can make the printer behave either as a LaserJet Plus or as a PostScript printer at the touch of a couple of switches. This is useful if you have software that does not know how to drive a PostScript printer, or applications in which a LaserJet can handle your printing more rapidly.

Note that in its LaserJet emulation mode, a multiple mode laser printer will not have any of the PostScript fonts available. Only 12-point Courier will be resident in the printer, just as with a real LaserJet. You can still download LaserJet fonts, of course. In most cases, a multiple-mode printer makes an enviable LaserJet Plus as it will have far more memory available than a typical LaserJet compatible.

It's probably worth noting that the process of switching between modes varies a lot between different multiple-mode printers. In some cases, such as with the NEC LC-890 I use, switching emulations involves nothing more than a few stabs at the front panel of the printer. Some laser printers that offer this feature require that you change several excruciatingly small, inconveniently located switches. If you spring for a multiple-mode laser, make sure that the procedure for changing modes is reasonable.

FOCUS ON THE HP LASERJET III

The current "real" LaserJet printer from Hewlett-Packard is the LaserJet III. There are actually several versions of this printer available at the moment, with varying capabilities.

The LaserJet III has several interesting characteristics that make it worthy of consideration. The most notable is a rather advanced print-engine design that generates variable size print dots. If you look closely at a diagonal line or a curve printed by a laser printer, you'll notice that the edge of the black area will be slightly irregular, due to to size of the printer dots. This characteristic is often called "the jaggies."

The LaserJet III's print engine cheats on the printer's 300-dot-per-inch resolution limit by adjusting the size of each printed dot. In situations where a full-size dot would make a line look noticeably jagged, it will shrink the dot. The result is 300-dot-per-inch output that looks very much tighter than that which is available from other 300-dot-per-inch lasers.

In many cases, conventional 300-dot-per-inch output is just a bit too rough to look like real typesetting, whereas the output of a LaserJet III seems just good enough to fool the eye.

A stock LaserJet III uses an enhanced version of the PCL language. This version, PCL 5, adds a number of interesting features to the basic PCL language we have discussed thus far, including an option for scalable fonts, much in the same way that PostScript handles its fonts. In time we should be seeing more software applications that make use of the new features of PCL 5. Until then, for most programs it's just a normal LaserJet Plus with tighter output.

One of the options available for the LaserJet III is a Post-Script cartridge. It costs less than $700. If you plug one in, your LaserJet III will become a PostScript printer— with the tighter output of the LaserJet III's tricky print engine.

It's worth noting two PostScript cartridges available for the LaserJet III. One is from Hewlett-Packard, and contains real Post-Script. The other, from a company called Pacific Data Systems, is in fact a PostScript clone.

The standard LaserJet III costs about $2500 list, or well under $2000 on the street. You'll probably also want at least a two-megabyte memory upgrade, which adds about another $300 to the price. It's a fairly slow printer, printing about seven pages per minute. You might want to have a look at the discussion of printing speed later in this chapter. The PostScript option costs about $700 dollars list, or about $500 on the street.

There is also a faster version of the LaserJet III, the LaserJet IIIsi, which prints seventeen pages per minute. It costs over $5000, though—a bit steep for home office applications.

Assuming that you can live with its uninspiring print speed, the LaserJet III is a superb, state-of-the-art laser printer. Even with its PostScript cartridge and a memory upgrade, its street price is typically under $3000, which makes it competitive with most PostScript printers. Its output is typically better than any other 300-dot-per-inch PostScript device as of this writing.

Figure 2.6 illustrates a LaserJet III printer.

Figure 2.6: A Hewlett-Packard LaserJet III, with optional envelope feeder (right). (Photo courtesy of Hewlett-Packard)

PRINTER SPEED—
LIES OF OUR CIVILIZATION

My NEC PostScript laser is rated at a print speed of twelve pages per minute. Of the over twenty thousand pages that have passed through it as of this writing, none have printed at anything like twelve pages per minute.

It is possible to set up a situation in which the printer will generate identical pages at a rate approaching twelve pages per minute, but the time it takes a laser printer to actually print something is determined by several factors, of which the speed of the printer's engine is usually only a minor one. The most important factor is usually the time it takes whatever is to be printed to download from your computer to the printer. For example, my printer will realistically print full-page graphics at a rate of about eight to ten pages per minute; but it takes about ten minutes to send the graphic to the printer. This is a rather extreme case.

In applications that involve printing text documents, downloading will include the downloading of fonts to the printer. In addition, when a PostScript printer receives a request to print some text in a particular font, it must scale the font to the size you need, which also takes time. Post-Script printers cheat on this a bit by doing what's called "idle time scaling." When a PostScript printer is sitting around with nothing to do, it amuses itself by scaling its fonts to sizes it thinks you might want to use later. If it turns out to have guessed right when you next send it something to print, the print time will be reduced somewhat.

After the initial font downloading and scaling are done with, text documents with one or two fonts can actually print at something approaching the rated print speed of a laser printer. Complex desktop publishing and drawing output usually prints very slowly indeed. As most of the time involved in printing these types of output is download time, a 4-page-per-minute printer probably won't take a lot longer than a 12-page-per-minute printer in these applications.

The download time of a document being printed will be affected considerably by the way your computer is interfaced to your printer. Most laser printers have both *serial* and *parallel* interfaces. You should be aware that a serial port operating at 9600 baud—the usual top speed for most laser printer serial interfaces—will move about half as much data to your printer as a parallel port in the same amount of time. A parallel interface is always preferable.

It's also worth noting that not all parallel ports print at the same speed. Higher-end computers usually have slightly faster printer ports, resulting in slightly better download times.

If you're uncertain whether you want a laser printer or a dot matrix printer, one thing you need to consider is the difference between the speeds of these two types of printers. Dot matrix printers are rated in characters per second rather than in pages per minute. Because of the very different natures of the two printing processes involved, there's no absolute relationship between the two values. However, as a rule of thumb, a dot matrix printer capable of 250 characters per second would print about as quickly as a laser printing at four pages per minute, all other things being equal.

CHOOSING A MACINTOSH PRINTER

Choice is a questionable thing. Having a lot of choices provides you with a lot of options, but it also leaves you with a lot of thinking to do to come up with an appropriate final decision.

The Macintosh offers far fewer choices for printers than a PC does. If you're even mildly familiar with Macintosh systems, it's probably not necessary to mention that the printers available to a Macintosh user represent the more expensive output options.

For practical purposes, all Macintosh printing must be done to printers that can communicate over *AppleTalk*. We'll have a more complete look at what AppleTalk is in a moment. The effect of this is that Macintoshes can only deal with printers that have AppleTalk ports.

Real Macintosh gurus will object to the preceding paragraph. There are actually other approaches to printing from the Macintosh. You can for example drive a LaserJet Plus from a Mac with some fairly exotic extra software. However, these alternatives are so complex and generally funky as to make them inadvisable for someone who isn't intimately familiar with the inner workings of a Mac. If you have chosen to work with

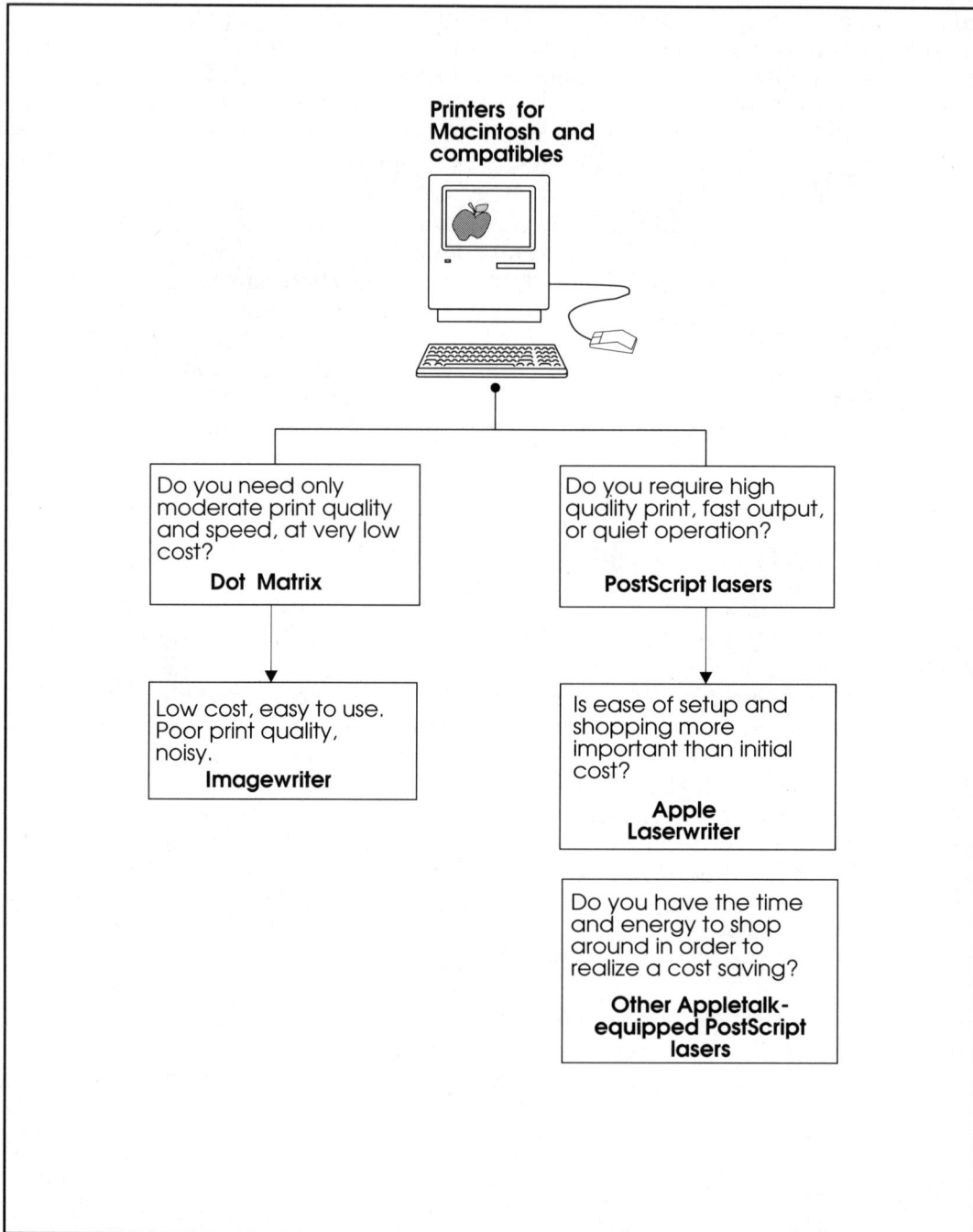

Printers for Macintosh and compatibles

Do you need only moderate print quality and speed, at very low cost?

Dot Matrix

Do you require high quality print, fast output, or quiet operation?

PostScript lasers

Low cost, easy to use. Poor print quality, noisy.

Imagewriter

Is ease of setup and shopping more important than initial cost?

Apple Laserwriter

Do you have the time and energy to shop around in order to realize a cost saving?

Other Appletalk-equipped PostScript lasers

a Macintosh system because it's easy to set up and use, this probably isn't the place to suddenly embrace complexity.

The only commonly available dot matrix printers that are equipped to communicate over AppleTalk are the Apple ImageWriters. These are fairly good, state-of-the-art printers and there's little more to say about them. An ImageWriter will produce dot matrix print that is acceptably tight and acceptably fast.

A Macintosh will deal with any PostScript laser printer that has an AppleTalk port. As such, you can use a real Apple LaserWriter or any of several dozen other PostScript lasers that also support AppleTalk.

Using MacWrite, the default word processor fro the Macintosh, you can select the font you want text to appear in. The font names are contained in a menu. When you're printing to a dot matrix printer, the actual font images that appear on the screen are used to drive the printer as well. If you print to a PostScript printer, the text on your screen will be printed in real PostScript fonts, as has been discussed in this chapter.

When it's editing a document, MacWrite has no idea what sort of printer that document will be printed to. As such, when you install a PostScript printer driver on a Mac, you'll also be installing fonts that correspond to the Times Roman and Helvetica fonts— among others— that live in a PostScript printer.

When you use these fonts in a MacWrite document, the same text with the same spacing and whatnot will print on both dot matrix and PostScript printers, although obviously it will look much better on a PostScript printer. The dot matrix version will be, in a sense, a picture of the image of the text on your screen.

With most PC applications, by comparison, the text to be printed is sent to the printer to be printed in whatever font it has been told to use. Thus, text sent to a dot matrix printer in draft mode will print with less resolution than text sent to a printer in near-letter-quality mode.

The important thing about all this is that a Macintosh has fairly coarse dot matrix print, tight elegant PostScript print, and nothing to speak of in between. The ImageWriter does have several density modes and there is a draft mode, but the example shown in Figure 2.7 is as close to letter quality as a Macintosh can manage on a dot matrix printer.

Sixth Annual Toy Drive & Fast Food Lunch
(A DIVISION OF THE EXTREMELY LARGE CORPORATION INC.)
1 PRESTIGE AVENUE
ARDWALLOW, CA
95092

Augustus P. Robes
1313 East Entwhistle Terrace
Ardwallow, CA
95010

Dear Mr. Robes,

Thanks massively for the fine collection of broadswords, crossbows and maces which you have so kindly donated to our annual toy drive. While I am certain that these items were donated in the kindest spirit of generosity, we most reluctantly cannot accept them. It has been our long standing policy not to provide the children with toys which require police permits.

I must also tell you that while we were all greatly entertained by the rhinoceros which you kindly included with your donation, this, too, cannot be used in our toy drive. Many of the children will be most disappointed by this, I am certain. However, the rhino has now speared a number of the neighborhood cats and a parked Toyota.

I am informed that California has some legal statutes regarding the keeping of endangered species by registered charities. I am not certain if this regards the rhino or the Toyota.

Thank you again for your thoughtfulness. I hope that we may look forward to your generosity next year.

Sincerely,

Paulina O'Blivion
Rejectionist

PO/mac

Figure 2.7: A letter printed on an Apple ImageWriter

APPLETALK—A BRIEF DIGRESSION

Before you can fully understand how the Macintosh deals with its printers, you should understand a bit about AppleTalk. With the exception of very ancient and now wholly obsolete "thin" Macintosh systems, all Macs talk to their printers over AppleTalk.

AppleTalk is what is called a "local area network," although it's a very primitive one by contemporary standards. It's also an elegantly simple one, and as such it doesn't require one tenth the sweat and aggravation that is traditionally the lot of network users.

A local area network is a way for multiple computers and printers— and occasionally other devices— to share their resources. In the case of a home office, it's unlikely that you'll actually want multiple Macintosh systems to share a printer, but should you wish, AppleTalk will allow you to make it happen painlessly.

The hardware to make AppleTalk go is part of every Macintosh and every Macintosh-compatible printer. In order to connect an AppleTalk printer to a Mac, all you need do is plug an AppleTalk connector into the AppleTalk ports of both devices and turn on the power.

Actually setting up a Macintosh to print to a printer over AppleTalk is a bit more involved than connecting the computer to its printer, but only just.

If you want to connect a second Macintosh to the printer, you can connect its AppleTalk port to the network and get to work.

AppleTalk cables are small and they're fairly immune to interference. You can run them for long distances without having to worry about degradation of your data over them.

AppleTalk is a bit brain damaged as full networks go, but it makes an exceedingly intelligent print manager. It allows users on a network with multiple computers and multiple printers to tell the network which of the printers to use. The network will keep track of which documents are to be output to which printer.

Most contemporary PostScript printers come with three interfaces, one of which is an AppleTalk port. Thus, a Macintosh need not be connected specifically to an Apple LaserWriter. Any AppleTalk-equipped PostScript laser will suffice. There are numerous PostScript lasers that offer more cost-effective printing than an Apple LaserWriter, which is a fairly expensive laser printer.

Chances are you will not be using AppleTalk for much more than as a way to connect a single printer to a single computer, so its various networking functions will not be important. For a single home office user, the most relevant aspect of AppleTalk is its unsurpassed ease of setup.

CHOOSING A PC PRINTER

There are a lot more choices to be made if you're thinking about a printer for a PC system. If you want very inexpensive printing and aren't too concerned about what it looks like, you should choose a dot matrix printer. You can fine tune your choice a bit— the very lowest price printing is available using 9-pin printers, although it looks awful. If you can afford a 24-pin printer the results will look somewhat nicer.

If the appearance of what you print, the time it takes to print it, the convenience of handling the pages, or the amount of noise your printer makes are more important than the price of the printer, you should consider either an inkjet or a laser printer. Inkjets are suitable for applications that involve primarily text on relatively few pages.

The decision in laser printers will lie between LaserJet compatibles and PostScript printers. The former are cheaper and suitable for applications that largely involve text. The latter are more capable— and considerably more expensive— but are a better choice for applications in which you anticipate using lots of fonts or extensive graphics.

COLOR PRINTERS

Thus far, all the printers we've discussed have printed in every color of the rainbow, provided it was black. There is a growing number of printers that can print in color. While color printing technology is still a bit primitive in some respects— and painfully expensive in others— it does exist for those applications that really demand it.

There are several strata of color printers. The least expensive are color dot matrix printers, of which there are quite a few. These also produce the least attractive results, of course.

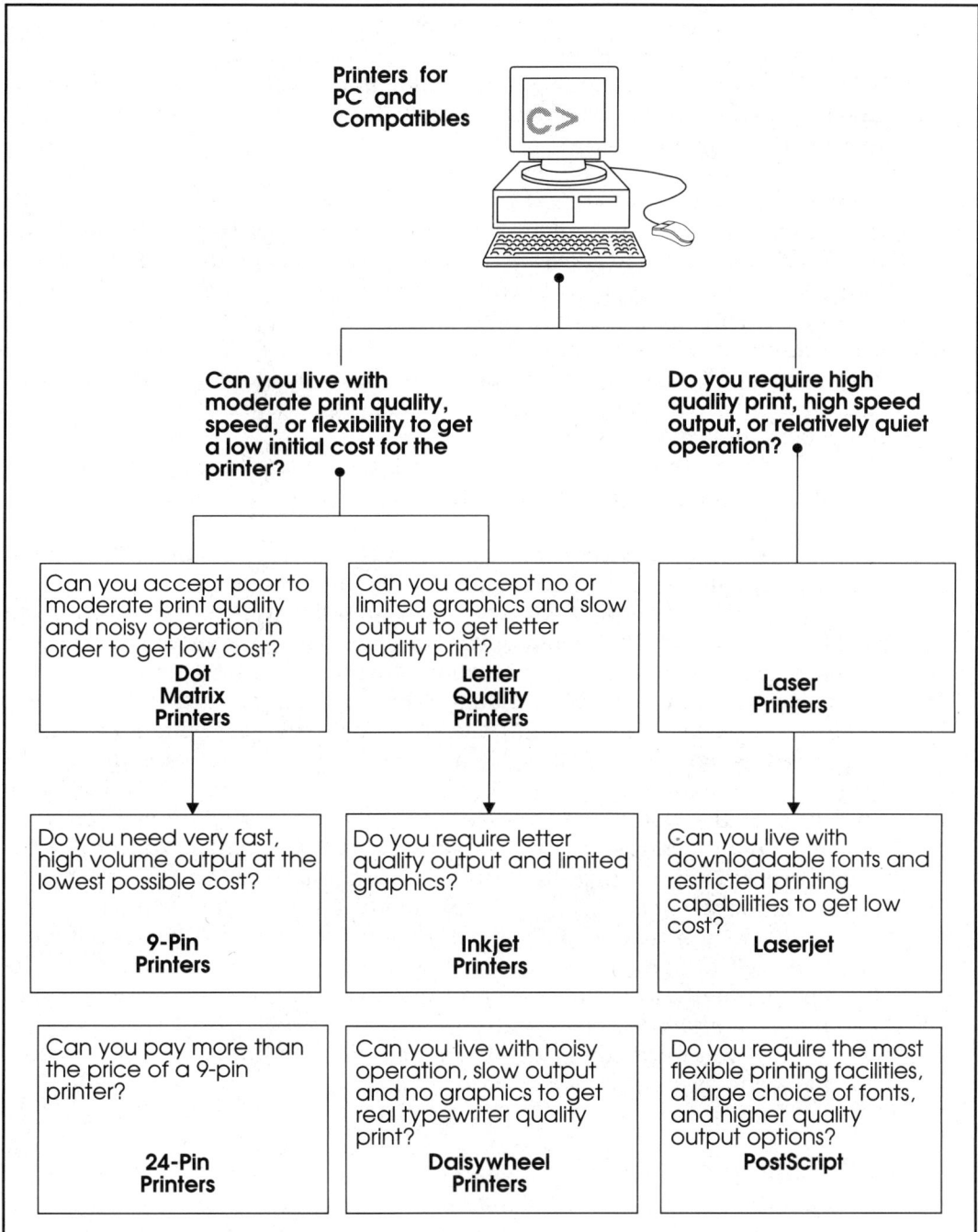

Printers for PC and Compatibles

Can you live with moderate print quality, speed, or flexibility to get a low initial cost for the printer?

Do you require high quality print, high speed output, or relatively quiet operation?

Can you accept poor to moderate print quality and noisy operation in order to get low cost?
Dot Matrix Printers

Can you accept no or limited graphics and slow output to get letter quality print?
Letter Quality Printers

Laser Printers

Do you need very fast, high volume output at the lowest possible cost?

9-Pin Printers

Do you require letter quality output and limited graphics?

Inkjet Printers

Can you live with downloadable fonts and restricted printing capabilities to get low cost?
Laserjet

Can you pay more than the price of a 9-pin printer?

24-Pin Printers

Can you live with noisy operation, slow output and no graphics to get real typewriter quality print?
Daisywheel Printers

Do you require the most flexible printing facilities, a large choice of fonts, and higher quality output options?
PostScript

Color dot matrix printers handle color printing with special ribbons having four colored bands. The four colors are black, cyan, magenta and yellow. Cyan is a medium blue color and magenta is somewhere between red and purple. These are, in fact, the primary colors used for commercial printing as well.

In theory, if you mix the appropriate amounts of these four primary colors you can arrive at any color you want. Unfortunately, a color dot matrix printer does not provide any way to mix colors per se. Some clever software is able to generate the illusion of other colors by "dithering" the four colors provided by such a printer. Dithering is a process whereby the appearance of color mixing can be achieved by printing patterns of colored dots. For example, if you wanted to produce a green color that was made up of 50 percent yellow and 50 percent cyan, you could arrive at this by printing an area in which every even numbered dot was yellow and every odd numbered dot was cyan.

This works reasonably well in theory, but it doesn't look that attractive on a dot matrix printer because of the fairly coarse resolution that such a printer provides.

Color dot matrix printers might be suitable for quick and nasty business graphs, but the results will rarely impress people.

The other end of the spectrum includes a number of very exotic color print engines. The most popular of these as of this writing is the QMS ColorScript 100, which starts at about ten thousand dollars. It's a PostScript printer that arguably produces the best color printing of any paper color output device available at the moment. It comes with 35 standard fonts, just as most conventional PostScript printers do. A modestly complex page can take several minutes to print, and when you figure in the cost of the supplies the ColorScript's output goes for about fifty cents a page.

If you want something beyond a color dot matrix printer but you aren't quite ready for a printer that costs as much as a new car, there is one option in between. The Hewlett-Packard PaintJet starts at less than a thousand dollars. It's actually a color inkjet printer, but its resolution is good enough to allow it to mix color by dithering with acceptable results. It's also popular enough to be supported by most of the software packages you might like to print color with.

If you need color output on a reasonable budget, PaintJets are a good place to start.

Alternatives to
Black Ink and White Paper

There are a lot of things you can do with a printer beside simply printing on sheets of paper. Many of these can open up new applications for your printer and your computer in general.

One of the most useful things to replace your paper with is labels. Sticky labels are available with tractor-feed backings to feed through a dot matrix printer and as sheets that can be printed with a laser. They come in a variety of sizes, and are ideal for things like address labels, file folder identifiers and so on.

My life changed forever when I realized I could load up the laser printer with a handful of Avery label sheets and never address another envelope again.

Many printers come with special envelope feeders that allow you to have your computer address a stack of envelopes with no further human intervention. This is even better— and cheaper— than using sticky labels.

Laser printers need not print on paper at all. You can get special laser printer acetate, allowing your laser to create overhead transparencies. Be warned, though— it gets quite hot inside a laser printer. If you attempt to print on conventional artist's acetate you'll probably find it has become part of the fuser roller of your printer, necessitating a trip to the shop.

Some types of laser printer toner cartridges are available with toner in colors other than black. You can, for example, have brown toner on buff laser printer paper, which looks pretty refined and executive. It's not practical to switch between multiple toner colors frequently, however. It takes quite a few copies to exhaust the toner that is currently in your printer so that the new color prints properly.

In this light, it's probably worth noting that not all paper is suitable for running through a laser. Photocopier paper will work fine, and there are all sorts of fancy papers that are specifically designed for use with a laser. However, choosing paper without some consideration of what it will be subjected to inside your printer can leave you with bad output at best and an ailing laser at worst.

Specifically, avoid very glossy paper. Toner doesn't stick to it very well, and the clay that's used to make it glossy can build up on the hot fuser roller of the printer, degrading subsequent copies. Paper with a very fibrous texture may tend to leave fibers behind, which will collect toner and leave streaks on subsequent sheets. Heavily textured paper doesn't collect the toner from the xerographic drum of a laser very well, resulting in irregular print.

AUTHOR'S CHOICE

There are a few situations left in which a dot matrix printer really makes sense. You might want one if you're really strapped for cash, if you plan to produce thousands of mailing labels, or if you need a small, rugged printer that you can carry around. Outside of these admittedly common and important situations, dot matrix only *looks* like a good deal. Its cost effectiveness is quickly being eroded by tumbling laser printer prices.

The best dot matrix printer I've used in the last few years has been the Panasonic KX-P1124, with the Roland Raven series of printers being a pretty close second.

Of the two inkjet printers we've discussed in this chapter, I'd choose the Hewlett-Packard DeskJet Plus. It holds lots of paper and will behave somewhat like a LaserJet for most applications.

If I had to buy another laser (well, pseudo-laser) printer I'd still choose the NEC LC-890 series printers. They do good work and they just never die. They also use exceedingly economical supplies.

The Hewlett-Packard LaserJet III is the best low-end laser I've encountered in a while. The additional print quality offered by its engine makes it worth the three or four hundred dollars more it winds up actually costing on the street compared to other low-end lasers. Being able to upgrade to PostScript for about five hundred dollars more makes it doubly attractive.

SUMMARY

As with choosing a computer, choosing a printer is a fairly logical process of defining your needs and locating a box that will address them. Unfortunately, weird little printers are far more common even than weird little computers. While some of these represent pretty respectable hardware, it's very difficult to know what's going on inside from the few words on the box.

Much of the software in use today makes some pretty serious demands on printers. Applications that print graphics— or use a printer's graphic modes to produce attractive text— are particularly intolerant of quasi-compatible printer emulations.

In addition, printers represent the most mechanically intensive part of a microcomputer system. There are more moving parts in most printers than in all the other hardware associated with them combined. Assume that sooner or later your printer will need some service, even if it's just a new print head or a replacement photoconductor cartridge. Those aforementioned weird little printers frequently turn out to be very hard to get parts for a few years later when you need them.

It's important to distinguish between printers that are really intended for casual, very low-volume home computer applications and those upon which you can rely for business uses. If you can't afford the time to deal with a quirky printer, it's worth buying one built by a manufacturer you've heard of.

3

THE OPERATING SYSTEM

The first aspect of your computer that you'll encounter after you've bought all the parts and plugged them together will be its operating system. For the Macintosh, this is the Finder, and for PC compatibles it is MS-DOS — usually just called DOS. There are, in fact, other operating systems for both these machines, but they're sufficiently exotic as to be beyond the scope of this book.

This chapter will walk you though the important parts of your operating system. When you're finished with it you will not know how to make it do all the tricks that fourteen-year-old computer hackers can manage; however, you'll be able to work with your computer with sufficient dexterity to use its basic functions.

You should not regard this chapter as being a replacement for the manual that accompanied your computer, although you might find it to be a convenient way to cheat on the manual a little. For example, although DOS now supports piping, drive substitution, and network management, you'll never use them. The manual for DOS explains them in copious detail, but all you have to know about them is that they're more than you need to know to operate your computer effectively.

This chapter will deal only with the parts of the PC and Macintosh operating systems that are actually germane to the basic functions of your computer. You may wish to refer to your manual later on if something comes up that you don't understand, or if you want to do something peculiar that isn't covered herein.

Either of the operating systems discussed in this chapter can be beaten into submission in about ten minutes if you only deal with the relevant aspects of them. We'll move to those directly after the following introduction.

HOW COMPUTERS WORK— THE VERY SHORT VERSION

When you first start a personal computer, it initiates a process called its "bootstrap," or "booting." This expression is derived from the notion of pulling one's self up by one's own bootstraps. In this case, the computer uses successively smarter chunks of its operating system to load still more chunks of its operating system.

After three or four levels of bootstrapping, a computer will have reached the point where you can see that it's finished starting up. In the case of a PC there'll be a C prompt on the screen and the cursor will be flashing. A Macintosh will have its desktop displayed and the mouse cursor will be free to scurry about the screen.

In its simplest sense, a computer consists of some memory and a processor. Programs are loaded into the memory. A program consists of a huge string of instructions to the processor in processor language, or, more properly, "machine language." The instructions are very primitive— they do things like adding two numbers together or moving things from place to place in memory.

The processor starts processing as soon as the computer is powered up, and never stops until it's turned off. It handles the bootstrap procedure, and when everything is ready for you to do some work, it waits by executing what's called a "loop." The loop that the processor waits in while you're trying to decide what to do next simply executes a few instructions over and over again.

Because the processor must always be processing instructions— because it must, in effect, always have a program to run— the last thing the bootstrap process does is to load the operating system into memory and set the processor to running it. The operating system is just a big program that, among other things, lets you choose the application program you'd like to run next. In the case of a PC, it does this by waiting for you to type a command. The Macintosh waits for you to click on the icon of the program you want to run. In both cases, the function of the operating system is the same.

When you run an application program— such as WordPerfect or MacWrite— the program is loaded into memory above where the operating system is. The processor loses interest in the operating system and begins to run your program. When you exit your program, the processor returns to running the operating system. While the recently executed copy of your program is actually still in memory where you left it, it has, as far as your computer is concerned, ceased to exist.

Figure 3.1 is called a memory map. It illustrates where things are in memory when a program is running.

You need not know anything about memory maps to use your computer. You might, however, find that a basic understanding of what's happening inside your system will be useful in making sense of what transpires when you hit the Enter key or click your mouse.

A computer can be thought of as having two sorts of memory. Its actual internal memory is very fast, but anything stored in it will vanish as soon as the power is switched off. In addition, there's a relatively small amount of it. The second sort of memory is disk storage. It takes more time to store or retrieve information from a disk, but disk data doesn't die when you turn your computer off. Furthermore, disks can hold thousands of times more information than internal memory. It's not uncommon to find a computer with a hundred megabytes of disk space. Computers with a hundred megabytes of memory are, as yet, relatively hard to come by.

Everything stored on a disk is stored as a "file." A file consists of a number of "bytes." The file that contained this chapter before it was

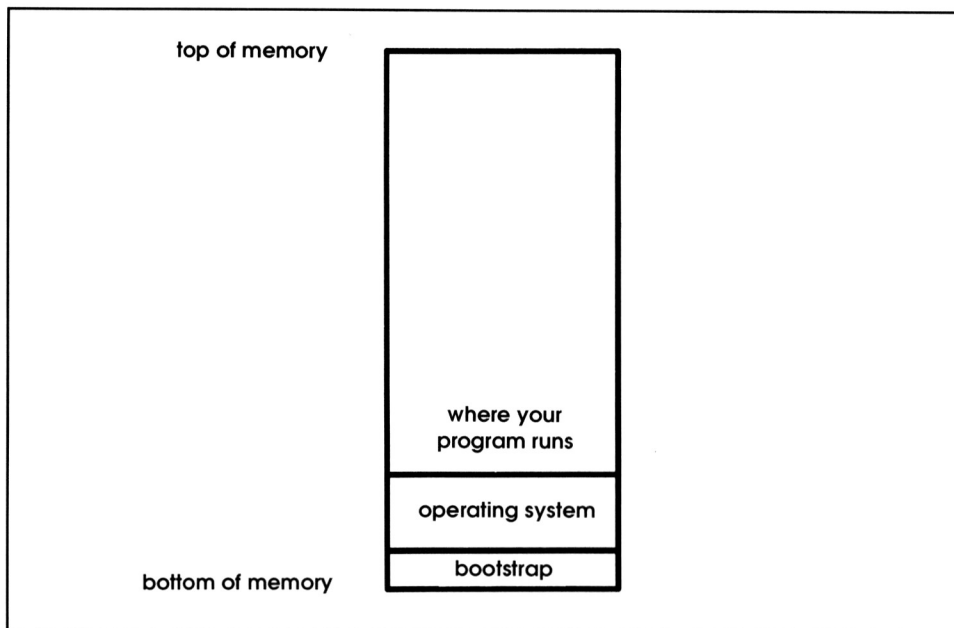

Figure 3.1: A very simple memory map

typeset and printed was a text *data file,* and each byte was a character. In a *program file,* each byte is an instruction to the processor. Other sorts of files use their bytes for other purposes, according to the nature of the file in question.

In general, disks do not know what to make of the contents of their files. Files are just long strings of meaningless bytes to a disk. The operating system will know how to deal with a limited number of types of files. Specifically, the operating system of your computer can tell which files are programs and which are not. Thus, it will not run a text file containing your ten favorite clam sauce recipes as if it were a program.

Operating systems are largely prohibited from knowing anything about files that are not actual programs, because these files pertain to other programs that you have for specific applications. The Macintosh cheats on this rule a bit by having a way to educate its operating system regarding certain types of non-program files.

The most important thing to keep in mind about your operating system as you read though the rest of this chapter is that it is a pretty simple beast at heart. All it wants to do is run programs. Programs are files of machine instructions. The programs, in turn, may use other files on your disk. Unless it has been put there in error, every file on your disk is either a program or a file that relates to a program in some way. A few will be files that relate to the operating system itself.

USING DOS

To begin with, DOS stands for "disk operating system." The PC environment seems to try to make up for what it lacks in simplicity of operation with easily understood acronyms.

The part of DOS that displays the C prompt and accepts commands typed at it is called its "command interpreter." Every time you type one or more words at the C prompt and hit Enter, it tries to use the first word as a command. All the words after the command are called "arguments." Arguments will be discussed in a minute.

The command interpreter has several built-in commands; that is, there are a few words it knows how to deal with without any further assistance. If the command you have typed is one of these, it will perform the appropriate function and then return you to the C prompt, awaiting another command.

All files on a DOS system are named with the following convention. The file name itself can be up to eight characters long. The file also has an "extension," which can be up to three characters long. The extension specifies the nature of the file to some extent. By convention, file names are written with the name and extension separated by a period. Hence, you might encounter files named COMMAND.COM, README.TXT, or DBASE.EXE.

As an aside, the command interpreter is stored in the file COMMAND.COM.

File names are usually written in uppercase characters only. The command interpreter doesn't care which case you use when you type a command. Hence, the command *TYPE* and the command *type* are identical to the command interpreter.

Files that contain programs that can be run have the extension EXE or COM. These stand for "executable" and "command," respectively. You can think of them as being interchangeable for the moment.

If the command you have typed is not one that the command interpreter knows how to handle itself, it looks at the disk to see if there is a file with a name corresponding to your command and the extension COM. For example, if you were to type the command "SING"—a command I just made up—the command interpreter would look for a disk file called SING.COM. If it found such a file, it would load it into memory and run it. When SING.COM was finished running, it would return control to the command interpreter, which would display a fresh C prompt.

If the command interpreter cannot find SING.COM, it then looks for SING.EXE, handling it as it would have done for SING.COM.

If its search turns up neither SING.COM nor SING.EXE, the command interpreter has one last thing to try. It can look for SING.BAT. The BAT extension stands for "batch." A batch file is a list of commands to the command interpreter. If it encounters SING.BAT, it will execute each command it finds in SING.BAT as if they had been typed at the C prompt by you.

If the command interpreter can't find SING.COM, SING.EXE, or SING.BAT, it will print "Bad command or file name" and return you immediately to the C prompt to have another try.

As you can see, this system is very flexible. If you take the proper steps to add a new program to your hard drive, it will immediately become one of the commands that the command interpreter knows how to deal with, simply by virtue of its existing in a searchable place on the disk.

The Structure of a Disk

The hard drive in my computer will hold a hundred and fifty megabytes. At the moment, there are over four thousand files on it. Even if it were possible to simply put them all together in one area of the drive, the resulting confusion would defy imagination.

In order to make keeping the files that relate to particular applications separate from those pertaining to other, unrelated functions, DOS allows you to structure your hard drive as a tree, or what the Macintosh refers to as a "hierarchical file system." Figure 3.2 illustrates the structure of part of my hard drive, as seen by DOS. Don't worry if some of this is a bit unclear as yet.

In this case, the roots of the tree are on the left side of the diagram and the tree has grown outward— an unlikely concept. Most people conceive of drive trees as growing straight down, which, when you think about it, is equally unlikely.

When you first turn on your computer and get a C prompt, you will be "logged into" the "root directory" of your hard disk. You can create what are called "subdirectories" that branch off from the root.

A subdirectory is a place to put files. Files placed in one subdirectory will not be visible from other subdirectories or from the root. Most people come to think of subdirectories as being rooms, with further rooms leading off them— a fairly workable analogy.

If you like the room analogy, you might imagine going to the word processing room to process words and to the database room to manage your data.

You might have cause to create sub-subdirectories in this model. For example, I use my word processor to write letters, to write magazine articles and, at present, to work on this book and one other. Rather than have the fifty or so files that all this entails in the subdirectory with my word processor, I have sub-subdirectories for each function, as shown in Figure 3.3.

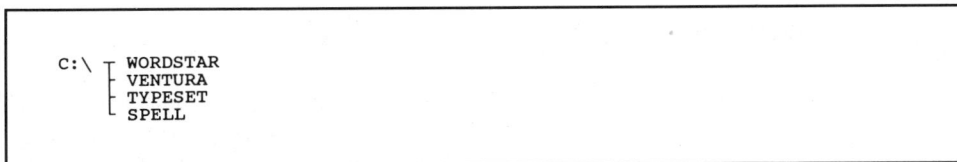

```
c:\ ┬ WORDSTAR
    ├ VENTURA
    ├ TYPESET
    └ SPELL
```

Figure 3.2: A drive "tree"

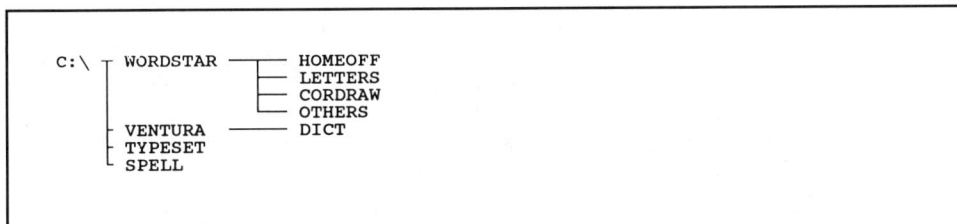

```
c:\ ┬ WORDSTAR ──────┬── HOMEOFF
    │                ├── LETTERS
    │                ├── CORDRAW
    │                └── OTHERS
    ├ VENTURA ─────── DICT
    ├ TYPESET
    └ SPELL
```

Figure 3.3: Sub-subdirectories

As with file names, subdirectory names can be up to eight characters long.

Under DOS, a file has a name, an extension—as we've discussed—and what's called a "path." A path specifies where on your hard drive a particular file is located. The text file for this chapter of the book you're reading is called CH03.WS. The name is CH03—Chapter Three—and the extension, WS, is one that I use to keep track of files that relate to the word processor I use, WordStar.

The CH03.WS file lives in the subdirectory HOMEOFF, which in turn lives in the subdirectory WORDSTAR, which lives on drive C.

If I were in the same subdirectory as CH03.WS, I could access it by its name alone. If you do not tell DOS that a file you're interested in has a path, DOS assumes that the file in question is in the same subdirectory as you are.

In order to work with the file CH03.WS in WordStar, if I was in the same subdirectory as the file, I would type

WS CH03.WS

For the moment, this also assumes that WS.COM or WS.EXE also exists in the same subdirectory. We'll get back that point in a moment when we deal with search paths. This command invokes WordStar and tells its to work with the file CH03.WS.

If I were somewhere other than in the same subdirectory as CH03.WS, I could still access the file by supplying a path to it. Here's the path and the file name in question:

C:\WORDSTAR\HOMEOFF\CH03.WS

This means that the file is on drive C—a letter with a colon after it always indicates a drive. The path from the root of drive C to the file is through the subdirectory WORDSTAR and from there into the subdirectory HOMEOFF.

Drive paths and subdirectories are a bit confusing at first, as their notation is a bit cumbersome. They're flexible, though, and you'll find that once you get used to them they represent a workable way to manage huge numbers of files.

It's also worth noting that there are several other bits of syntax in creating paths. We won't deal with them here, as they aren't really necessary for the basic operation of DOS, and they'd only serve to make things even more confusing at this point.

The Basic Commands

You can think of DOS commands as falling into three groups. The most elementary of them are the ones that the command interpreter will know how to interpret by itself. These are often called "internal" commands, as the intelligence to perform their functions resides within the command interpreter itself. The other two groups fall under "external" commands. They reside in files on your disk.

The operating system itself comes with a large number of small programs that are usually referred to as "utilities," the first group of external commands. These perform commonly used functions that are specific to the operating system. They were not included in the command interpreter mainly because there wasn't room for them.

The second group of external commands are those that you specifically add to the system. These represent the commands that will execute your applications software. These might, in fact, be COM, EXE or BAT files. You need not keep track of which is which, because, as when you type the command to run a program, the command interpreter will check for each.

A Few Good Commands

You will need to know relatively few of DOS's commands to make it work. You'll find that these few, at least, are fairly mnemonic and should be pretty easy to remember.

You will also need to know a bit about the way DOS structures its command syntax. This is also pretty easy to remember, but it's not all that obvious.

As we discussed previously, when you enter words on the DOS command line, the first one is interpreted as a command and the remainder, if there are any, are passed as "arguments" to the command.

An argument is something to tell the command what to do. Not all commands can respond to arguments, and in some cases the arguments will be optional.

In the command line

JUMP UP AND DOWN

the command JUMP would be run— presumably as JUMP.COM, JUMP.EXE or JUMP.BAT— and it would be passed three arguments, to wit, "UP," "AND," and "DOWN." This is hypothetical— there is no command called JUMP that comes with DOS.

Having your computer jump up and down will invariably void its warranty.

Most of the commands that come with DOS relate in some way to disk files. There is a particular syntax for dealing with multiple disk files that can save you a lot of time. This syntax uses asterisks and question-marks as "wild cards." You should make a point of understanding it, as it gets around a world of typing.

> **DOG*.CAT** This means "all files with names starting with DOG and having the extension CAT." This would include such files as DOGFOOD.CAT, DOGTAGS.CAT and DOGNOSE.CAT. It would also include DOG.CAT.

> **DOG*.*** This means "all files that start with DOG and have any extension at all." It would include all the foregoing files as well as DOGFOOD.WS, DOGTAGS.EXE and DOGNOSE.BAT. It would also include DOGFACE, that is, a file with the name DOGFACE and no extension.

> ***.*** This means, simply, all files.

We'll look at some practical uses of wild cards in just a moment.

It's important to remember that command arguments that specify file names can also have paths. For example,

C:\WORDSTAR\HOMEOFF\CH*.WS

would mean all the files that start with CH and have the extension WS that are in the subdirectory HOMEOFF, which is in the subdirectory WORDSTAR, which is on drive C.

You'll find that the commands we'll be discussing will be a lot easier to keep track of if you turn on your computer now and try them out as they come up.

Subdirectory Commands

As we've gotten fairly heavily into the lore of subdirectories, let's start with the basic commands for working with them. We'll begin by creating a new subdirectory from the root of your hard drive. This will not hurt your hard drive, and you'll be able to dispense with the new subdirectory momentarily.

The command for creating a new subdirectory is MD, for "make directory." We'll call this directory WOMBAT. Actually, you can call it anything you like, so long as it's eight letters or less in length.

To create this directory, type

MD WOMBAT

To enter this directory, type

CD WOMBAT

The CD command stands for "change directory." You are now in the subdirectory with the path C:\WOMBAT.

If you type CD without any arguments, DOS will tell you what your current directory path is. In this case, DOS would respond with

C:\WOMBAT

You can make another directory within the subdirectory you have just created, a sub-subdirectory. Let's call this one AARDVARK. Type MD AARDVARK, and then CD AARDVARK to change to that directory. If you subsequently type CD with no arguments, DOS will respond with

C:\WOMBAT\AARDVARK

You're now two levels down in your subdirectory path. The procedure for moving down a path should be pretty obvious by now. Moving back up may not be. The command to move from the AARDVARK directory back up to the WOMBAT directory is

CD ..

That's CD with a space and then two periods. There is a reason for this, but it's complicated and there's no useful reason to get into it here.

If you back up to the WOMBAT directory you can try the last of the three subdirectory commands, the one that removes directories. It is, as you might have suspected, RD. To remove the AARDVARK directory when you're in the WOMBAT directory, type

RD AARDVARK

If you now attempt to issue the command CD AARDVARK, DOS will not find a directory called AARDVARK, so it will say "Invalid directory."

You can't use RD to remove a directory if there are files or other directories in it. You must delete the files and remove the lower directories first. Finding and deleting files will be discussed in a moment.

At this point you might want to move back up the root directory and use RD to delete the WOMBAT subdirectory.

Here's a last bit of syntax you might want to remember. The following command will return you to the root of your current drive no matter how many levels deep in its subdirectories you happen to be:

**CD **

Changing Drives

Your computer will have at least one floppy drive and at least one hard drive "partition." The floppy drive will be drive A, and there may be a B floppy as well. The first hard drive is usually drive C.

Depending upon the version of DOS that's on your hard drive, the size of your drive and the way DOS has been set up, your hard drive may all be drive C or it may be split up into several partitions— sections— of which the first will be drive C, the next drive D and so on. Under DOS version 3.3 and earlier, partitions could be no larger than 32 megabytes. Drives larger than this had to be split into multiple partitions. From DOS version 4.0 on it was no longer necessary to do this, but many users find having multiple partitions to be a useful way to organize a large hard drive whether they have to be there or not.

If you have a drive with several partitions, you can treat it as if it were several distinct disk drives.

When your computer first boots up, you will be logged into drive C. If you want to work with a program or files that are located on drive D, you must log into drive D. The command for this is

D:

As soon as you hit Enter, you'll be returned to a prompt. However, rather than being a C prompt it will be a D prompt. The letter in the prompt indicates the drive you are logged into.

Depending upon how your system is set up, your prompt may also indicate your current drive path.

There are few instances in which you will want to log into drives A or B, that is, your floppy drives, but you're free to do this. Make sure there's a disk in the drive first and that the door is closed. If you attempt to access a drive that has no disk in it, DOS will say

Not ready error reading drive A
Abort, Retry, Fail?

In this case, either put a disk in the drive and hit R to have another shot at whatever you did to provoke this message or hit A to abort and return you to whatever disk you were logged into before this message cropped up.

If you attempt to access a hard drive partition that doesn't exist—drive H, for example, when you only have drives up to G— DOS will say

Invalid drive specification

It's important to note that neither of these messages is particularly catastrophic. They don't indicate that any files have been corrupted or that your computer has been damaged. They're simply DOS telling you that you've done something it doesn't understand. Despite appearances to the contrary, DOS is very careful about letting you do something you'll regret later.

Finding Files

Every directory, including the root directory, maintains a list of the files and subdirectories it contains. You can look at this list whenever you'd like to see what's in a particular directory. The command for this is

DIR

This will probably be among your most used DOS commands. If you type DIR, a listing like the one in Figure 3.4 will appear. The file and subdirectory names will be different for your computer.

Note that the DIR listing separates the names and extensions of files with one or more spaces to make its listing look attractive. In any other notation, the file

AUTOEXEC BAT

would be written AUTOEXEC.BAT.

```
Volume in drive C is STEVE C
Directory of   C:\

DOS            <DIR>        4-05-90    4:13p
VENTURA        <DIR>        2-21-91    8:56a
TYPESET        <DIR>        2-21-91    9:02a
WINDOWS        <DIR>        2-21-91   10:32a
COMMAND  COM     47845      4-09-91    5:00a
HIMEM    SYS     11552      4-09-91    5:00a
CONFIG   SYS       128      5-16-90    5:30p
AUTOEXEC BAT       296      5-17-91   10:47a
TRADSONG TXT      7936      1-17-91   11:04a
              9 File(s)     1284096 bytes free
```

Figure 3.4: A directory listing for Drive C

The numbers immediately to the right of the file names are the number of bytes occupied by each of the files. The names that have <DIR> after them are subdirectories. In the above directory I could type CD DOS to enter the DOS subdirectory.

The times and dates in this list indicate when the files and subdirectories in question were initially created or, in the case of files, last modified.

In most cases you'll find that this form of the DIR listing will tell you more than you want to know if you're just looking for a file. An alternative form of the DIR command is

DIR /W

This will produce a wide listing with only the file names displayed. You'll be able to see more names at a glance.

If you want to look at the DIR listing for a directory having lots of files, you might want to use this version of the command:

DIR /P

This will cause the listing to pause every 24 lines. Hitting any key will get it rolling again.

Here's something important to remember. Any DOS command can be interrupted by holding down the Ctrl key on your keyboard and striking the Break key. This is useful if you type DIR in a heavily populated directory and find several miles of file names cruising past your monitor.

The DIR command will also accept arguments. Here are a few common ones:

DIR A: Look at the files on drive A.

DIR *.COM Look at all the COM files.

DIR A:*.COM Look at all the COM files on drive A.

**DIR ** Look at all the files in the root directory of the current drive.

DIR DOS Look at all the files in the subdirectory called DOS, assuming there is one.

Deleting Files

You can delete files from your directories with the DEL command. For example, if there's a file called DELETE.ME that you no longer want, you would delete it by typing

DEL DELETE.ME

The DEL command also accepts wild cards. Here are a few examples of their use:

DEL *.DBF Delete all the files having the extension DBF.

DEL WORD*.* Delete all the files having names starting with WORD.

DEL *.* Delete all files in the current directory. If you issue this command, DOS will ask you if you really want to do so.

You should be very careful about using the DEL command. While deleted files can in most cases be undeleted if you do so immediately— this will be discussed in Chapter 12—you shouldn't count on being able to do so all the time.

You can use the DEL command to delete all the files in a subdirectory. If you have a subdirectory called OLDFILES, you can delete all the files therein by typing

DEL OLDFILES

DOS will ask if you really want to do this before proceeding.

Renaming Files

You can rename a file under DOS using the REN command. To rename the file READ.ME so that it will be named DELETE.ME, you would type

REN READ.ME DELETE.ME

DOS will refuse to rename a file if a file with the new name already exists in the current directory.

Copying Files

There are two commands for copying files between disks or directories under DOS. The simplest one is COPY. To copy the file READ.ME from your current directory to a floppy disk in drive A, you would do this.

COPY READ.ME A:

There are a lot of variations on the arguments to the COPY command. Here are a few of them.

COPY A:READ.ME   Copy the file READ.ME from drive A to your current directory.

COPY READ.ME A:DELETE.ME   Copy the file READ.ME from the current directory to drive A, but call it DELETE.ME when it gets there.

COPY *.ME A: Copy all the files in the current directory that have the extension ME to drive A:

COPY READ.ME DELETE.ME   Copy the file READ.ME in the current directory to a new file, called DELETE.ME, also in the current directory.

Note that COPY will overwrite existing files if you tell it to copy a file into a drive that already contains a file of the same name.

There is a second command, XCOPY, which performs the functions of COPY, but in a more intelligent way. Unlike COPY, the XCOPY command is not part of the DOS command interpreter— it exists as a file called XCOPY.EXE— so you may have to create a search path before you can use it. This will be discussed shortly.

The XCOPY command accepts the same syntax as the COPY command, but it works faster if you're copying lots of files using wild cards, or if you copy files that are larger than 65,535 bytes. (This is a round number to a computer, even if it doesn't look like one to a human being.) The XCOPY command also accepts all sorts of extra arguments and options, but we won't get into them here.

Search Paths

There's a fairly important—and unfortunately, fairly complicated—aspect of paths that you should be aware of early on. It involves what's called the "search path."

Earlier in this chapter we discussed how DOS looks for a COM, EXE, or BAT file when you type a command that it does not recognize as being part of the command interpreter. As it comes out of the box, this really means that DOS only looks for these files in whatever directory or subdirectory you happen to be logged into. This can be a problem on a large hard drive. For example, if you want to use the XCOPY command in a subdirectory other than the one it's usually stored in, you would have to copy it to the directory it's needed in. This would be very tedious.

You can tell DOS to look elsewhere. Specifically, you can establish one or more subdirectories that contain programs you might want to run from anywhere on your disk and tell DOS to look there for commands that it can't find in your current subdirectory. The process of telling it to look in specific directories is called setting up a "search path."

Most DOS users place all the COM and EXE files that come with DOS and that serve as extra commands in a directory called DOS on their C drive. To create a search path that tells DOS to look here, you would issue the command

PATH C:\DOS

Having done this, all the COM, EXE, and BAT files that were located in the DOS directory on drive C would be visible to DOS from anywhere on your system. You could, for example, use the XCOPY command from within any subdirectory even though XCOPY.EXE was not in that subdirectory.

To make this a permanent feature of your system, you must add this command to the file AUTOEXEC.BAT in the root of your C drive. This is a batch file that DOS automatically runs each time your system starts up.

A Word About DOS Shells

If you bought your computer with DOS already on your hard drive, it might have come with a DOS "shell" program. The shell might already be installed so it runs automatically, such that you do not start off with a C prompt.

Shells are programs that ostensibly make your use of DOS less complex. Rather than having to remember the syntax for copying files, changing directories, and so on, a shell program allows you to use menus or function keys to handle these common DOS operations.

Starting with version 4.0, DOS came with its own shell program. There are also a lot of commercial shell programs, including PC-Tools, Norton Commander, XTree, and so on.

Shell programs certainly can make learning to use your computer less intense at first—you get to learn how to use a shell, rather than how to use DOS. Most shell programs have less demanding manuals and even on-screen help.

There are several drawbacks to shell programs. (Nothing useful on a computer ever comes without a price.) Overall, shells are easier to use than the DOS command line, but slower. More troublesome than this is that most shell programs are memory pigs. If you attempt to run a large program from within a shell, you'll probably find that it has much less memory available to it than you'd expect, because much of your system memory will be tied up by the shell.

There are two ways to get to a C prompt from a shell—you can quit or you can shell. Quitting a shell program will return you to DOS as it is normally, that is, with almost all your system memory available for running applications in. Shelling out of a shell program actually causes the shell to run a second copy of the DOS command interpreter, COMMAND.COM. In this case, the memory map in Figure 3.5 will apply, and much of your computer's memory will be unavailable.

If you're uncertain whether you've quit a shell program or merely shelled out of it, type EXIT. If nothing happens and you return immediately to a C prompt, you weren't in the shell: there's no shell to exit to. If you suddenly find yourself back in the shell, you had only shelled out, and EXIT has exited you back to the shell.

Shell programs aren't the only programs that allow you to shell out to DOS. A great many application packages allow you to shell out to DOS as well. This is a handy way to get to a DOS prompt to copy or delete a few files or run some other small applications. However, the restricted memory map from Figure 3.4 applies to these situations as well.

top of memory

the memory left
to a shelled program

partial copy of
operating system

where your
program runs

operating system

bootstrap

bottom of memory

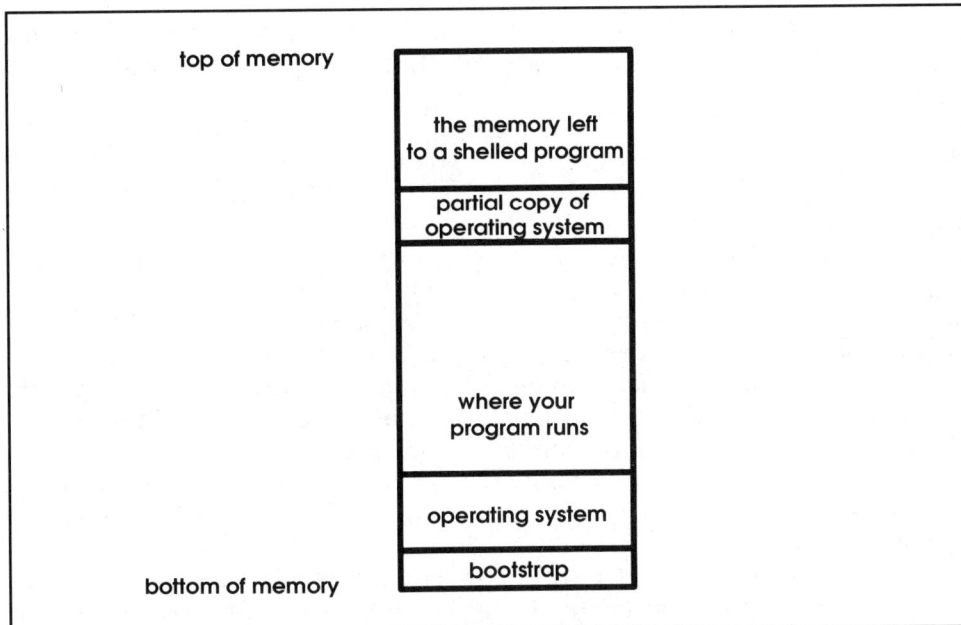

Figure 3.5: Memory usage when "shelling out"— rather than exiting— to
another program

DOS shells are an acquired taste, and one you might wish to think carefully about before acquiring. Giving up half your system memory to a program that does nothing much beyond relieving you of the necessity of typing might turn out to be a bit extravagant.

A more complete discussion of DOS shells appears in Chapter 12.

It's probably also worth mentioning that Microsoft Windows is in a sense an extremely powerful DOS shell. There's a good argument for using Windows when you want to work in a user-friendly environment and DOS when you need all the power of your system at your disposal. A traditional DOS shell—which is a bit of both—will probably be superfluous in this context.

A Word about Resident Programs

Calculators are among the most mysterious types of electronic technology. While not manufactured with any sort of feet, they still learn how to move from where you put them and hide in places that no human would ever think to look.

A calculator that could not possibly be misplaced would be almost magical. In fact, there are several such calculators that you can make part of your computer. Hit a special combination of keys, and a window pops up over whatever you're doing and behaves like a calculator for as long as you need it.

There are similar arrangements for pop-up calendars, note pads, reminders, games— the list of pop-up programs is almost endless. These programs are called "resident utilities," or TSRs. TSR stands for terminate and stay resident.

A resident program works by loading itself into the memory of your computer and telling DOS that the first free part of memory will thereafter be above where it resides. The memory map in Figure 3.6 illustrates how memory looks with a resident program in place.

Once it's loaded, a resident program hides in memory and watches the keyboard. If its special combination of keys appears, it pops up, opening a window on the screen and taking control of your computer until you tell it to stop, whereupon it goes back into hiding. Resident programs typically use key combinations that would not ordinarily appear in normal applications.

Resident programs are extremely handy, and a lot more will be said about them later on in this book. However, there are several serious catches to their use. The biggest one is the memory they occupy. Load up

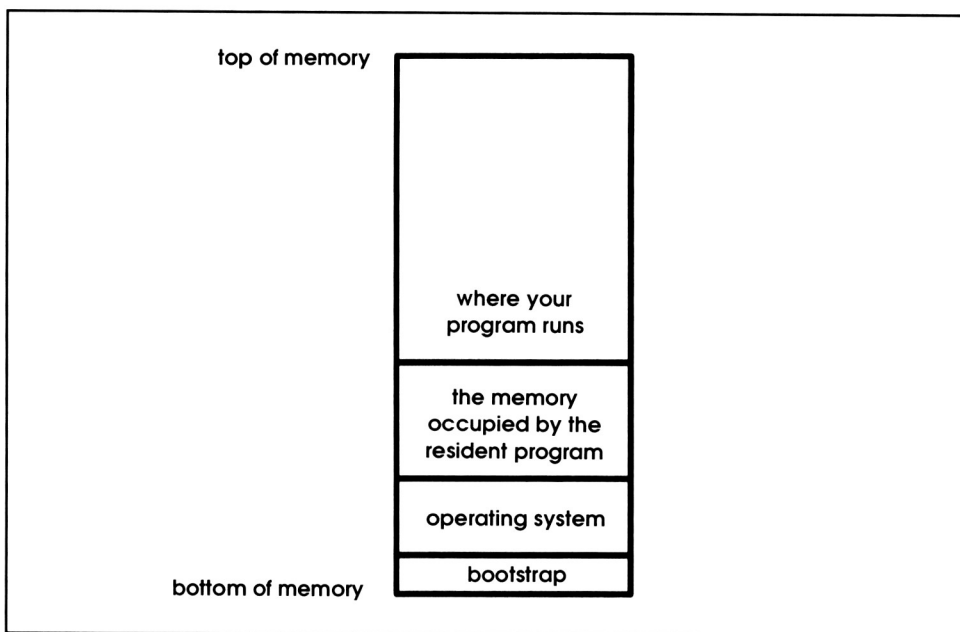

Figure 3.6: A memory map with a resident program loaded

a resident calendar, a note pad, a few pop-up games and so on— and pretty soon you'll find that a few hundred kilobytes of system memory is tied up with these clever little monsters. Applications that formerly ran in your available system memory may suddenly decide that they no longer have enough of it.

A second potential problem is in the way resident programs work with the keyboard and with internal bits of your computer. Some resident programs pretty well assume that they'll have exclusive dominion over these things, and become cranky if this turns out not to be so. Devotees of resident programs frequently discover that they have two or more resident programs that each insist on being the last resident program to be loaded into memory.

Depending upon your system requirements, you might find that a few well-chosen resident programs are worth the memory they tie up. Bear in mind that resident programs are, in a sense, a band-aid solution to the nature of DOS, which doesn't really allow you to have two things going at once. If you need this facility— if you want to be able to flip from a word processor to a calculator to a database manager to a phone book manager and so on— you should consider a multitasking operating system like Windows, which performs this function well and without all the limitations inherent to resident programs.

If you bought your computer from a dealer who configured it for you, you might want to check to see if there are any resident programs being loaded automatically when the system powers up. These are handled by the AUTOEXEC.BAT file. If you start running into memory problems, removing dispensable resident programs from your AUTOEXEC.BAT file is a good place to start in trying to overcome them.

USING THE MACINTOSH FINDER

The Macintosh Finder is arguably a lot easier to use than DOS for much the same reason that it's easier to choose a Mac than it is a PC compatible. There are far fewer choices involved, and there is far less to remember.

It's worth noting that in the recent evolution of the Macintosh, a lot of bits of optional system software have cropped up. These are things that the Finder can be made to attach to itself when your computer boots, providing you with all sorts of colorful screen blankers, keyboard macros, and, on some of the higher-end Macintosh systems, sound effects. One of the Macs that I work with has been beset by sound effects. It makes twanging noises every time a window opens and laughs insanely if an error message appears.

Using the Mouse

The Macintosh mouse cursor should track the movement of your mouse across your desktop. If you have a particularly smooth desk you might find that a rubber mouse pad will make the mouse more responsive and less likely to slip.

The Macintosh mouse, by virtue of its single button, can do relatively few things. The payoff for this apparent limitation is that there is little to keep track of. (Actually, these days the PC crowd is finding plenty of opportunity to use mouses with similar ease.) Specifically, you can do the following with a mouse:

Click   Place the mouse cursor on something and click the button once.

Double-click Place the mouse cursor on something and click the button twice very rapidly.

Drag   Place the mouse cursor on something, hold down the button and pull the mouse cursor across the screen, dragging the object in question with it.

We'll discuss exactly what gets clicked and dragged over the course of this section.

When your Mac first boots up, you should see something like one of the screens shown in Figure 3.7. Note that the names of things will most likely be very different on your Macintosh.

The first screen in Figure 3.7 represents a Mac with the window for its hard drive closed. The picture in the upper right corner is the hard drive. This is called an "icon." The Mac uses icons like this to represent almost everything. If you double-click on it, it will open into something like the window in the second screen.

Under normal circumstances, Macs always remember how you left their Finder windows from session to session. As such, if you open the hard drive window now, it will remain open indefinitely unless you explicitly close it some time in the future.

All activity on the Macintosh takes place in windows, that is, in rectangular areas. In some cases, a window may encompass the entire screen. In most cases you can adjust the size of windows.

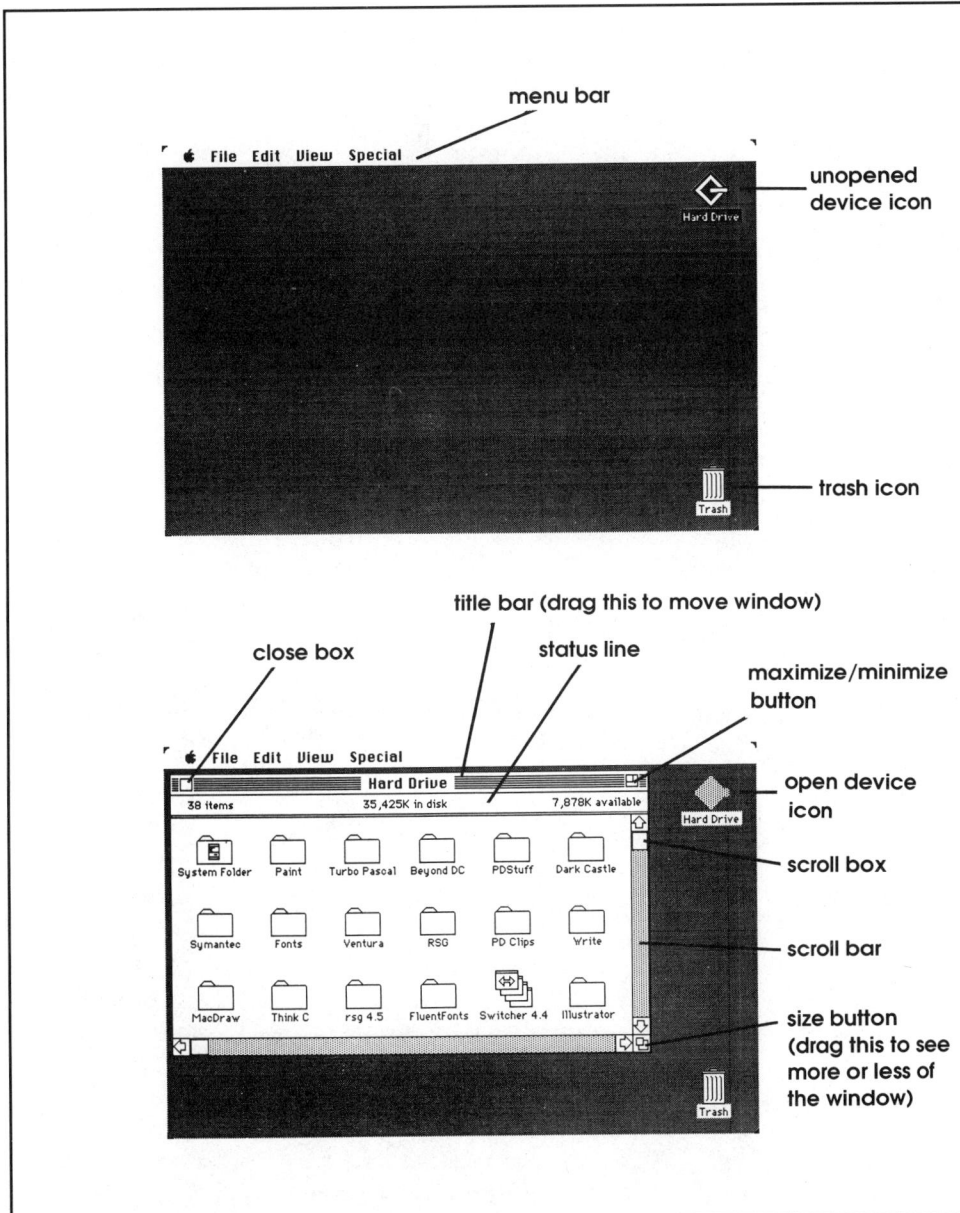

Figure 3.7: After booting up a Macintosh

Windows on the Macintosh have varying characteristics and elements to suit their varying functions. Figure 3.7 illustrates several of them, and the names of their parts.

For the sake of this discussion, a Finder "device" corresponds to a disk drive. As your Mac first boots up, there'll be one device, and hence one window if it has been opened. If you put a floppy in the Mac's floppy drive, another device icon will appear at the right side of your screen. If you double-click on it, a second window will appear, as in Figure 3.8.

The frontmost of any set of windows is said to be the "active window." Things can happen only in the active window, the one that is not overlapped by any other windows. If you click in an inactive window—any rearward one—it will come forward and become the active window.

Windows such as the ones used by the Finder for its devices can be moved, resized, and closed. To move a window, place the mouse cursor somewhere on its title bar—as shown in Figure 3.7—and drag it to a new location. To resize a window, place the mouse cursor on its size button—also shown in Figure 3.7—and drag the box around until the window is sized the way you want it. Finally, to close a window, click in its close box.

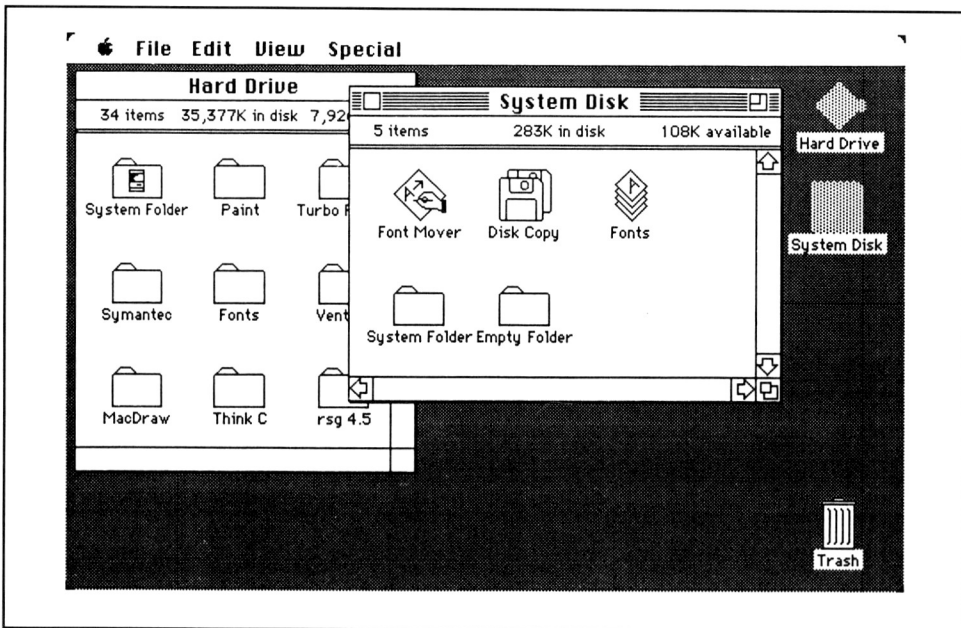

Figure 3.8: Two devices and two windows

In the the case of a Finder window, closing it will make it, in a sense, deflate back into its parent icon until you open it again by clicking on the icon in question.

Finder Icons

The icons in a Mac's Finder windows represent files and folders. These are analogous to files and subdirectories for PC systems. Files can be applications, word processing documents, spreadsheets, pictures of packrats, or bits of the Mac's operating system, among other things. Folders contain files, just as traditional cardboard folders contain traditional paper documents. Because you will typically have a lot of files on a hard drive, you should use folders to keep all the files associated with each application you use separate from whatever else is on your drive. For example, my hard drive has a folder called Write, another called Paint, another called Ventura, and so on. Each of these contains an application and the files that go with it.

You can open a folder by double-clicking on it. This will cause a window to open, showing you what's inside the folder. Every folder defaults to displaying its contents as normal Finder icons. However, you may find it convenient to change this. You can introduce your mouse to the Mac's "menu bar" in the process.

If you place the mouse cursor over the word *View* at the top of the screen, a boxed list of features and changes— a "menu"— will appear. Drag the mouse cursor down and the items in the menu will be highlighted as the cursor passes over them. If you select, for example, *by Small Icon* and then release the mouse button, the icons in the current Finder window will all shrink. You'll be able to see more of them at a glance. You can also select *by Name*, which is how many Macintosh users prefer to keep their folders.

Assuming that you have the items in your current Finder window displayed as icons, you can move them around to suit yourself. Simply place your mouse cursor over the icon you want to move and drag it to its new location. You will probably want to place the icons for things you use frequently at the top of their respective windows.

Once you have moved some icons around, you can select the *Clean Up Window* item from the Special menu if you like. This will tidy up the icons in the currently active window. If you can't find this item in the Special menu— but you do find *Clean Up Selection* instead— you have more than one icon selected in your current window. This will be indicated by the icons in question being reversed black for white. If you select *Clean Up Selection*, only the selected icons will be affected. Click in the blank space between the icons of a window to unselect the selected ones.

We will discuss the uses of selected icons shortly.

Moving Icons

Icons—and the files or folders they represent—can be moved around on the Macintosh almost effortlessly. For example, to move a file from one folder to another, all you have to do is drag it from where it is to where it is to go.

If you want to move several icons at once, you can do so by selecting them. Click and hold the mouse above and to the left of the icons you're interested in. Drag the mouse down and to the right—a "selector box" will appear behind it. When you release the mouse, the icons contained within the box will be selected, that is, they'll be reversed black for white. Drag any one of the icons to its new location, and all the others will follow.

If you move a file between different devices—such as from a folder on your hard drive into a folder on a floppy drive—the file will actually be copied, rather than simply moved. That is, a copy will appear on your floppy disk, but the original file will remain where it was.

You can move folders just as you would individual files. If you drag a folder into a different folder, the folder and all the files—and perhaps additional folders contained with it—will come with it.

Here's a useful shortcut to keep in mind when you're dragging files from folder to folder. You can move an icon into a folder without opening the destination folder. Simply drag the icon to be moved to the icon of the closed destination folder. It will find its way into the folder by itself.

If you have many icons in a folder you'll probably find that it has become too full to see them all. One way around this is to simply make the window bigger, but you'll run out of screen space in time. In this case, you can "scroll" more icons into the window by using the scroll bars.

Scroll bars are always visible in a Finder window. If the number of items in the window exceeds the window's capacity to let you view them all at once, the scroll bars will be active. If all of a window's contents are visible, the scroll bars are inactive. This is indicated by the background areas of the scroll bars in question being white.

Either or both of the scroll bars may become active if there are enough icons in a window to warrant it, or if you resize the window to make it too small to display all the icons that are present at once. To cause the window contents to scroll in a certain direction, click on the appropriate arrow of the appropriate scroll bar.

The arrows of a scroll bar will cause the window to scroll by a small amount. Finally, if you grab the scroll box of a scroll bar and drag it to a new location, the window's contents will follow the movement of the box.

Deleting Files and Folders

Deleting things on a Macintosh is actually handled as a special case of moving them. If you glance the screen of your Mac, you will find the trash can icon, as you saw in Figures 3.7 and 3.8.

To delete a file or folder, simply drag the offending item to the trash, and it will be deposited in the trash automatically. (Trashing several files at once is more convenient if you first open the trash can into a window—by double-clicking on it.)

Once trashed, items in the trash can window will remain in existence until you next run an application, until you power down your Macintosh, or until you explicitly tell your Macintosh that you no longer want them around by selecting *Empty Trash* from the *Special* menu. Until that time, if you trash a file or folder and then realize that you shouldn't have done so, you can rescue it by simply opening the trash can window and dragging the item in question back onto your desktop. You can almost hear rescued files sighing with relief.

Using the Finder's Menus

Many of the items in the Finder's menus will also appear in most Macintosh-based applications. If you take a moment to read through this section, you'll have a good head-start on the applications you will eventually be using on your Mac.

In each case, you can select menu items by clicking on the appropriate item of the menu bar and dragging the mouse down over the resulting menu until the item you're interested in is highlighted. Releasing the mouse will select the item and cause whatever action is associated with it to transpire.

There are a few variations on basic menu items that you should be familiar with. For example, if you pull down the File menu, you should find that the *Print* item is grey, and cannot be selected. This is called a "disabled" menu item. Disabled items are disabled because it would be inappropriate to perform their associated functions in the current situation. In the case of the *Print* item of the File menu, there's nothing to print just now.

Some menu items are "toggles"; that is, they represent things that can be turned on and off. You will have already encountered this in the View menu. The current view mode for the currently active window is indicated by a checkmark. If you select a different view mode, the checkmark will move to indicate that item.

Finally, some menu items will have icons associated with them. You will not find any of these in the Finder, but they do crop up in applications from time to time. These menu icons behave differently from the other icons you've seen in that they are wholly decorative—their associated menu items behave just as they would had they been text only.

You will notice that most menus have at least one horizontal line. These serve to separate the menu items into convenient, logical groups of functions, but serve no other purpose.

Some menu items, such as the *New Folder* item in the File menu, have symbols beside them. Specifically, there'll be a curly thing and a letter to the right of the item's text. The curly thing is the symbol for the Command key. You'll find the same symbol on one of the keys of your Mac's keyboard.

Menu items that include command keys can be run from the keyboard as well as with the mouse. The *New Folder* item, for example, can be executed by holding down the Command key and hitting *N*. As you get used to the Finder and the applications you run under it, you'll probably pick up those command keys that represent frequently used operations.

The Apple Menu

The Apple menu is the leftmost item in the menu bar. It doesn't show its name, only a symbol—an Apple with a bite missing. If you click in this menu, you'll be able to select About the Finder and some "desk accessories."

The *About the Finder* function tells you things about the version of the Finder software you're using and how much memory is available on your system. It's illustrated in Figure 3.9.

The remainder of the items in this menu are desk accessories. Desk accessories are little applications that you can pop up over whatever you're currently running on your Mac. They provide you with functions such as a calculator, various windows to help set up your Macintosh, a game or two, and so on.

The File Menu

The File menu performs functions that relate more or less to files, which as far as the Finder is concerned includes folders and applications. Most applications have File menus too, with equivalent items to some extent.

New Folder   This item will create a new folder in the currently active window. It will be called *Untitled.* You can change this to reflect its eventual

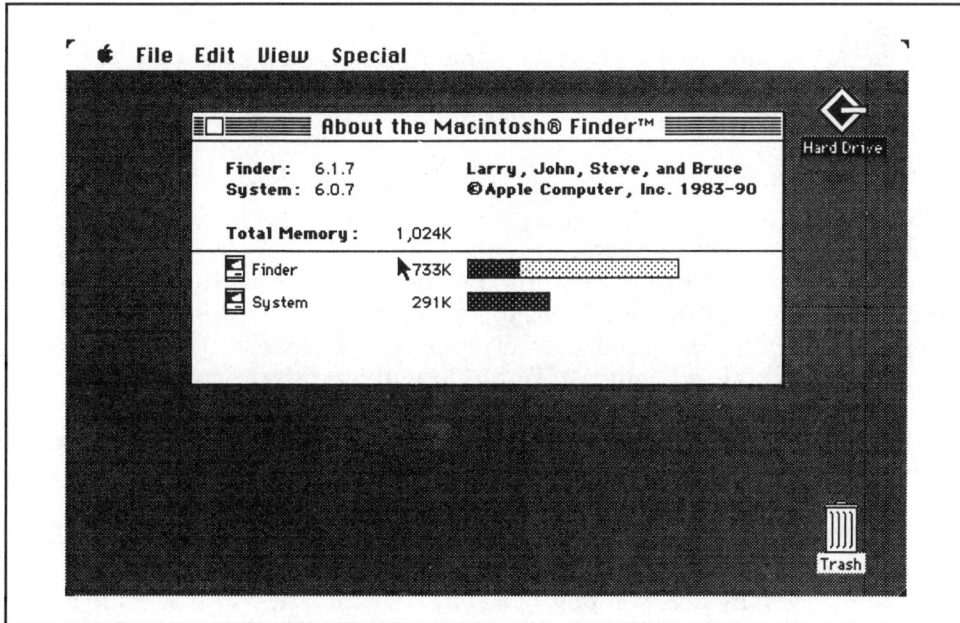

Figure 3.9: "About the Finder"

contents by hitting the Delete (or Backspace) key and then typing in a new name for it. The text you type will appear beneath the folder's icon.

You can change the name of a folder or file icon any time you like by placing the mouse cursor over the name and clicking. Anything you type will appear in the name area. You can use the Delete key to dispose of the existing text if need be.

Open   You will probably have no cause to use this item—normally, you would simply double-click on things instead. If you select a folder and then select *Open*, the folder will open as if you had double-clicked on it. If you select a file and then this item, an application will open.

Print   This item may take a while to understand properly. If you select a document—such as a word processing file or a picture—and then select *Print*, the application that originally created the document will open up and print the document to whatever printer you have currently told the Mac to use. You might want to leave this one alone for now.

Close   Selecting this item is equivalent to clicking in the close box of the currently active window. It's included for much the same reason that the Open item is— i.e., for the rare window that doesn't offer a clickable equivalent— and you probably will have no cause to use it.

Get Info   If you select one or more icons and then select this menu item, windows will open to tell you about the icons you have selected. Examples of these windows can be seen in Figure 3.10.

   The large empty box at the bottom of each of these windows can include comments. Type in something about the file in question and it will remain attached to the file until such time as you decide to change it. This is a useful way to leave yourself reminders about what's in a file, or what it was created for.

   When you no longer wish to see a Get Info window, click in its close box to dispense with it.

Duplicate   If you select one or more icons and then select *Duplicate*, the Finder will create copies of whatever the icons represent. The names of the new files will be preceded by "Copy of." As such, if you had a file called "Picture," the new file would be called "Copy of Picture."

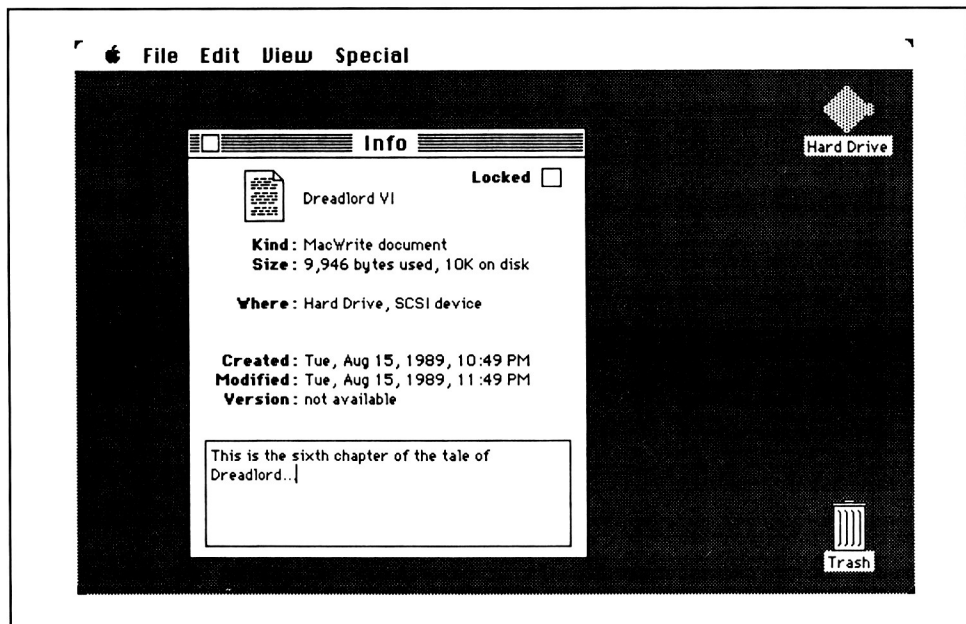

Figure 3.10: A Get Info window

You can duplicate folders, but note that this will duplicate the folder *and* all its contents. This can take up a considerable amount of disk space if the folder contained a lot in the first place.

Page Setup   This will pop up a window to set up any options that are appropriate to the printer your Mac is currently set up to print to. The nature of the Page Setup window varies among printer types.

Print Catalog   This will print a catalog of the files and folders in the currently active window to your currently selected printer. In effect, this will be the entire contents of the window as they would appear on your screen, except that anything that would have required scrolling to be visible will be printed too.

Eject   Once you insert a floppy disk into a Macintosh, there is no obvious way to get it out again. In fact, the Mac must condone its release, at which point it will spit the disk out without any human intervention.

When a floppy disk has been inserted into one of your Mac's drives and an icon for it has appeared at the right side of your screen, you can tell the Mac to spit it out in one of several ways. The absolutely correct way is to select the disk's icon and then select *Eject* from the File menu. The slightly less correct way is to drag the disk's icon to the trash, which will also cause it to pop out.

The Edit Menu

All Macintosh applications— including the Finder— are supposed to have an Edit menu. Many of the functions that might appear in an Edit menu will not mean much in the context of the Finder, and some of them will be disabled all the time.

The only items that you'll probably ever have cause to use from the Finder are *Select All* and *Show Clipboard*. The *Select All* item will select all the icons in the currently active window, just as if you'd drawn a box around them with your mouse. This includes icons that aren't visible because they've scrolled outside the visible area of the window.

The *Show Clipboard* item will open a window to display the current contents of the Mac's "Clipboard." We have not discussed this yet, but it will crop up in conjunction with several of the Macintosh applications discussed in this book. Very briefly, the Clipboard is a place where Macintosh applications can temporarily store fragments of things for later use. There is seldom any cause for even really inventive Mac users to want to get at it from the Finder.

The View Menu

The View menu tells the Finder how to display the icons in the currently selected window, as discussed earlier in this chapter.

The Special Menu

The Special menu is really a collection of all the Finder functions that didn't have anything to do with any of the previous menus. It does things that are largely specific to the function of the Finder itself and hence to the Mac's hardware.

The *Clean Up Window* item of the Special menu has already been discussed, as has the *Empty Trash* item. Note that *Empty Trash* will be disabled if there's no trash to empty.

The *Erase Disk* item is used to erase the contents of floppy disks, something that you will not usually have to do. Other useful items are described below.

Shut Down   This item will tidy up your Macintosh—putting files away, emptying the trash, and so on. On some Macintosh systems, it will clear the screen and tell you that you may safely turn the system off. More recent Macs have the power switch under computer control, and selecting this item will actually turn the computer off.

You should always power down your Mac by selecting this item, even if you thereafter have to turn off the juice manually. This gives the system a chance to do any last-minute housekeeping that might have been left undone.

Restart   This item will cause your Mac to "reboot" itself, that is, to assume the state it was in immediately after you first turned it on. It's infrequent that you will want to use this function, but in some cases you must restart the system to make certain low-level changes in the system software take effect. The software in question will tell you when to restart your Mac.

Running Applications

The Macintosh deals with its applications and the files associated with them in an unusually convenient way. To cause an application to run, you locate its icon and double-click on it. A window encompassing the entire screen will open and the application you have selected will appear within it a few seconds later.

When a Macintosh application creates a file—what is properly called a "document" in Mac terms—the file itself knows what application it belongs to. For example, when MacPaint creates a file, the file knows that MacPaint was its creator. If you double-click on a file, it will tell its parent application to run and then load the file you clicked on.

Figure 3.11 illustrates a Finder window with an application—MacPaint—and several MacPaint files. Let's assume that you want to edit the one called Sunburst. You *could* do this by double-clicking on MacPaint and then opening the file Sunburst from within MacPaint. However, you could simply double-click on the Sunburst file icon you see here, which would get you the same results with somewhat less clicking.

There are a few sorts of documents that do not have applications associated with them. If you attempt to double-click one, a box will appear to tell you that this is the case.

The System Files

There will be one folder on your hard drive that will look a bit different than all the others. It will usually be called System Folder. Even if it

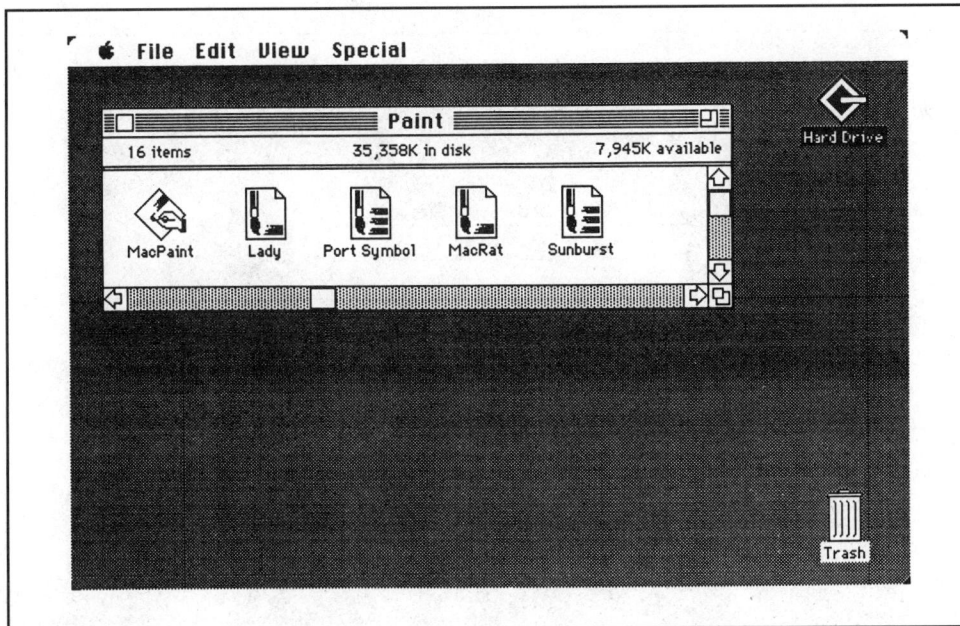

Figure 3.11: MacPaint and some picture files

isn't, you can tell it's special because it has a very tiny Macintosh drawn in it. Figure 3.12 illustrates this folder.

The Macintosh's operating system is contained in two principal files, called System and Finder. The function of the Finder is probably fairly clear by now— it handles the desktop for you, gives you a convenient way to work with files and folders, provides a place from which to run applications, and so on.

The System folder contains all sorts of low-level things for the Mac to use. It also contains the system's "resources." While the Mac uses the concept of resources to mean all sorts of things, the important ones found in conjunction with the System folder are fonts and desk accessories.

All the fonts that are available to Macintosh applications are stored in the System folder. You can add fonts to the System folder using a special program that comes with the Macintosh system software called Font/DA Mover.

Desk accessories can also be added to the System folder with this program— the "DA" in Font/DA Mover stands for desk accessory. Desk accessories will be discussed briefly in the following section.

Adding lots of fonts and desk accessories to the System does not tie up extra system memory, but it can make the System folder pretty

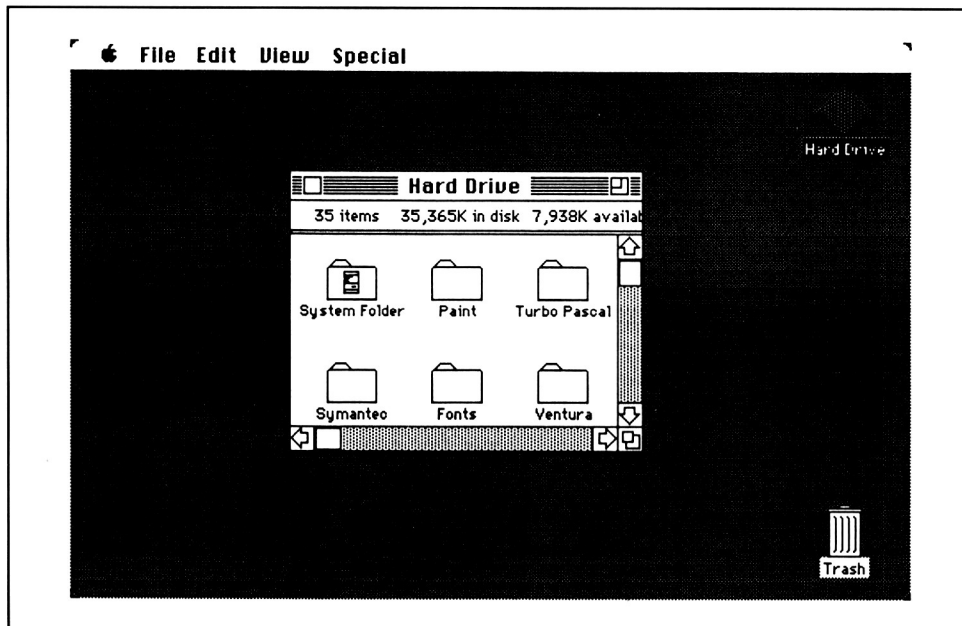

Figure 3.12: The system folder and others on the hard drive

obese. The System folder on my Macintosh is about a megabyte it size, mostly due to its overabundance of fonts.

A whole book could be written about the System folder, and several probably have been. For the most part, you will be able to leave these files alone until you've become a lot more familiar with the workings of your Macintosh.

Desk Accessories

It's difficult to discuss desk accessories in detail, in part because there are so many of them. In addition to the ones that come with the Macintosh, there are commercial desk accessories for every conceivable function. Many software developers have sought to overcome the fairly limited multitasking facilities of the Mac by providing everything you might want to multitask in the form of desk accessories instead.

This section will look at the bare minimum of desk accessories. As you get more familiar with your Macintosh, you'll undoubtedly want to add more desk accessories to it.

The Apple menu, from which desk accessories are called, is available under most Macintosh applications just as it is under the Finder. (You will find that most applications replace the *About the Finder* item, however, with an About box relevant to themselves.)

Chooser

Perhaps the most fundamental desk accessory is the one called Chooser. The Chooser is used to tell the Macintosh which sort of printer to send your documents to. In most cases, you will have a choice between ImageWriters and LaserWriters, the latter in fact being any sort of Apple-Talk-compatible PostScript printer. The Chooser is shown in Figure 3.13.

The left side of the Chooser will contain icons for one or more types of printers. The Mac that the Chooser in Figure 3.13 resides on is connected to my NEC LC-890 PostScript printer, which it thinks is a Laser-Writer. It's also connected to an unspeakably ancient ImageWriter, which has survived three Macs now. It predates the existence of AppleTalk. Fortunately, there are quite a few of these dinosaurs around and Apple has seen fit to continue supporting them in the Chooser.

To select a printer, begin by double-clicking on the icon that represents the type of printer you wish to print to. If you have only one printer—the usual state of affairs—this will be pretty easy.

If you select a printer that communicates with the Mac over AppleTalk—also the usual state of affairs—the Chooser will look out across

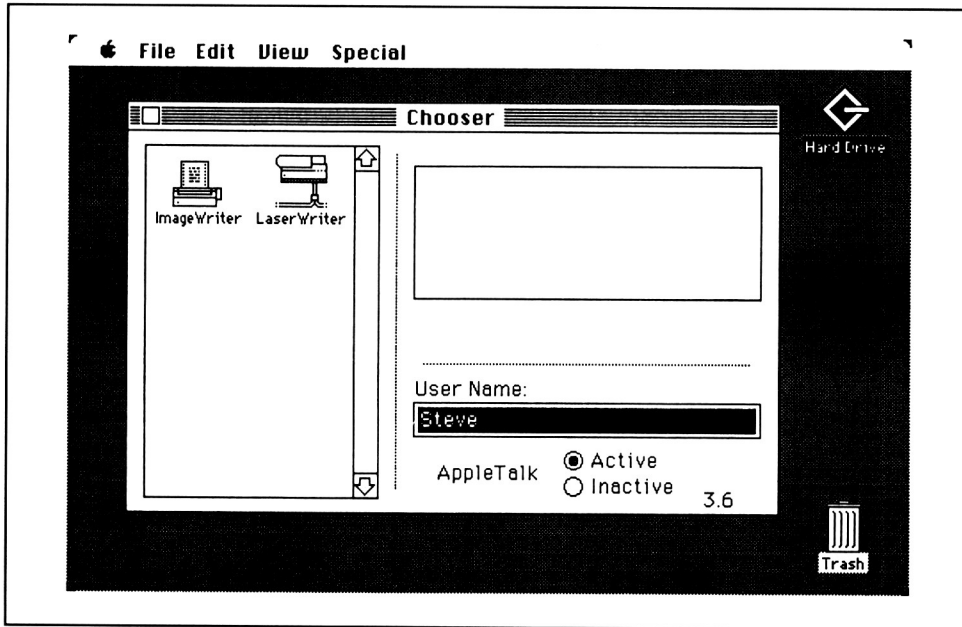

Figure 3.13: The Chooser

the AppleTalk network and see how many printers of the type you've selected are about. It will only be able to see those printers that are turned on. In the case of multiple-mode PostScript lasers, such as my NEC LC-890, it will only see those printers that are both turned on and set up to use their AppleTalk interfaces.

After a few seconds of AppleTalking, the Chooser will display a list of available printers in the upper right corner of its window. Under Apple-Talk, each printer has a name. These usually default to the product names of the printer, such as "LaserWriter," or, in the case of my NEC printer, the vastly inappropriate "SilentWriter." If you have several laser printers made by the same manufacturer, you can change their names to make it possible for the Chooser to distinguish them. This will be covered in the documentation for your printer.

Select the printer you want to print to.

The box in the lower right portion of the Chooser's window tells the Chooser who you are, or, more specifically, what the name of your Macintosh is as it relates to printing. This is important if you'll be using your Mac on a network with other Macs and printers, as every name on the network must be unique. You needn't worry about it if you have only one Mac connected to one printer—just put your name here.

In the bottom right corner of the Chooser box you'll find a control to make AppleTalk active or inactive. This should be set to active if you will be dealing with your printer over AppleTalk.

Once you've used it to initially configure your Macintosh for printing, you will probably not have to open the Chooser again unless you want to change the way your Mac prints, to select a different printer, or to add a printer to your system.

Control Panel

The Control Panel serves as a catch-all of things you might want to configure on your Mac. Virtually every software designer who writes graphical-user-interface applications such as those for the Mac will tell you that a well-designed program should not need such a box. Virtually every one does, though.

In fact, the Control Panel desk accessory allows you to access any number of actual sets of controls. When you first open it you'll find yourself looking at the main Control Panel, as shown in Figure 3.14.

The box down the left side of the Control Panel will allow you to scroll through and select additional, specialized control panels if any have

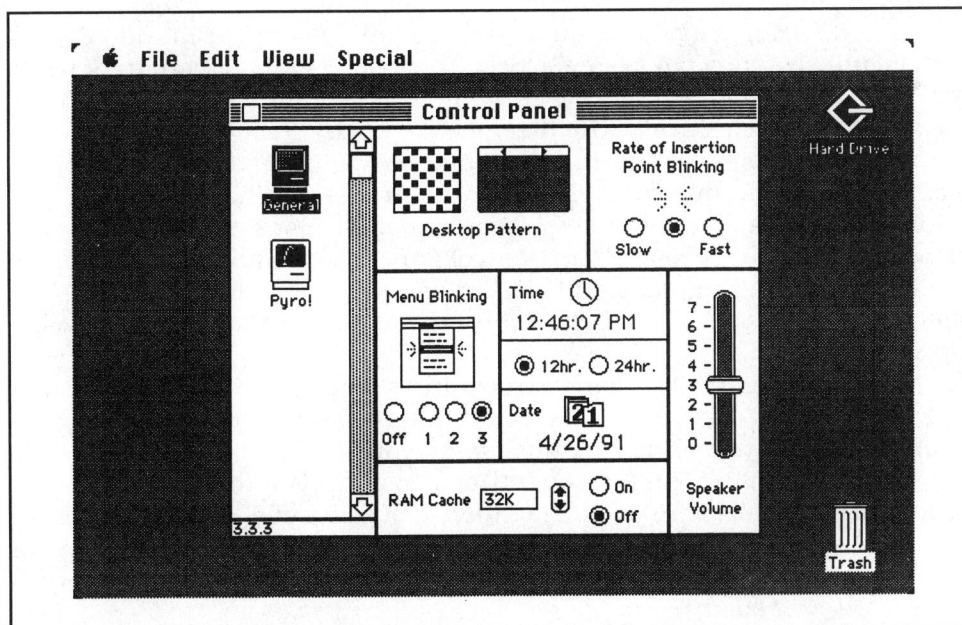

Figure 3.14: The main Control Panel

been installed in your system. The only one visible in Figure 3.14 is Pyro, which controls the characteristics of a program that blanks the screen on my Mac after a period of inactivity.

More recent and complex Macintosh systems typically have more control panels available. These include panels to deal with such phenomena as color monitors and sound effects, and how certain features will behave when the computer boots up, and so on. We will not be discussing these here, as they get pretty complex pretty quickly.

The main Control Panel allows you to fine tune a number of the overall characteristics of your Macintosh. The *Desktop Pattern* area lets you choose the pattern that will be displayed behind the desktop area of your Mac's screen. It defaults to a grey pattern. If you click in the left box of this area, you can turn pixels on and off and create a custom pattern. If you click near the two small arrow heads at the top of the right box, you can step through an assortment of canned patterns. Avoid patterns that will make your screen primarily white, as this can get a bit hard on your eyes after a while.

The *Rate of Insertion Point Blinking* option allows you to decide how quickly the text editing cursor will blink. This cursor appears whenever you have to type something. Likewise, the *Menu Blinking* option allows you to tell the Mac what to do when you select a menu item. By default, the text will flash a few times before the function it indicates begins.

The time and date functions allow you to set the time and date of the Macintosh's internal system clock. The clock is run by a battery when the Mac is switched off; so, once set, the time should remain correct. To change one of the values in the time or date fields, click on the number. A box with two arrows— one pointing up and one pointing down— will appear to the right of the numbers. Click on the arrows to change the selected number. Note that in adjusting the time value, the clock will be frozen until you select something else in the Control Panel. Consequently, you can set the time to something just a bit ahead of the correct time, wait for your watch to catch up with the value set on the Mac, and then start the Mac's clock going again.

The *Speaker Volume* control adjusts how loud your Mac's speaker will get overall. It behaves exactly like the stereo slider control it looks like. Grab the slider knob and move it to where you want it.

Finally, the *RAM Cache* setting can allow you to improve the performance of your hard drive at the expense of some memory. When it's active, a RAM cache attempts to anticipate the parts of your hard drive your applications will call for and keep them in memory. Because memory is hundreds of times faster than a hard drive is, retrieving part of a file from memory takes very much less time than it would to retrieve the same data from your hard drive.

Every time the cache guesses correctly, it obviates the need for your applications to actually access— and wait for— the hard drive.

In order to function, the cache must tie up some memory to store the parts of your hard drive it thinks your applications might need frequently. As this cache "buffer" gets bigger, the number of times the cache guesses correctly will improve.

A modest size cache of at least a few hundred kilobytes will make a notable improvement in the performance of your Macintosh for many sorts of applications. As you get used to your system, you should make a point to adjust the cache size and see if it makes a meaningful difference in your work.

It's worth noting that not all applications actually derive any real benefit from the existence of a cache. A database manager, for example, accesses so many parts of the disk so frequently that it will typically do it better without the existence of a cache. A word processor, which will usually keep its files wholly in memory, will hardly notice a cache.

The RAM cache situation is complicated a bit because in times of memory shortages the Mac may move parts of its applications on and off the disk. If the memory shortages are caused by half your system memory being tied up in a cache, the cache will only be contributing to the problem it was intended to solve.

Find File

As your hard drive has more and more files added to it, you may find that locating a specific one can be a time-consuming process, especially if it turns out not to be where you expected it. The Find File desk accessory, as seen in Figure 3.15, will help you out in this case.

To find a file, type as much of the name of the file as you can recall into the *Search For* box and either hit Enter or click on the walking man icon (for "Proceed"). Find File will look into every folder of your hard drive, searching for files that match what you've typed. Case (uppercase or lowercase) does not matter. For example, if I entered "Mac" into this field on my hard drive, Find File would tell me about all file and folder names that contain those three letters in any part of the title.

Clicking on the stop icon or closing the Find File window will interrupt a search at any time.

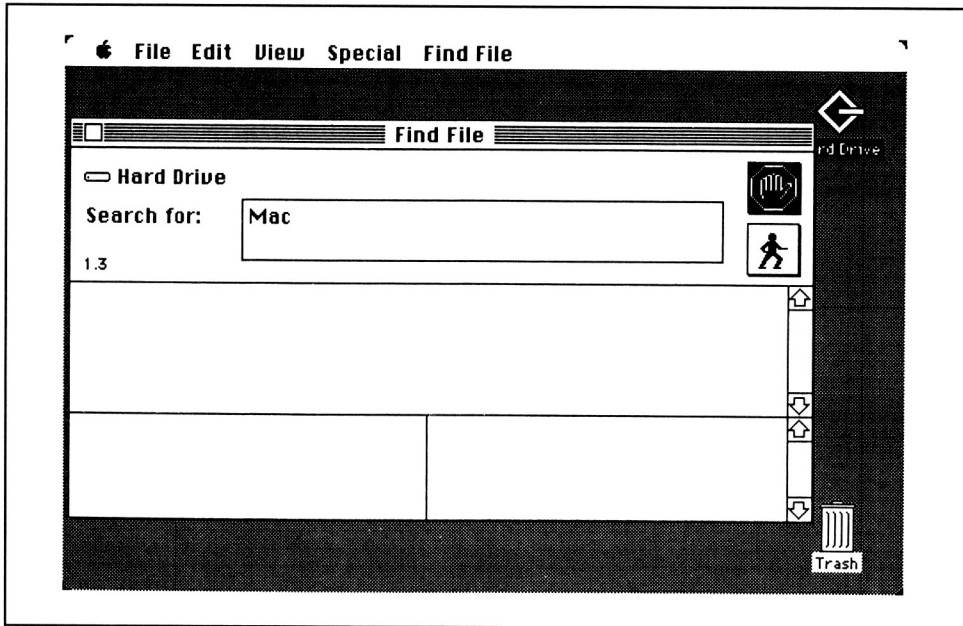

Figure 3.15: The Find File desk accessory

Calculator

The Calculator desk accessory is pretty much what it purports to be: a four-function calculator. It isn't very powerful, and you'll find that there are commercial and shareware replacements that will prove more productive, but it's good for simple math.

SUMMARY: PERSONALIZING YOUR COMPUTER

In a sense, as you add applications and tools to any computer, you personalize it to suit your requirements. This is so much the case that most people find it difficult to sit down at someone else's computer and know how to perform even simple functions. We all tend to name things, locate things, and set things up in ways that are intuitively obvious to ourselves.

The Macintosh, despite its rather sterile, homogenized appearance at first, allows for more personalization than you might have imagined possible. Aside from the applications you add to your hard drive, you can provide yourself with a wealth of desk accessories and, likewise, of fonts. Don't be afraid to structure your hard drive in a way that makes sense to you, especially if no one else will be using your computer. In time you'll probably find that maintaining a computer is less a matter of organization and more one of interior decorating.

If this notion appeals to you, you'll probably be interested in the next chapter of this book. It deals with Microsoft Windows, a program that, among other things, allows you to set up a PC in much the same way as a Macintosh.

CHAPTER

4

4

MICROSOFT WINDOWS

One of the arguable drawbacks to Apple's Macintosh computers is that they impose a tradeoff: convenience versus power. This point is arguable, as was discussed in Chapter 1 of this book, because there are many users who are quite happy to pay in terms of power for the convenience of a Macintosh's user-friendly environment.

As it comes out of the box a PC does not have anything like the user-friendliness of a Mac, but an equally friendly environment can be added to it. The result of such a transformation will leave you with what could be seen as the best of both worlds—a single computer that lets you choose when to have power and when to have user-friendliness.

While there are several "bolt-on" user-friendly environments—packages that are made part of your system after the fact—the most popular and the most powerful is unquestionably Microsoft's Windows 3 software. It provides much of the user-friendliness of a Macintosh, more power than a Macintosh in many respects, and a convenient interface both to special Windows applications and to the countless thousands of existing DOS-based programs. It's inexpensive and easy to learn, and in some cases you may find that it supplants more expensive software in the process.

As of this writing, the street price of the complete Windows 3 package was well under a hundred dollars.

There are two principal drawbacks to Windows. The first is that it's hardware hungry—the real extent of its voracity will be discussed later in this chapter. The second is that almost no one seems prepared to really explain, in words of a manageable length and simplicity, what Windows will do for you. This chapter will solve the second problem starting now.

AN INTRODUCTION TO WINDOWS

To make understanding Windows easy—and to help you decide whether Windows suits your requirements—this chapter will deal with the issues somewhat out of order. The hardware requirements of Windows will be dealt with second, after we've had a chance to tour through Windows itself.

This discussion will assume that Windows has been installed on a fairly high-end computer and that it has sufficient memory and disk space available. (You'll be able to pin down the exact magnitude of that word "sufficient" later on.)

When a computer with Windows first boots, one of two things happens, depending on how the system is set up. Many Windows users prefer to work in Windows all of the time, so they have the system come up with Windows running. Others want to be able to choose whether to run Windows or not each time the computer starts up, so they begin with the DOS prompt and later type WIN to run Windows. In either case, the main screen of Windows—the "Program Manager"—will look something like the one in Figure 4.1.

Unless your system is set up exactly like my system, your main Windows screen won't look exactly like the one in Figure 4.1. One of the

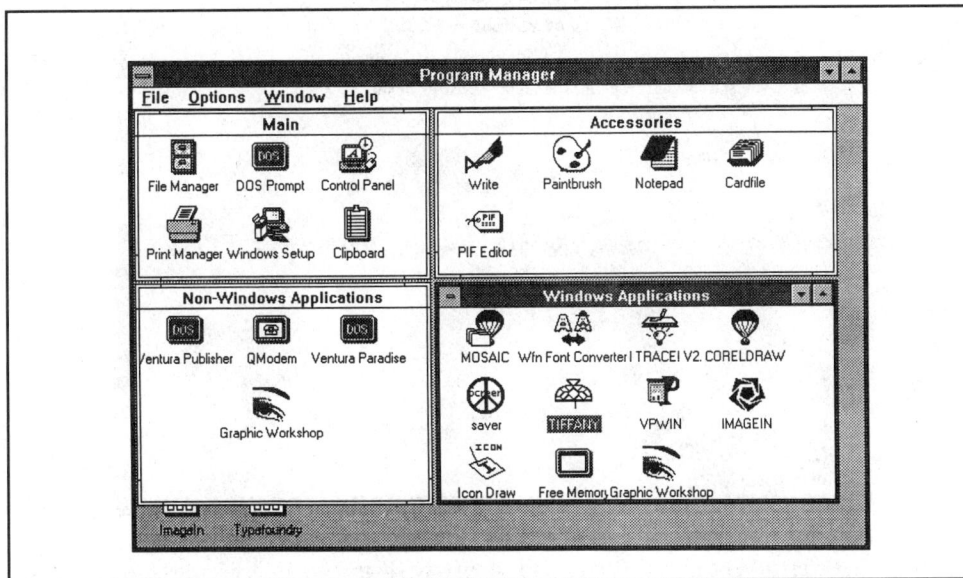

Figure 4.1: The main screen of Windows

nice things about Windows is that you can arrange things on its screen to suit yourself.

The basic elements of a Windows application screen are the same as those for a Macintosh application, and are used in the same way. For example, the small "icons" on the Windows screen represent applications. Rather than typing a command name to run a program, Windows allows you to move your mouse pointer to the appropriate icon and click twice—"double-click"—to start the application you'd like to run.

For example, to do some word processing under Windows you would double-click on the Write icon. After a moment or two to boot up, a window with a word processor in it would open on your screen, as in Figure 4.2.

Windows Write is included with the Windows package. It's pretty powerful for a little word processor. It allows you to use multiple fonts and to include pictures with your text. It's also very easy to use.

Under DOS, in order to do something different from what your current program enables you to do—for example, if you decide in the middle of a word processing program that want to create some graphics—you would have to get out of your word processor and run a drawing or paint

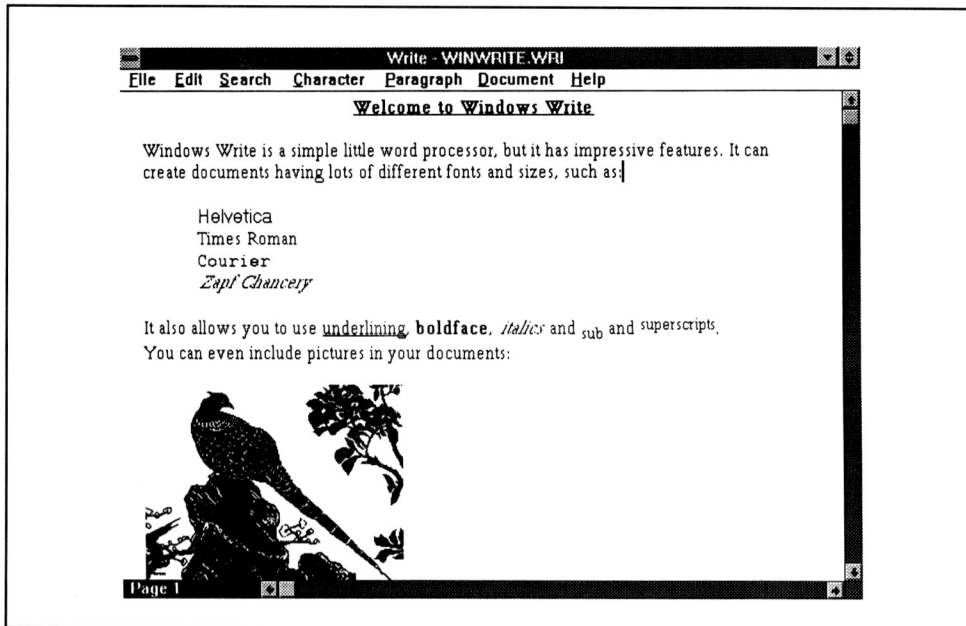

Figure 4.2: The Windows Write word processor

program. Under Windows, you can merely click outside the Write window to bring the Program Manager forward, then double-click on Paint. The Windows Paint program, which also comes with Windows, will appear as in Figure 4.3.

Inasmuch as Write allows you to create letters and reports that include both text and pictures, it's quite likely that you will find yourself in a situation where you'd like to use both Write and Paint at the same time. This is where Windows proves to be more than mere window dressing. When you clicked outside the Write window to get back to the Program Manager, Write didn't disappear. It merely went to sleep, being hidden behind the Program Manager. You can bring it forward. In fact, you can make it coexist with Paint, such that you can move effortlessly between the two. Figure 4.4 illustrates these two programs together.

You can have multiple applications running at one time, moving between them as required. You can tell Windows to make the programs you're not using at the moment go to sleep until you need them, or you can have them active even though you aren't actually working with them. For

Figure 4.3: Windows Paint

example, you could have a program doing complex, time-consuming calculations in the "background" while you bring up the Write window and
catch up on your correspondence.

Windows likes to regard applications as running in either the
foreground or the background. The program that you're working with at
the moment is in the foreground, and will always be foremost in the
layered windows on your screen. In Figure 4.4, for example, the Write
window is foremost. All windows that are not the foreground program are
considered to be in the background. Their applications may be running
or sleeping, as you prefer.

Windows also refers to its current foreground application as
being "active" and its background applications as being "inactive."

There are several ways to move between multiple programs running at one time. If you arrange the screen to have at least a bit of each window visible, you can simply click somewhere in the window of the program
you want to bring forward and it will come to the top of the stack.

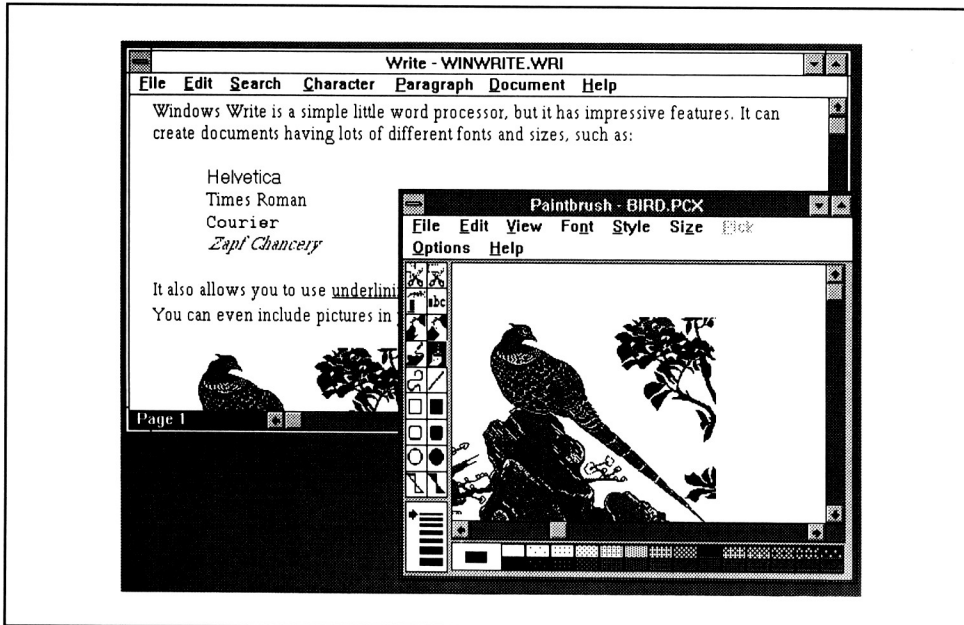

Figure 4.4: Using Windows Write and Paint simultaneously

In some cases it's more convenient to have each program running in a window that occupies the whole screen, such that the foremost window always obscures all the windows behind it. For example, Write allows you to see more text on the screen at once when you do this. In this case, you switch windows by holding down the Ctrl key and hitting the Esc key. A box like the one in Figure 4.5 appears, allowing you to select a new foreground application.

Windows allows you to run both applications especially written for Windows and regular DOS programs. This means that if you want to do word processing with Windows Write or one of the other word processing packages written especially for Windows, you can do so with all the power and flexibility of Windows. If, on the other hand, you find that you like a non-Windows word processor, such as PC-Write or last year's version of WordPerfect, you can still use such a program under Windows. When you run a non-Windows program from within Windows it behaves just as it would had you run it from the DOS prompt.

This means that you can use any PC software you like under Windows, with a very few exceptions.

Using Windows Software

The Windows package comes with a number of small programs. These include several Windows-related utilities to help you set up and use Windows. There are some games. There are also a number of remarkably useful business applications, such as the aforementioned Write and Paint programs.

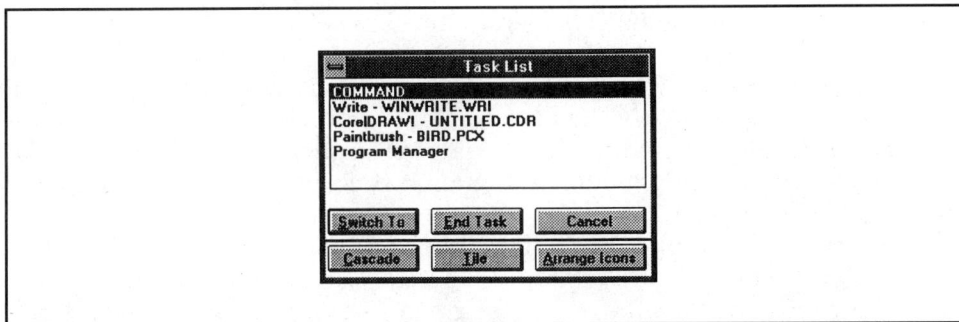

Figure 4.5: The Program Manager's Task List box, showing the programs that are currently available in the foreground and background

A growing number of very good applications are being written by third parties for use in the Windows environment. A brief survey of Windows applications includes

CorelDRAW   Among the best drawing and type-manipulation packages available for any system

Word for Windows   An extremely powerful word processor

Ventura Publisher   The most powerful desktop publishing package. (A DOS version also exists.)

Excel   This is the spreadsheet program to end all spreadsheets.

This list could be expanded for pages.

It should be noted here that while for many sorts of PC software applications you can choose between Windows and non-Windows packages, there are some for which the best software is based on Windows and so you'll need Windows to use it. Examples of such programs are CorelDRAW and Excel. Nothing else can touch them and they both insist on running under Windows.

The thing that makes learning Windows software so agreeable is that, like Macintosh applications, all Windows applications are constrained to have a consistent user interface. Figure 4.6 illustrates the main screens of each of the aforementioned applications. While each program does something different, each one has effectively the same elements. The menus behave identically, and you deal with the dialog boxes and commands of the programs in the same way. Thus, once you learn one application, you'll have a pretty good leg up on all of them. It's worth observing that the Windows Program Manager is itself a Windows application. Everything that pertains to Windows applications such as Write or Excel will also apply to the Program Manager.

Windows applications usually function through *menus*, which are boxed lists of commands. Menus are accessed via the *menu bar* at the top of an application's window. To select a menu item or command you would click and hold the mouse on the menu name in the menu bar. The menu will appear below the name. Click on the item you're interested in.

A Windows application will usually need to communicate with you from time to time to ask you for information or to tell you what's happening. This typically happens through the use of *dialog boxes*, or "dialogs."

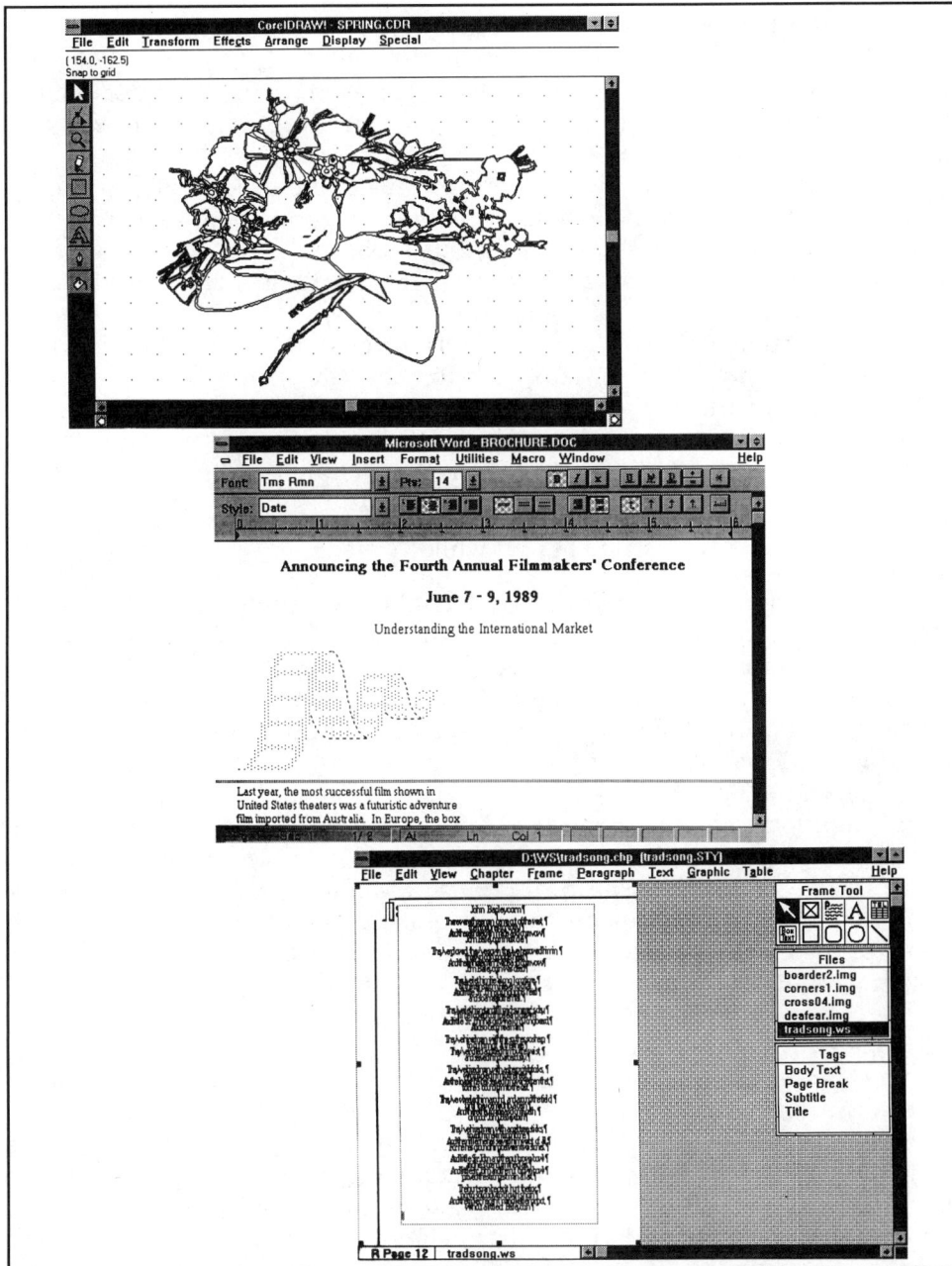

Figure 4.6: The main screens of CorelDRAW, Word for Windows, and Ventura Publisher for Windows

If its purpose is to ask for information, there'll be an appropriate way for you to enter that information in the dialog box. If it's there just so Windows can tell you something, it will usually just present you with information, possibly with a button to click to tell Windows that you've read the message and no longer require the dialog.

Every application will generate dialogs that are specific to its particular function. However, dialogs all behave in much the same way and there are few distinct types. You'll find little difficulty in knowing what to do when you're confronted by one. Figure 4.7 illustrates several dialog boxes from various Windows applications.

Any dialog that expects input from you will have at least one button, usually called "OK." You can click on the OK button to indicate that you're done with the dialog. You will also find a "Cancel" button in many dialogs. The Cancel button allows you to back out of any function that you discover you've arrived at in error, or that you change your mind about.

Windows Help

The rightmost menu for most Windows applications is entitled "Help." It's not an exaggeration to say that once you're familiar with the basic operation of Windows applications in general, you'll be able to use this menu in lieu of program manuals to work your way through many of the programs you later acquire. You may also find Help to be useful in learning Windows in the first place.

The Windows Help function is *context-sensitive*. This means that the information available under the Help menu changes to suit the application you're working with. An index of the topics available for the application you're using—or for the Windows Program Manager, if that's what you're using at the moment—can be called from the Help menu. Figure 4.8 illustrates the Help menu for the Program Manager. Note that there's an item to help with using Help, just in case you become really lost.

Whenever you select an item from the Help menu, a Help window will appear. The one illustrated in Figure 4.9 represents one page of help. The page is actually longer than the window is—you can scroll up and down to read the whole thing.

Help uses what's called a "hierarchical" or tree structure. This means that a page of help will usually lead off into several subpages—which may, in turn, lead off into sub-subpages—to allow you to query the Help system for more information about specific topics. For example, the help

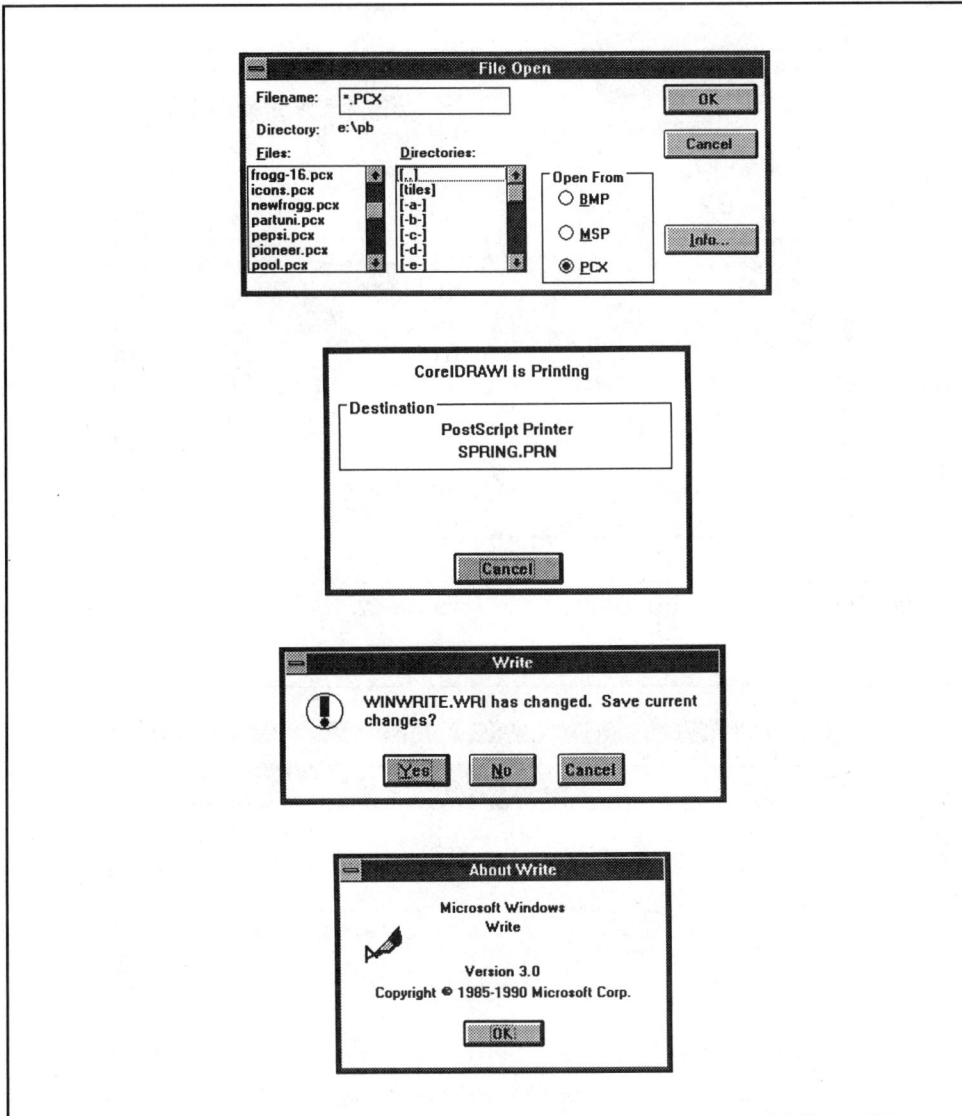

Figure 4.7: Windows applications dialog boxes: A file name chooser, a
message to indicate that printing is taking place, a prompt
to ask you to save a file before quitting, and an About dialog

page in Figure 4.9 appeared when I asked the Help system in Windows
Write for help in using the Edit menu of that application. By clicking on one

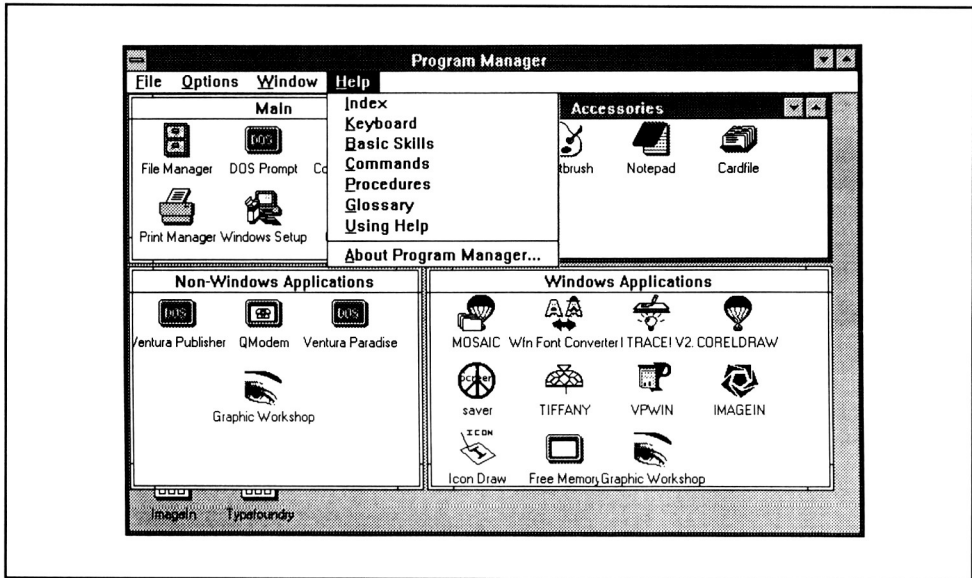

Figure 4.8: The Program Manager's Help menu

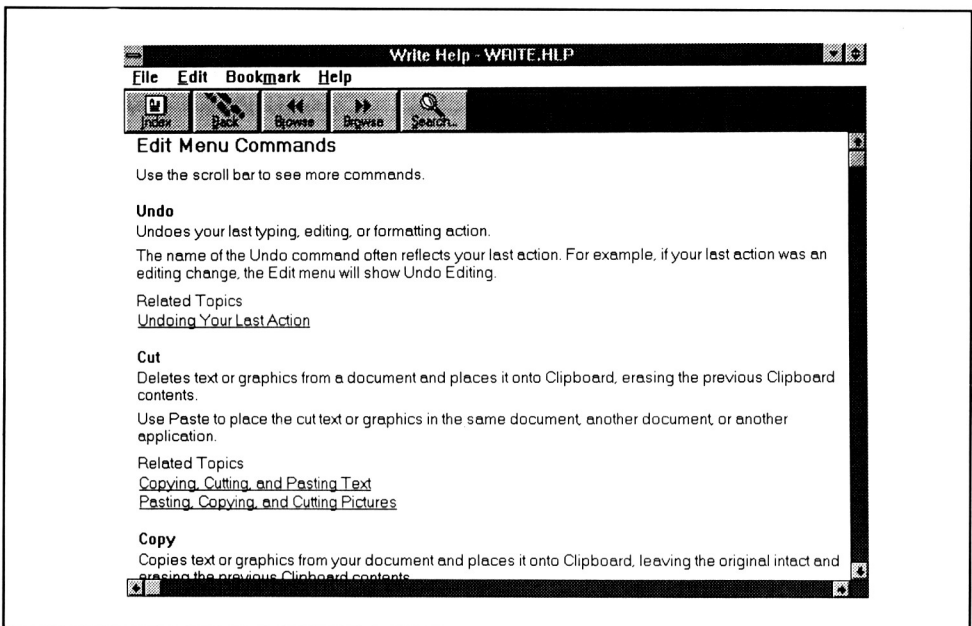

Figure 4.9: One page from the help for Windows Write

of the underlined bits of text—such as "Undoing your Last Action"—I could get detailed help about that topic.

The grey buttons at the top of the Help window allow you to navigate through the help. The Index button will return you to the main index of Help topics for the application you're working with. The Back box—the one with the footprints—lets you work backwards one at a time through the pages you've viewed. The Browse buttons allow you to move quickly through all the available help pages. The Search button lets you find help about specific topics you're interested in.

Once you have even a rudimentary understanding of Windows, you'll find the help to be intuitive to use and comprehensive.

Windows—The Good and the Bad

There are few software restrictions to Windows. It is a very well crafted package, and one that you'll find to be easy to learn and intuitive to use.

If you're a bit nervous about DOS and all its commands, Windows will probably be ideal for you. It lets you have the cost-effectiveness of a PC with the convenience and ease of use of a Macintosh-style interface. In addition, DOS will still be there behind Windows, available for those times when you need its facilities or for the day when you simply want to learn to use it.

The multitasking facilities of Windows make it better suited to a home office environment than any of the other choices discussed in this book. Unless your work is extremely streamlined, you will invariably find yourself jumping between tasks frequently—usually about once every time the phone rings. Being able to just click your way instantly into another application rather than having to quit your current program and run a new one is a facility of inestimable value.

Most of the drawbacks to using Windows will become apparent in the next section of this chapter when we discuss the hardware it requires to run effectively.

HARDWARE CONSIDERATIONS FOR WINDOWS

The box that Windows comes in states that Windows will run on any AT-compatible or better computer with at least 640 kilobytes of memory. This is technically true, but it ignores many of the real-world considerations of using Windows.

The limitation in most personal computers is one of memory. Memory is required to store data and also to hold programs while they're running. Windows was designed with this limitation in mind. It trades disk space for memory by moving parts of itself and programs running under it onto and off of your disk. If Windows moves a program out of memory and into a disk file while it isn't being used, the memory it formerly occupied will be released for more pressing tasks.

The process of moving things between memory and your hard drive is time consuming. All other things being equal, a computer with more memory will run Windows and Windows-based applications faster because it will entail less of this "swapping" to and from your disk.

The speed issue is more than just one of convenience. On a machine with no more than 640 kilobytes of memory—the bare minimum for running Windows—larger applications may run so slowly as to be unusable.

There are four principal considerations in buying a computer on which to run Windows:

1 The speed of its processor

2 The amount of memory it has

3 The size of its hard drive

4 The type of display it offers

These issues were touched upon in Chapter 1, but they're worth dealing with specifically as they relate to Windows. As a rule, you will need a much more powerful computer to run Windows than you would to run most other applications.

Windows turns your PC into something like a Macintosh. In addition to affording it the convenience and intuitive environment of a Mac, it also besets it with the same sorts of hardware tradeoffs. You will have to buy a lot more computer to support all this convenience, and a good part of it will do nothing more than run Windows. However, if your objective in using a computer is to get things done effectively, rather than to get them done with the least possible outlay of cash, you might well decide that it's worth paying for a bit of extra hardware to have the convenience of Windows.

All this is relative. Memory, processor speed, a high-end video display and hard drive space are not all that expensive anymore, and they're commodities that are cheaper still for a PC than they are for a Macintosh. The difference between a very economical low-end computer and one that will run Windows efficiently may be less than a thousand dollars. If your time is valuable, this may be a pretty reasonable price for freeing up a lot of it.

As with computer hardware choices in general, you may find that you can't make the ones that pertain to Windows right away. Some of them will be determined by the nature of the software you'll be running, and you might not be too clear about this until you've gotten further into this book.

Processor Speed

Windows will function on an AT-compatible running at 8 or 10 megahertz—but not well. I would not want to use such a system and after a week or so you wouldn't either. Such a computer is really too slow to use Windows effectively.

High-end AT-compatible systems running at 20 megahertz will run Windows acceptably well. However, in most cases the difference between one of these computers and an 80386 machine running at 16-megahertz will be pretty negligible, and, in fact, the latter is a better choice for Windows.

A high-end 25-megahertz 80386-based system will run Windows at a very respectable speed. This, unfortunately, is not just a few dollars more than a 16-megahertz 80386SX system. You'll have to weigh the value of your time against the cost of what will be a pretty expensive piece of hardware.

Aside from being faster, an 80386 series processor is more suited than the 80286 to the way Windows wants to use memory. This has several benefits. It allows Windows to provide more memory to some non-Windows applications running under Windows. It also lets Windows juggle its internal memory requirements more efficiently in some cases, which usually results in your getting more performance out of your computer with less memory.

There are a few other clever things that Windows can do using an 80386 series processor, but they're sufficiently esoteric as to be beyond the scope of this discussion.

Memory

Two megabytes is the bare minimum memory allotment for running Windows and moderate to large Windows applications in a business environment. You can do a lot with this if you have a fast machine and a large, fast hard drive.

Four megabytes of memory will certainly improve the performance of Windows and especially the performace of large, memory-hungry Windows-based applications such as CorelDRAW and Excel. With either of these applications, you won't really start to feel the pinch of inadequate memory until you've used it for a while and gotten to the point where you're working with lots of data.

Increasing the memory in your system past four megabytes will improve the performance of Windows and Windows-based software further still, but probably not until you really start making some serious demands on Windows. In all but the most involved Windows sessions, eight megabytes of memory will absolve Windows of ever having to write temporary files to the disk. It will be able to handle everything in memory. As a rule, every operation that involves Windows working with a temporary disk file will slow the application in question down by two or three hundred percent for as long as it takes to deal with the file. Eliminating this potential bottleneck can really enhance the performance of Windows.

There are a few other memory considerations to keep in mind. For one, you can improve the performance of many Windows-based applications by using a disk cache. The use of a disk cache will be discussed in Chapter 11. An effective disk cache will need at least a megabyte of memory, and its effectiveness will improve as you add still more memory to it.

Hard Drive Space

There are a few fairly simple rules that might help you decide how big a hard drive you'll need to run Windows and Windows-based applications. To begin with, Windows itself will refuse to install on your hard drive unless it sees a minimum of six megabytes of free space. In addition, prior to installing Windows, you will need the better part of a megabyte for DOS— make that two megabytes for DOS 5—and its utilities.

Most large Windows applications such as CorelDRAW, Microsoft Word, Excel, and Ventura require at least two megabytes each to get sprawled out and comfortable. In some cases this is a bit conservative— CorelDRAW can easily take up twice this much room without half trying— and in others you won't need quite this much real estate until you've used the software for a while.

Windows also requires some free disk space to use for temporary files. Two megabytes should be considered a bare minimum for this, with twice this much better still. The amount of temporary file space Windows requires will be determined in part by the amount of memory you have in your system, the applications you run, and the number of applications you like to keep running at the same time. (There are Windows users who will tell you that after you have come up with a number based on the above rough guidelines, you should double it. There's a degree of sense to this idea—you'll probably find that there are a lot of things to run under Windows that won't occur to you now but will seem awfully handy in six months.)

Display Type

You can run Windows on some pretty low-end display hardware, such as a monochrome Hercules card, as was discussed in Chapter 1; however, as with running it on a slow, low-end AT-compatible computer, you really wouldn't want to.

In a business environment where you'll need to get a reasonable amount of work done, you shouldn't consider running Windows on anything less than a VGA card. A super-VGA card is better. Among other things, it gives you a larger "desktop" to spread out Windows and its applications on. Figure 4.10 illustrates several screens from Windows running in the standard 640 by 480 pixel mode of a VGA card and in the 800 by 600 pixel mode of a Paradise Professional super-VGA card.

You can get super-VGA cards and drivers with still higher resolutions, and Windows will have still more space on your screen. However, as a display's screen gets bigger it also takes longer to update. A display that is snappy and quick to work with at 640 by 480 pixels may seem lethargic at 1024 by 768 pixels. A high-end display really needs a high-end computer to drive it.

You can cheat on this. Once you get familiar with Windows you'll learn how to keep "drivers" for several screen modes on hand. While the process of changing modes is inelegant, it allows you to use the 640 by 480 pixel mode when you want things to run at maximum overdrive and, for instance, an 800 by 600 pixel mode when you need some extra screen space to manage multiple applications.

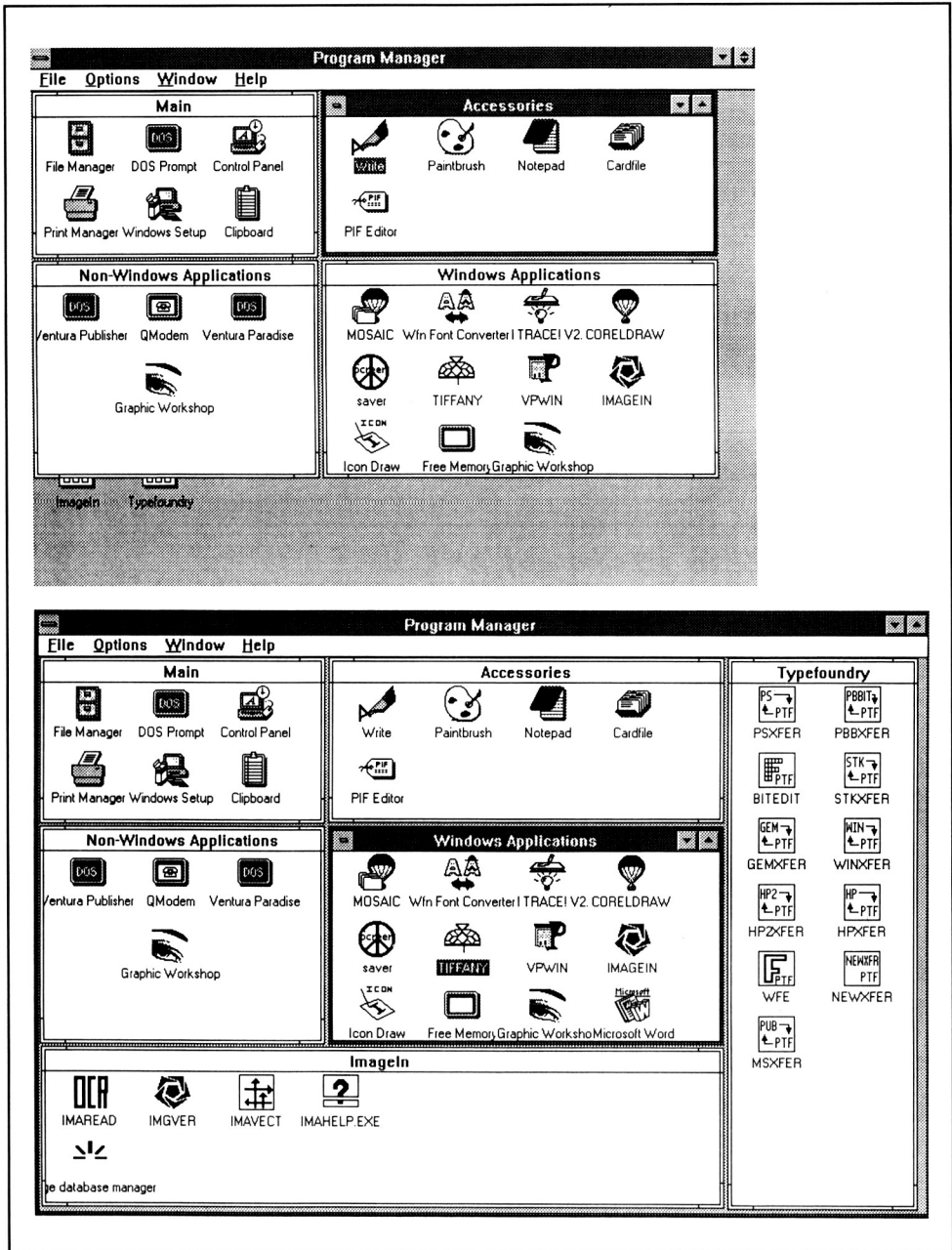

Figure 4.10: Standard and super-VGA modes running Windows

AUTHOR'S CHOICE: WINDOWS HARDWARE

Windows applications just naturally tend toward obesity. Whereas DOS programs are constrained to fit in a limited amount of memory—and hence tend to be restricted as to how much hard drive space they'll take up—Windows applications can include all the features their authors can dream up, and can thus get as big as is necessary. If you read the ads in computer magazines you'll observe that software manufacturers love having lots of features to announce, whether or not they'll ever be used.

To buy a business computer with a hard drive of less than a hundred megabytes is to delude yourself. My system has a 150-megabyte hard drive in it, which is now full. I wish I'd sprung for the next step up, 220 megabytes.

You can get by with a smaller hard drive by moving things off to floppies, faithfully cruising through your subdirectories and killing unnecessary files every few days and so on, but all this housekeeping takes time. If your time is valuable, consider that a bigger hard drive will demand less of it.

The Dell 325 computer that the above hard drive lives in—a 25-megahertz 80386-based computer—is a fast, comfortable place to run Windows. I've had the opportunity to use Windows on several lesser systems that I've been loaned to write magazine reviews about, most of them 16-megahertz 80386SX computers. As a rough approximation, for the sort of work I do under Windows, the Dell 325 allows me to do 25 percent more in a given period of time than an 80386SX-based computer.

From a business perspective, once again, this gets down to what your time is worth. Most of the 80386SX systems that have been through this home office actually cost less than half what the Dell cost. You might have to put in a lot of hours before the additional cost of a really high-end computer actually makes sense.

From a personal perspective, even if you aren't in a hurry it's a lot more rewarding to work on a fast computer that rarely expects you to wait for anything. There are some situations where the speed of your computer can really affect the quality of your work. A slower machine may make you reluctant to add a bit more detail to a graphic or to try a few more permutations of a spreadsheet.

My Dell 325 came with four megabytes of memory, which ran Windows acceptably. Eight megabytes runs it a lot better, and considering what the extra four megabytes of memory actually cost, I wish I'd bought it sooner. If there were room on the motherboard I think I'd try four more.

The Dell 325 came with a Paradise Plus VGA card, which I subsequently updated to a Paradise Professional. The latter card allows Windows to run with 256 colors, which is a feature that only really matters if you're doing full-color graphic design in a program like CorelDRAW. The Paradise VGA cards are very fast and well engineered, and a good choice for pretty well any sort of Windows application.

A number of other Windows users hereabouts use ATI VGA Wonder cards. Especially in their 16-color business graphics modes— the modes that most users will run Windows in— it would be hard to say that one was preferable over the other.

I'd like to say that all the computer hardware I've bought in the last few years has been as a result of careful consideration and research— but it's not entirely true. Much of it has been bought in moments of frustration with its predecessors. However, despite this it has all paid for itself handsomely. There's a definite relationship between the power of the computer hardware you use and the amount of work you can get done.

In addition, it's worth noting that nearly everything I bought a year ago because it was state of the art and interesting— as opposed to practical or necessary at the time— has found new software appearing to make use of its resources. A computer that is more powerful than you need at the moment won't stay that way very long.

As an aside, one of the computer "accessories" that has proved to be very important to the efficient operation of Windows has been an air conditioner. High-end personal computers eat a lot of power and consequently generate a lot of heat. They have a lot less tolerance than less powerful machines for an environment that is too hot or too humid. I can recall first-generation XT systems that would run comfortably all day in the middle of August in conditions that would kill anything more sophisticated than a transistor radio. This is rarely the case for an 80386-based system.

SUMMARY

This chapter has not really told you very much about how to use Windows; the program itself comes with documentation that will perform this task pretty well. However, having read the chapter you should have a good idea of what Windows offers you. You should also know—in real-world terms—what you'll need to make Windows into a useful part of your home office.

CHAPTER

5

5

WORD PROCESSING

Most home office applications will require some recourse to word processing, and it may be that a great deal of what you do will center around your word processor. Word processing is one of the more diverse areas of applications software. You can buy word processors with as little or as much power as you need and fine tune your choice to suit your requirements.

Of necessity, a discussion of word processing will at least touch on the subject of desktop publishing, something that won't be dealt with in detail until the next chapter. However, despite the complex formatting available under desktop publishing software, the words on a desktop published page have to start somewhere, and the usual place is in a word processor. If you plan to use a desktop publishing package, you'll probably import words into your desktop publishing documents from word processing files.

As with choosing computer hardware, it's not all that easy to fully understand what your requirements of a word processor will be until you've used one for a while. Fortunately, if you choose a package that turns out to be less than what you need you'll be dealing with the replacement of a hundred dollars worth of software rather than several thousand dollars worth of hardware. However, although replacing one word processor with another is a fairly painless undertaking, the files you created with your old package might not be usable with your new one. We'll discuss this issue in greater detail later on in this chapter.

WORD PROCESSING FACILITIES

A word processor can be anything from a sort of muscular electric typewriter right on up to a complete typesetting house and art department on a disk. The more powerful ones represent a considerably longer learning curve, however. If you envision writing nothing but letters, a high-end word processor will probably be much more than you need. It will take up more disk space than it should, it will need more memory, it will offer you more controls, and it will take longer to learn and subsequently to use.

If you envision creating complex documents with multiple columns, elaborate typography, and inset pictures you will find that high-end word processors and true desktop publishing packages maintain an uneasy alliance, with the former very often having designs on functions that might be better performed by the latter. If your applications for word processing involve complex page designs you might find that you can't really make up your mind about the software you need until you've gotten through the desktop publishing chapter of this book too.

The simplest sorts of word processors are those that merely process words. You might think of such a program as being an electric typewriter with some additional features. The screen and memory of your computer behave like a tremendously long sheet of paper under such an application, but one with rather more convenient characteristics than are found in real paper. Having typed some text into a word processor, you can move around the page adding and deleting words, editing what you've written, moving blocks of text about, and so on, without having to retype the rest of the text. When you're finished with your document you can save it in a disk file to call it back and work with it again some time in the future. When it's ready to appear on real paper—as "hard copy"—it can be printed with no typographical errors or applications of liquid paper.

This entire book was written using this sort of word processor. It was subsequently sent to its publisher, which made changes to it using another word processor. In fact, it was sent to the publisher over a phone line rather than by Federal Express, but that part of things will have to wait for a while.

The text that you're reading at the moment is set in what is called "proportionally spaced" type. This means that every character takes up only as much space on its line as it has to, with characters such as the letter *i* being typically much thinner than characters such as the letter *M*. Thus, there's no fixed number of characters per line. The number of characters depends on the aggregate widths of the characters in question.

When you type text into a word processor, the word processor will impose automatic line ending, or "word wrap." This means that when the text you type exceeds the right margin of the word processor's page, it will move down to the next line and allow you to keep going. Experienced word processing users don't even notice this process—you need only hit Enter at the ends of paragraphs.

In a very simple word processor—such as the one I use to write books—all the characters are assumed by the word processor to be of the same width, and the word processor in turn assumes that its text will be printed to a printer that supports characters of equal widths so that what gets printed will look like what appeared on your screen. This means that the word processor need not measure the widths of all the characters. It will know that its right margin is set at the sixty-fifth character position, for example, just like a traditional typewriter.

These sorts of word processors are often referred to by the people who use them as "text bashers." Such a program is capable of quickly entering and editing text, but it has only rudimentary formatting capabilities. In fact, they're so rudimentary that they can be listed here without taking up very much space. A simple word processor can do the following things to a document:

— It can underline text by printing it with the underscore character.

— It can print text in bold face by printing it twice. This doesn't work if the output is to a laser printer.

— It can do crude automatic right-margin *justification* by padding out the spaces between words until all the lines end at the same position.

This is a tiny fraction of what more sophisticated word processors can handle. Simple text basher word processors exist for two reasons. To begin with, they're very easy to use and once you've learned their few simple commands you can use them with astounding speed. Second, they're ideally suited for creating relatively "pure" text files to be used in desktop publishing chapters. The nature of a pure text file will be discussed later in this chapter.

There are very few simple PC word processors of this sort. One of these, WordStar, is no longer readily available in its simplest, most useful form (version 3.3). The packages that most PC users who need this sort of facility turn to is one called PC-Write. The PC-Write software is actually distributed as "shareware." Shareware will be discussed in detail in Chapter 12.

There are no really simple word processors of this sort for the Macintosh.

Figure 5.1 illustrates a document produced by a simple word processor. You might want to keep this in mind to compare it with the documents output by more advanced software.

WYSIWYG Word Processors

The apparent typographical error in the foregoing heading is one of the more interesting of contemporary computer acronyms. Pronounced "wizzy-wig" on those occasions when it must be pronounced at all, it stands for "what you see is what you get."

Two simple WYSIWYG word processors are MacWrite for the Macintosh and Windows Write for the PC. While they don't offer all the high-end features of the packages to be discussed in the next section of this chapter, they let you use most of the special type effects you could ask for and are not terribly complicated.

MacWrite and Windows Write both work in graphics mode and they both support proportionally spaced type such as the text you're reading now. In fact, driving laser printers, they could both have created pages like the one you're reading. They can certainly do first-class letters and reports.

With this sort of word processor, you can select a variety of fonts and font sizes in which to set your text. Having typed some text, you can use your mouse to change the font and/or other attributes for one character or for several paragraphs. All you need to do to change some text to, say, boldface is to drag the mouse cursor over the text in question and select *Bold* from one of the menus.

You can learn to use either MacWrite or Windows Write from a standing start in well under an hour. Both are masterpieces of intuitive software.

Figure 5.2 illustrates a document that was produced by Windows Write. An identical page could have come from MacWrite. You'll notice an element that has not been discussed thus far, that of a picture in the text.

Both MacWrite and Windows Write allow you to include pictures with your text. In both cases this facility is decidedly crude by comparison with more advanced word processing and desktop publishing facilities, but it's still quite useful. You can, for example, have your letterhead printed as part of your documents. You can include charts and tables, scanned photographs, and other descriptive graphics within the body of reports. In both cases, the pictures you use can come from a variety of sources, most of which will be discussed more fully in the next chapter.

The contemporary version of MacWrite is a more powerful word processor than Windows Write. This may not be surprising, as MacWrite is

Dreadlord & Leech
Parrot Mongers
1511 East Igneous Court
Coppertown, CA 94716

Preston Brett Hatbox
612 Silicon Road
Coppertown, CA 94720

2 May 1991

Dear Mr. Hatbox,

Let me begin by thanking you most superficially for your recent order. I should like at this time to offer you a reply to your various questions regarding the care and maintenance of parrots.

1. <u>Oven temperature:</u> We do not recommend keeping parrots in an oven, as such a habitat would be dark and not conducive to the well-being of the bird.

2. <u>Tensile strength:</u> I've consulted with our technical people and have discovered that no attempt has ever been made to test the tensile strength of a parrot. It was universally agreed that it would be very low, and we strongly suggest that no attempt be made on your part to test it, either.

3. <u>Footcandles:</u> I confess I had to look this one up. As I understand it, this is a measure of light output. None of our people can imagine a way to cause a parrot to emit a measurable amount of light, and I for one do not wish to consider it.

I regret that we are unable to be of much more assistance regarding your numerous other points, such as <u>permeability</u>, <u>leftist tendencies</u>, <u>electrical resistance</u> and so on. None of these are areas which we, as parrot dealers, have had much experience.

Your letter gives us rise to question whether you are aware of the requirements of the birds you have ordered.

Please also be informed that we are not able to sell parrots by the pound.

Sincerely yours,

Cyrus P. Dreadlord
President

CPD/xf

Figure 5.1: A document produced by a simple word processor

Dreadlord
PARROT MONGERS
&Leech

1511 EAST IGNEOUS COURT - COPPERTOWN - CA - 94716

Preston Brett Hatbox
612 Silicon Road
Coppertown, CA 94720

2 May 1991

Dear Mr. Hatbox,

Let me begin by thanking you most superficially for your recent order. I should like at this time to offer you a reply to your various questions regarding the care and maintenance of parrots.

1. Oven temperature:

We do not recommend keeping parrots in an oven, as such a habitat would be dark and not conducive to the well-being of the bird.

2. Tensile strength:

I've consulted with our technical people and have discovered that no attempt has ever been made to test the tensile strength of a parrot. It was universally agreed that it would be very low, and we strongly suggest that no attempt be made on your part to test it, either.

3. Footcandles:

I confess I had to look this one up. As I understand it, this is a measure of light output. None of our people can imagine a way to cause a parrot to emit a measurable amount of light, and I for one do not wish to consider it.

I regret that we are unable to be of much more assistance regarding your numerous other points, such as *permeability*, *leftist tendencies*, *electrical resistance* and so on. None of these are areas which we, as parrot dealers, have had much experience.

Your letter gives us rise to question whether you are aware of the requirements of the birds you have ordered.

Please also be informed that we are not able to sell parrots by the pound.

Sincerely yours,

Cyrus P. Dreadlord
President

CPD/xf

Figure 5.2: A document produced by Windows Write

a commercial, paid-for package while Windows Write comes free with Windows. The pagination tools of both packages are pretty impressive. You can have MacWrite or Windows Write print a long string of text as neatly formatted pages, specifying the page length to suit your requirements, and each page can have a header and a footer if you like—however, under Windows Write the headers and footers can only include text and the page number. Under MacWrite they can also include things like the time and the date.

The spelling checker of MacWrite is arguably its most notable advantage over Windows Write. Spelling checkers will be discussed in the next section.

Spelling Checkers—A Digression

My life runs on word processors, but it has been saved by spelling checkers. While I could probably write with a typewriter in the absence of a word processor—what a ghastly thought—I still wouldn't be able to spell. There's nothing like being brought up with two languages to make one incapable of spelling either correctly.

Spelling checkers exist either as stand-alone programs or as integrated, built-in features of some word processors, such as MacWrite. The function of a spelling checker is very easy to understand. It maintains a very large dictionary of words. Given some text to check, the software steps through it one word at a time comparing each to its dictionary. Words that are found to exist in the dictionary are ignored. Words that aren't in the dictionary are brought to your attention, because they might be misspelled. Alternatively, it might just be that they're not in the dictionary yet.

Having found a suspect word, a spelling checker will typically allow you to enter the correct word. Most spelling checkers will suggest a number of similar words so you can quickly pick a likely replacement. If the word turns out to be correctly spelled but simply unknown to the spelling checker, you can have it added to a supplemental dictionary so that it won't have to be questioned again the next time it occurs. In this way, your spelling checker can learn specialized terms and names that you use often.

Wonderful, blessed things that they are, spelling checkers embody several important limitations. The first is that they will not catch incorrect usages of homonyms. For example, if you use "their" or "there" when you meant to use "they're," your spelling checker isn't going to raise any flags, since any one of them is a correctly spelled word.

Having a spelling checker built into your word processor is exceedingly handy. MacWrite is a delight to use in this respect, although its spelling checker is fairly slow as these things go. You can quickly check a letter you've just written, and MacWrite allows you to check only selected portions of a document if you like. Microsoft Word, to be discussed in the next section of this chapter, also features an integrated spelling checker.

Stand-alone spelling checkers are typically faster and smarter than those built into word processors. Because you can insert the correct spellings into documents from within a spelling checker, you don't have to get back into your word processor.

There are two other software packages that often come up when spelling checkers are discussed. The more useful of these is the electronic thesaurus, which will quickly find words of similar meanings when you're stuck for something different. The other is a grammar checker. In practice, neither of these things will ultimately do you as much good as you might expect.

An electronic thesaurus typically has only a fraction of the facilities of a traditional paper one. Although spelling checkers can hold tens of thousands of words in their dictionaries in what seems to be nowhere near the space all those words should take up (because there's a way to compress the list of words), there's no comparable way to compress the list for a thesaurus.

Grammar checkers can be downright offensive. They have very parochial notions of grammar, and complain about all sorts of perfectly acceptable sentences that don't conform to their standards. Unless you know when to ignore its advice or decline its suggestions, a grammar checker can very quickly water down the impact of some of your most important sentences. While its results may be better than the text of a lot of business correspondence, it restricts your expression somewhat.

HIGH-END WORD PROCESSORS

The word processors that get the most advertising are not the simple applications we've discussed thus far. The best way to sell software is to give it more features than its competitors, and a word processor is an ideal program to tack more features onto.

The most popular high-end word processor for PC environments is a package called WordPerfect. The relative merits of WordPerfect can frequently be heard discussed at high volume levels among its adherents and detractors. WordPerfect can do almost everything anyone can imagine a word processor doing, but it always seems to find the least intuitive way of doing it. Its designers were enamored of the PC keyboard's function keys, and as a result a large number of the functions of WordPerfect are accessed through the function keys themselves or combinations of the function keys with Alt, Shift, and Ctrl. The F7 key, for example, is used to exit WordPerfect. There's no obvious reason for this choice—you just have to remember it.

Of the plethora of high-end word processors available, perhaps the most applicable one for a home office is Microsoft Word. Available in versions for a PC running DOS, a PC running Windows, or the Macintosh, it presents a consistent user interface that can be quickly mastered. It can do almost as much as WordPerfect and other high-end word processors, but it doesn't take half your lifetime to make it worthwhile. Though not quite a desktop publishing package, Microsoft Word features a lot of the high-end facilities that make desktop publishing powerful.

Figure 5.3 illustrates two versions of Word. I'll be using Word in this section as a very good representative of what is available with high-end word processors.

Word is in many respects a much more powerful version of the WYSIWYG word processors discussed in the previous section. If MacWrite or Windows Write seemed like what you want but didn't quite have enough features, Word will probably be perfect. It will display a document on the screen exactly as it will be printed, that is, the bold and italics will appear as such, the relative sizes will be displayed, and so on. You can change fonts by selecting the text you wish to affect and then selecting a new font from a menu.

Word provides powerful text formatting capabilities. You can define the sizes of the margins of each page, where headers and footers will appear and what they'll contain, how headings and subheadings will look, and so on. You can also insert pictures into documents.

Word has a first-class spelling checker. It's dictionary is large enough to be really comprehensive and it's quite fast. You can check all or part of a document. The Macintosh version of Word has a word count facility, which is handy if you have to fill a defined space with text. The Windows version offers one of the previously disparaged electronic thesauruses—its installation is optional.

One of the most powerful features of Word for working on larger projects is that it allows you to open multiple documents at once. This means, for example, if you write a report with three chapters in it you can have each one in its own window and move quickly between them. You can cut and paste blocks of text from one to another. The Windows version will actually keep track of which documents you have open from one session to another, making it easy to resume where you left off. When you first boot it up, the File menu will have a list of your most recently used files.

Another powerful feature of Word is its ability to use *macros*. A macro is a key combination that, when struck, will cause something more complicated to happen. For example, you might assign your name and

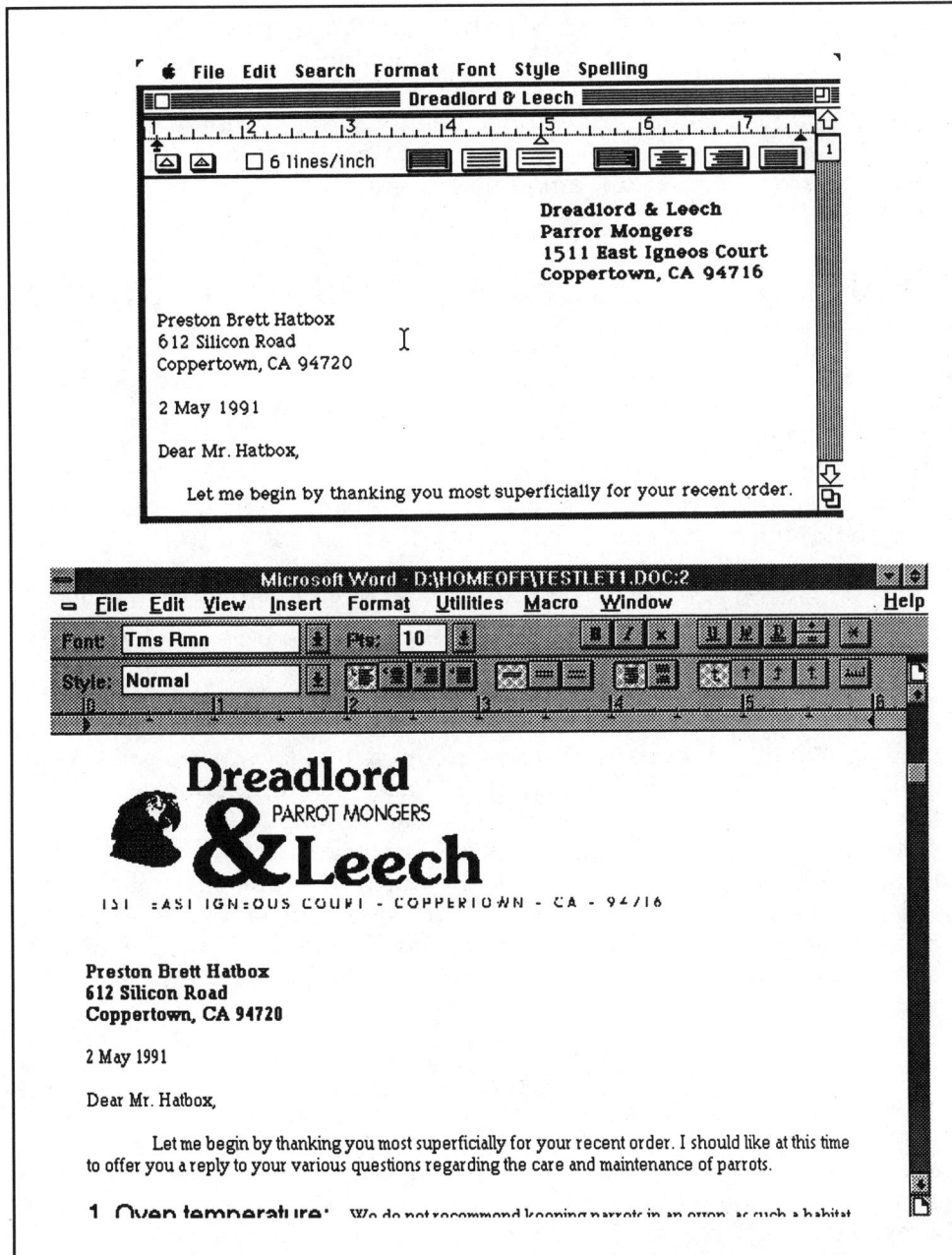

Figure 5.3: The Macintosh and Windows versions of Microsoft Word

address to the key combination *Ctrl-N* under Word. Thereafter, whenever you hit *Ctrl-N* you would have your name and address automatically typed into whatever document you're working on. Macros can also be used to do things like jump around between documents, insert headers and footers, and so on. As you get more proficient with Word you'll find that its macro facility can save a significant amount of typing.

WORD PROCESSING FILE FORMATS

When you save a file under a word processor, the text you've written will be stored on disk in a format that is specific to the word processing software you're using. Aside from the words you write, in most cases your document will include some special codes to indicate that certain words are in boldface or italics, that there are font size changes, that pictures are to be inserted in the text, etc. The format for a document saved by Microsoft Word would differ from that saved by WordPerfect, and a Word file would be of little use to WordPerfect.

As word processing has become more powerful and more widely used, the authors of the predominant word processing packages have recognized the need for people using different word processors to be able to exchange files. Consequently, the Windows version of Microsoft Word for example will actually open files from a variety of other word processing packages, including Windows Write and WordPerfect, and Windows Write will save its files to either its own special format or the Microsoft Word format.

At such time as you begin to look at desktop publishing software, you should take particular care to make sure that the desktop publishing package you want to use will accept the native document format of your word processor. In many cases there are conversion programs that will squeak past file incompatibilities, and you can usually work with pure ASCII files in a pinch, but neither of these solutions is terribly convenient if you have to use it a dozen times a day.

ASCII Text Format

There is a standard format for "raw" text, that is, text that includes absolutely no formatting. It's informally called an "ASCII" file. The acronym ASCII stands for American Standard Code for Information Interchange, and really just refers to the way text is coded on a computer.

An ASCII word processing file consists of nothing but text, tab characters, and, at the ends of paragraphs only, carriage returns—the result of hitting the Enter key.

None of the word processors discussed in this chapter work directly with pure ASCII files, although they will all read and produce them on command should you find yourself confronted with one. The drawback to a pure ASCII file is that a document saved as one will lose all its font and format changes and so on.

The PC-Write word processor mentioned early in this chapter works with files that are very close to being pure ASCII. The others don't even come close.

CHOOSING A WORD PROCESSOR: MACINTOSH

This chapter has only discussed two word processors for the Macintosh, these being MacWrite and Microsoft Word. There are quite a few others, of course. They all seem to have gathered in the high end of the Mac word processor market, struggling to dislodge their competitors.

Packages such as FullWrite and WriteNow, which look very impressive in their respective magazine ads, tend to be as much desktop publishing packages as they are word processors. They have fairly steep learning curves. They certainly have their place, but their mix of features isn't really ideal for a home office.

If you plan to write nothing but letters and perhaps some small reports, MacWrite will probably be all the word processor you'll ever need. If you envision handling larger documents or producing more complex pages, you should choose Microsoft Word. If you have designs on handling really involved pages with multiple columns, lots of graphics and such, you should be looking at two separate programs: a desktop publishing package and a simple word processor.

Although desktop publishing software will be dealt with in the next chapter, there's a useful consideration to note here. One of the Macintosh desktop publishing packages that will be discussed will be the Macintosh implementation of Ventura Publisher. As of this writing Ventura for the Mac was still quite a new application, and it would not import MacWrite text files. It does, however, handle Microsoft Word files, something to keep in mind if you're choosing a word processor for the Macintosh to use with Ventura.

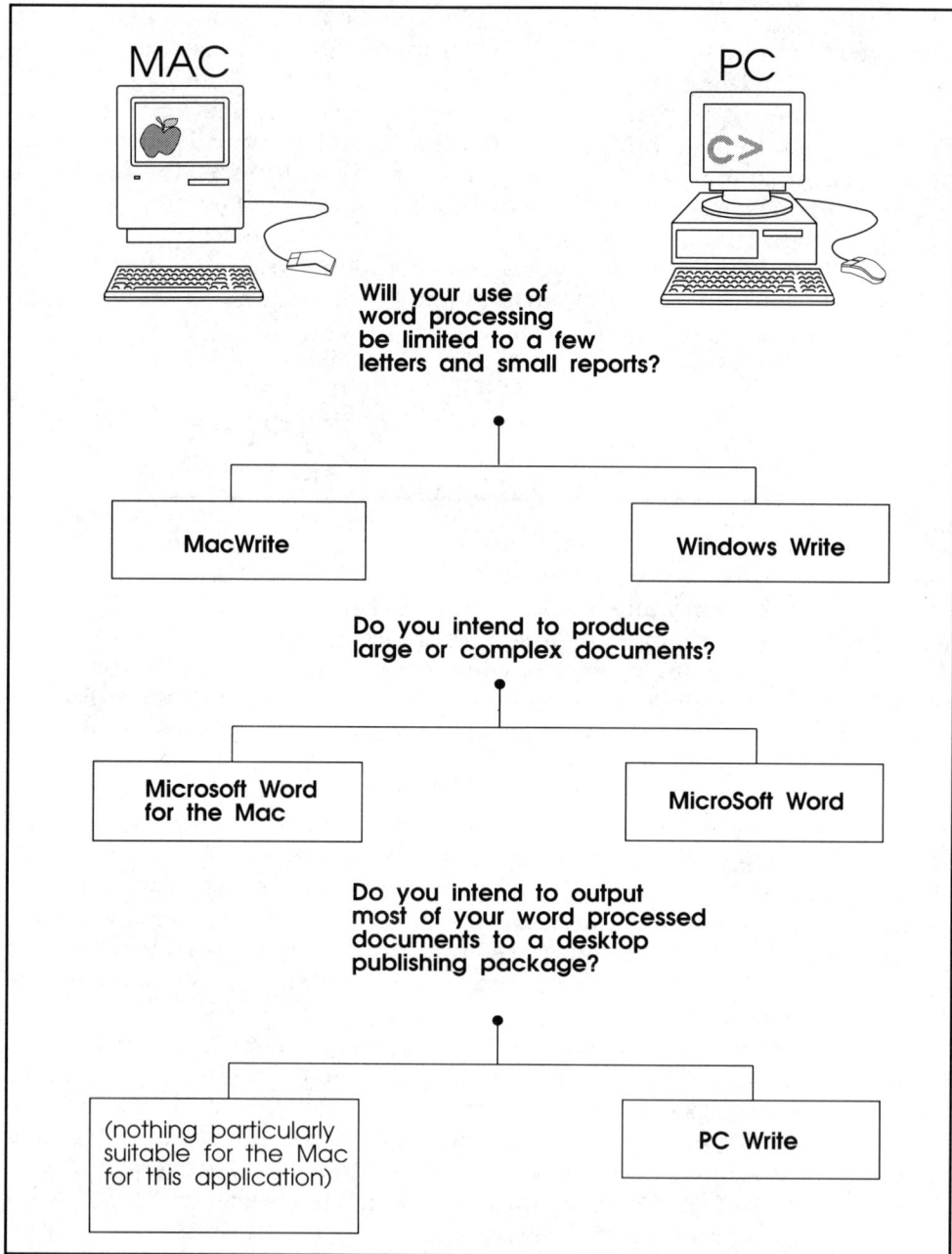

MAC   PC

Will your use of
word processing
be limited to a few
letters and small reports?

MacWrite	Windows Write

Do you intend to produce
large or complex documents?

Microsoft Word for the Mac	MicroSoft Word

Do you intend to output
most of your word processed
documents to a desktop
publishing package?

(nothing particularly suitable for the Mac for this application)	PC Write

CHOOSING A WORD PROCESSOR: PC

The decision tree for choosing a word processor for the PC is a bit more involved than the one for the Mac. Once again, there are countless other contenders that could have appeared here. The packages that have been omitted from this chapter aren't necessarily bad word processors—they just aren't ideally suited for use in a home office.

If the majority of your writing will ultimately wind up being desktop published, you can use a small, inexpensive text-only word processor such as PC-Write. The PC-Write word processor bashes text and does little else.

If you plan to write a few letters and perhaps some small reports and you want a word processor that will be very easy to get into, the Windows Write application is ideal. If you were going to buy Windows anyway, the price is right too—Windows Write comes with Windows at no extra charge.

If you'll be generating longer reports or other documents with moderately complex formatting, you should probably spring for Microsoft Word, either in its DOS or Windows manifestation. It's worth noting that inasmuch as Word for Windows can open Windows Write files, you can start with Write and later step up to Word if you find you need it with what must be one of the most painless transition processes available in PC software.

Should you plan to produce newsletters, fliers, advertisements, complex multi-column reports or other really sophisticated pages, you'll really need a desktop publishing package. In this case, you can probably choose any one of the three word processing packages discussed here. If you'll be doing nothing but desktop publishing you'll find PC-Write to be just about perfect. If you envision doing a few letters and other sorts of documents that will be printed directly from your word processor in addition to desktop publishing, Word is a good choice. The Word file format is readily accepted by most desktop publishing software.

6

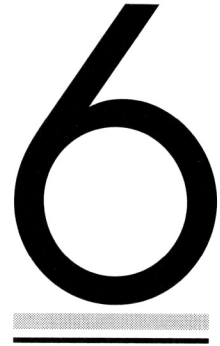

DESKTOP PUBLISHING
AND GRAPHICS

No matter how brilliant your words are, few people will want to read them if they're hand written. Not too many people will be interested in reading them if they're merely typed, either. Typeset text, on the other hand, carries with it a sense of authority and purpose. It implies that your words are at least sufficiently important to command the cost of printing.

Expressive typography is largely beyond the capabilities of simple word processors. As was discussed in the last chapter, you can squeeze a certain amount of desktop publishing from a word processing package like Microsoft Word, but the results will rarely be quite as tight as what a proper desktop publishing package could have done. In addition, you frequently have to go to some pretty involved lengths to trick Word into doing things that a real desktop publishing package such as Ventura Publisher could do with a few mouse clicks.

Desktop publishing will avail you of things that were the province of commercial production houses a few years ago. It will give you the facility to create newsletters, advertisements, fliers, reports, and all sorts of other professional documents. Furthermore, it will allow you to create them in hours instead of weeks.

The first part of this chapter will discuss desktop publishing in general. The second will deal with graphics. In most cases you'll use graphics software to supply images to a desktop publishing package, just as a word processor supplies it with words. However, there are certainly applications for stand-alone graphics. If yours is one of them, you might want to skip the discussion of desktop publishing and go straight to the graphics section.

DESKTOP PUBLISHING—WHAT IT DOES

The easiest way to think of a desktop publishing package is to see it as an analog for an art department. Before there were laser printers, people would produce newsletters like the one in Figure 6.1 by writing or typing the words and snapping some pictures, taking the pages and pictures to a design house, and then taking the art boards from the design house to a printer.

A graphic artist confronted with the raw materials of the newsletter in Figure 6.1 would "mark up" the text for typesetting. This involved indicating the typefaces, sizes, and effects to be used in typesetting the text. The marked-up copy would then be given to a typesetter, who would type the text into a typesetting machine. Some while later—usually a day or so in busy commercial art departments—the type would emerge as a long strip of type one column wide, called a "galley."

In the mean time, the graphic artist would make PMTs of your photographs. These are reproductions which replace the greys of conventional photographs with screens of dots. You can see these if you look carefully at a photograph in any newsletter or newspaper.

When all the components of the newsletter were ready to assemble, the graphic artist would wax them—the wax served to make them stick to whatever they were to be assembled on—and then paste the whole works onto art boards such that the type was assembled in columns, the pictures were stuck down to appropriate parts of the page, and so on. Rules were either drawn in by hand or applied using specially made tapes.

A desktop publishing project starts with the computer equivalents of the same things. The words are, of course, a word processing file. Pictures can come from all sorts of places. They can be drawn in a graphics package, as will be discussed later in this chapter. They can be "scanned" from photographs. They can also be "exported" from other applications. For example, if you wanted to create a desktop published report that contained a graph derived from a financial spreadsheet, you would export the graph to a drawing file and then import it into a desktop publishing "chapter."

A desktop publishing chapter can be thought of as being the framework that holds all the disparate elements of your newsletter, report, or other publishing project together. It's a most accommodating frame. If

Alchemical News

SPRING 1991 • UPDATES FOR ALCHEMY SHAREWARE

Desktop Paint 256™

Desktop Paint 256 is a powerful super-VGA paint program which will allow you to create and edit full colour pictures. It can load and save to several popular image file formats, making it suitable for a wide variety of graphic applications. Desktop Paint 256 is a superb tool for picture collectors, artists, desktop publishers and for anyone who just likes to draw or meddle with images.

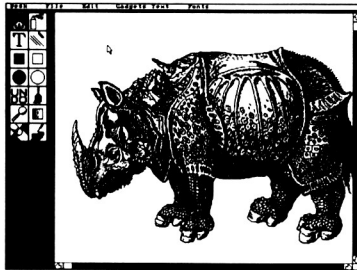

In addition, Desktop Paint 256 supports a grey scale mode for use with desktop publishing software such as Ventura Publisher and PageMaker.

Desktop Paint 256 has a full range of drawing tools and effects. It will perform basic drawing functions such as adding lines, rectangles, ellipses and so on to a picture. You can zoom in and edit details and draw freehand with colour brushes. You can also cut and paste image fragments, as well as importing and exporting them. There's an undo function to deal with mistakes.

A variety of special effects are also available under Desktop Paint 256. You can rotate, flip and invert areas of a picture. You can also stain, smudge, posterize, sharpen and soften parts of a picture... the latter effect is particularly effective at reducing the effects of moiré scanning aberrations.

Desktop Paint 256 also allows you to add text to a picture. It comes with a selection of fonts, and you can add more to it if you like. The optional font toolkit provides additional fonts and a selection of utilities to convert fonts from Macintosh FONT resources, GEM/VDI font files and Windows FNT files.

The intuitive user interface of Desktop Paint 256 makes it exceedingly easy to learn, even if you don't usually read the documentation for software before you boot it up. Complete EMS support means that it will work on pictures of any size, as long as you have enough extended memory to contain them. Pictures of 640 by 400 pixels or less can be edited without EMS.

Current users of the monochrome version of Desktop Paint will find that Desktop Paint 256 has many of the same features and a similar feel and user interface.

Hardware and Software

Desktop Paint 256 will read and write image files in the following formats:

- PCX (as used by PC Paintbrush®)
- GIF (from CompuServe®)
- TIFF (Monochrome, grey scale and colour)
- IFF/LBM (as used by Deluxe Paint®)

Please note that due to the variations in the way TIFF files are structured, Desktop Paint 256 will not read *all* TIFF files.

Desktop Paint 256 requires a Microsoft compatible mouse and driver and one of the following super VGA display adapters:

- Paradise Plus® (256K on board)
- Paradise Professional® (512K on board)
- ATI VGA Wonder® card (256K or 512K on board)
- Headland Video7® or 1024i card (256K or 512K on board)

Cards which are genuinely compatible with these are also suitable. For example, there are numerous cards which use the Western Digital chip set and are thus effectively Paradise cards. The OEM VGA cards supplied with Dell computers behave as Paradise cards, for example.

Desktop Paint 256 does not run in the "standard" 320 by 200 pixel VGA mode. Drivers for additional super-VGA cards are in the works.

Please note that the Desktop Paint 256 font toolkit is identical to the font toolkit for the monochrome version of Desktop Paint. You only need one copy.

Registration

Desktop Paint 256 is available for a shareware contribution of $35.00. Please specify 5 1/4 or 3 1/2 inch disks.

ALCHEMY MINDWORKS INC. • P.O. BOX 500 • BEETON • ONTARIO • L0G 1A0 • CANADA • (416) 729-3831 • FAX (416) 729-4156

Figure 6.1: A desktop published newsletter

you think of the text that will fill your pages as being fluid, you might describe it as being "poured" into the frame of your page. For example, you might decide that you want the text to appear in three columns. The desktop publishing package will "flow" the text into the appropriate areas. If you want to place a picture on the page, the text will flow around the picture. If you make some of the text bigger, the remaining text will flow further along to accommodate it.

These are all things a graphic artist formerly would have done with a sharp knife and multiple trips to the typesetting department.

One of the less appreciated aspects of desktop publishing is that, aside from giving you finished documents in a short time, it gives you compete control over what they'll look like. It also gives you complete responsibility for them, of course—you can no longer describe what you want in vague terms and have a graphic artist choose type and design elements for you. However, once you have developed a sense of how to express your ideas in design and typography, you'll be able to do so without having anyone else interjecting their ideas.

Pages and Chapters

There are two sorts of desktop publishing packages, and although these areas overlap considerably in real-world applications, you'll do well to determine exactly what your purposes are if you're to choose the best one for your types of projects. The two areas are pages and chapters.

Desktop publishing applications that are fine-tuned for producing individual pages—such as flyers and advertisements—make it easy to place a few words where you want them and to quickly integrate graphics with your text. Packages that are designed to produce multiple-page chapters—books, reports, newsletters, and so on—have their strengths in flowing large text files through multiple pages. They make dealing with lots of headings and stylistic elements easy. Such a package will typically manage things like footnotes, an index, a table of contents, and other elements of a large publication automatically. We'll discuss software of both types in this chapter. Specifically, this chapter will deal with Ventura Publisher and Ready-Set-Go on the Macintosh and Ventura Publisher and PageMaker for the PC environment. Ventura is a package that leans toward producing longer documents, and the strength of Ready-Set-Go and PageMaker—as the name of the latter might imply—is in producing shorter publications, especially single-page documents that integrate text and graphics.

These categories are by no means exclusive. Ventura can build pages and Ready-Set-Go and PageMaker can both build longer publications. They're just not ideally suited for these tasks.

It's worth noting that a version of PageMaker also exists for the Macintosh—in fact, it was born there. It won't be discussed in this chapter, however, since I believe Ready-Set-Go is a better choice for the sorts of desktop publishing you'll be likely to do in a home office environment.

The desktop publishing software to be discussed in this chapter represents a small fraction of the applications available to perform these functions. Specifically, there are a lot of low-end desktop publishing packages, such as Publish It! by TimeWorks, that offer some of the power of higher-end desktop publishing software, but with a lot of limitations. For most serious applications, the money you'd save buying Publish It! over, say, Ventura would get spent many times over in the time you'd have to spend to get things done. Worse still is the time you have to spend with low-end desktop publishing software only to find that your software isn't capable of doing what you want it to do.

Ventura, PageMaker, and Ready-Set-Go are all a bit expensive, but they work well and are suitable for use in a serious home office environment.

Using Tags

One of the fundamental differences between a page creation package such as Ready-Set-Go and a chapter creation package like Ventura is the use of "tags." Tags make producing long documents easy, and if you understand them you'll probably be well on your way to being able to decide which sort of software your applications call for.

Periodically throughout this book you have encountered subheads—a few words in bold type that serve to break up the text of each chapter into logical sections. In fact, there are three levels of these subheads, called A, B, and C. The one you just read was a C-level subhead.

In a desktop publishing package which uses a tag system, each of the levels of subheads would be given a tag. For example, if I'd been typing this chapter with the intent of pouring its text file into a Ventura Publisher chapter, I would have typed the foregoing head like this:

@SUBHEAD C = Using Tags

The @SUBHEAD C = is a Ventura tag. It identifies this subhead and all other C-level subheads in the chapter as having the same typeface, size, and other typographic characteristics. It does not actually define what they are—only that they're consistent. (Note that when you print a Ventura chapter the tags themselves do not appear in the printed output. Likewise, they don't show up on the screen when you're working with a Ventura chapter.)

Having finished writing this chapter, I would have imported its original WordStar file into Ventura and selected one of the C-level subheads. Ventura allows each tagged item to be given a specific typeface, size, and so on. There are, in fact, dozens of parameters that can be associated with each distinct tag in a chapter, although many are usually left to their default values and never explicitly set.

Changing the typographic characteristics of one instance of the @SUBHEAD C tag automatically changes them all. Thus, rather than having to select all the C-level subheads in the book one at a time and change them, Ventura will make all the changes. This eliminates a lot of work, of course—it also eliminates the possibility of missing a few.

The complete set of tags, along with the page margins and other stylistic elements of a particular Ventura chapter, are called its "style sheet." Style sheets are interchangeable. For example, having created the style sheet for the first chapter of this book under Ventura, I could ensure that all the subsequent chapters looked the same by simply instructing Ventura to use the same style sheet for them all.

If you produce, for example, a lot of reports, you can apply the same style sheet to them all. This really means that having designed the first one all the subsequent ones will require little more than pouring their text into Ventura and a quick trip to the laser printer.

It's worth noting that Ventura does allow you to select some text with a mouse and change it, just as MacWrite, Word, and Windows Write did. Likewise, you should also know that the current version of PageMaker implements tags and style sheets, although these facilities are considerably more developed under Ventura. Competition has forced most of the major desktop publishing packages to borrow heavily from each other.

VENTURA PUBLISHER

We'll have a look at Ventura first, because it's available for both PCs and Macs. In fact, there are three implementations available, because there are two different versions for the PC—a Windows version and a non-Windows version. The basic features of the three implementations are largely consistent, so, with a few fairly obscure exceptions, talking about one will cover them all.

Figure 6.2 illustrates the three implementations of Ventura Publisher. In this case, each has opened the chapter which contains the first page of the newsletter from Figure 6.1.

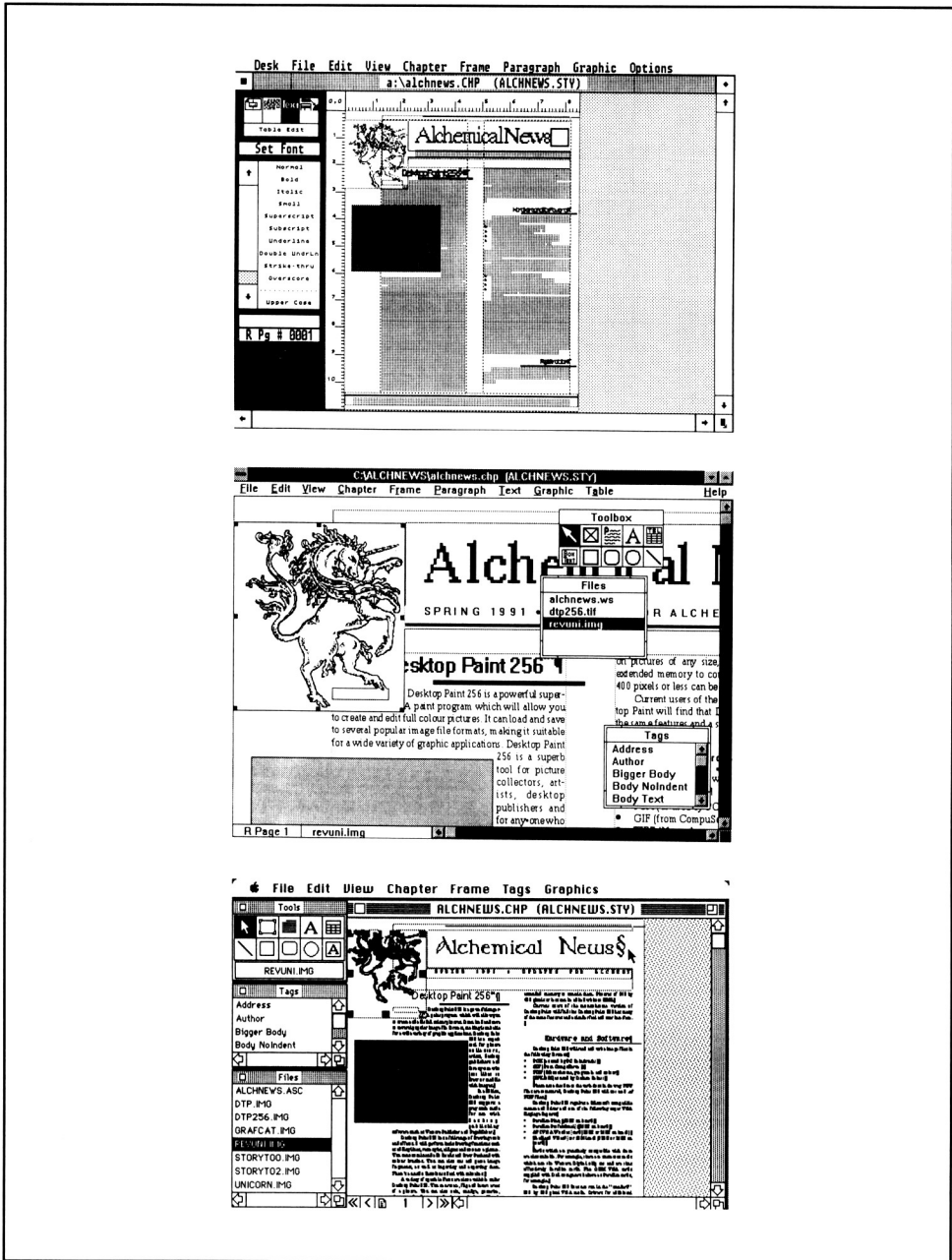

Figure 6.2: The GEM, Windows, and Macintosh versions of Ventura Publisher

The first version is the one that runs directly from DOS. The GEM designation refers to the software this implementation of Ventura uses to manage its windows, menus, and so on. GEM is a little like Microsoft Windows, though nowhere near as sophisticated. In any case, you'll never actually have to deal with GEM directly in using Ventura; it's built into the package.

The Windows version of Ventura was written to run under Microsoft's Windows 3. If you know how to use other Windows applications you won't have much trouble learning Ventura for Windows, because the style of its menus, dialogs, and so on will be familiar to you.

There are positive features to recommend either of these two versions:

— The GEM version is notably faster than the Windows version. It's able to use downloadable printer fonts—as discussed in Chapter 2—in a much more convenient way. It has been around longer, and has fewer bugs and problems than the Windows version.

— The Windows version offers the same advantages of other Windows applications. You can use it concurrently with other programs, popping between them as needed. It has the same user interface as other applications, making it easier to learn. It also takes up substantially less disk space than the GEM version, as many of the things that the GEM version must provide for itself are available from the Windows software for the Windows version.

The drawbacks to the Windows version of Ventura are worth noting. It's quite slow, even on a fairly high-end machine. For practical purposes it can't use downloadable PostScript printer fonts as of this writing—it's limited to those fonts that are resident in your printer. It also has a number of shortcomings in what it can do, since the current version was rushed to market when Windows 3 was initially released.

No matter which implementation you use—Gem, Windows, or Macintosh—the chapters you create with one version can be opened by all the other versions. In the case of the Mac implementation, however, you'd need a way to physically move the chapter files between a PC and a Mac. In the case of Figure 6.2, the chapter was opened over a network connecting several Macintosh and PC systems.

One of the things that endears Ventura to its users is that it's able to accept files from a large number of sources. For example, it can accept word processing documents in any of the following formats:

ASCII files

WordStar

WordPerfect

XyWrite

Multimate

DCA

Microsoft Word

Xerox Writer

It can also handle text files created by other sorts of applications. Your Ventura chapters can therefore include spreadsheet and database data. One popular use for the latter is in publishing directories.

Ventura is equally flexible in working with pictures.

Ventura handles imported text and picture files in a way that is markedly different from most other desktop publishing packages. For example, the newsletter in Figure 6.1 consisted of the following files before Ventura got hold of them.

NEWSLETR.WS   A WordStar text file

RHINO.TIF   The picture of the rhinoceros on the front page

UNICORN.IMG   The picture of the unicorn

APRIL.TIF   Another picture later in the newsletter

In creating the newsletter, Ventura generated four files constituting the actual chapter information, as well as a style sheet file and a file to specify where the pictures appeared. It didn't modify any of the source files.

Because NEWSLETR.WS remains a WordStar file, I can edit it with WordStar even after Ventura has incorporated it into a chapter. If I'd created NEWSLETR as a Microsoft Word file, Ventura would maintain it as a Microsoft Word file in the same way. In addition, if I make changes to NEWSLETR.WS from *within* Ventura—for example, if I notice a spelling error and fix it on the screen—Ventura will save the result back to NEWSLETR.WS as a WordStar file. Likewise, I can change the pictures and they'll reflect the changes when the chapter is next opened.

The result of this arrangement of files is that you'll have a lot more files to keep track of. Ventura gets upset if you create a chapter and subsequently rename, move, or delete one of the files it expects to be present. However, it also means that you can easily modify the contents of a chapter using the tools you initially used to create it. (While Ventura has some rudimentary word processing facilities—as do all desktop publishing packages—you'll invariably find that it's easier to use a true word processor to edit text.)

While it's beyond the scope of this book to get into the details of using Ventura, here are a few general observations which might help you decide whether it's appropriate for your applications:

— Ventura is the most involved package to learn of any of the desktop publishing applications discussed in this chapter. It is also the least likely to produce anything useful until you do learn it.

— Ventura is the most powerful of the desktop publishing packages for creating larger or more complex documents.

— Ventura has the best selection of import features, making it able to accept text and graphics from a wide variety of other applications.

— Ventura's chapter structure makes its documents the easiest to maintain and update.

— Ventura's system of tags and typographical codes makes it possible to extensively pre-code a text file. This means that documents such as reports and even extensive databases can be poured into Ventura and printed without any manual font changes from within Ventura itself.

ALDUS PAGEMAKER

Aldus PageMaker is widely regarded as being the first true desktop publishing package. Originally a Macintosh application, it was ported to the PC for Windows quite some time ago. There is no non-Windows version for the PC.

The pages of this book were actually laid out using PageMaker.

PageMaker was originally a sort of very sophisticated word processor. For example, font changes were handled as they would be under Microsoft Word, that is, by highlighting some text with a mouse and using menu selections to change the characteristics you were interested in.

More recent versions of PageMaker have seen it acquire a tag system similar to that of Ventura Publisher. It's possible to pre-tag text, and to implement global changes to tagged objects.

Whereas Ventura speaks the language of typography, PageMaker is more versed in that of graphic arts. It has been written to be used by the graphic artists discussed earlier in this chapter who have found their knives and rule tapes being replaced by computers and laser printers.

Figure 6.3 illustrates a screen from PageMaker. You'll note that it's not unlike the Windows version of Ventura in its basic layout.

Assembling a document under PageMaker is somewhat more interactive than it would be under Ventura. This means that you will be called upon to specify where things go to a greater degree. For example, to create the newsletter in Figure 6.1 under PageMaker, I would have begun by "placing" the text onto a blank page and then defining where the columns would go. Under Ventura, the text is poured into a blank page that has already been told to work with a defined number of columns with a certain space or "gutter" between them and so on.

Under PageMaker there's a great deal more mousing around required to get these simple things done, but there's also a lot more freedom to do certain sorts of things. For example, producing a document having

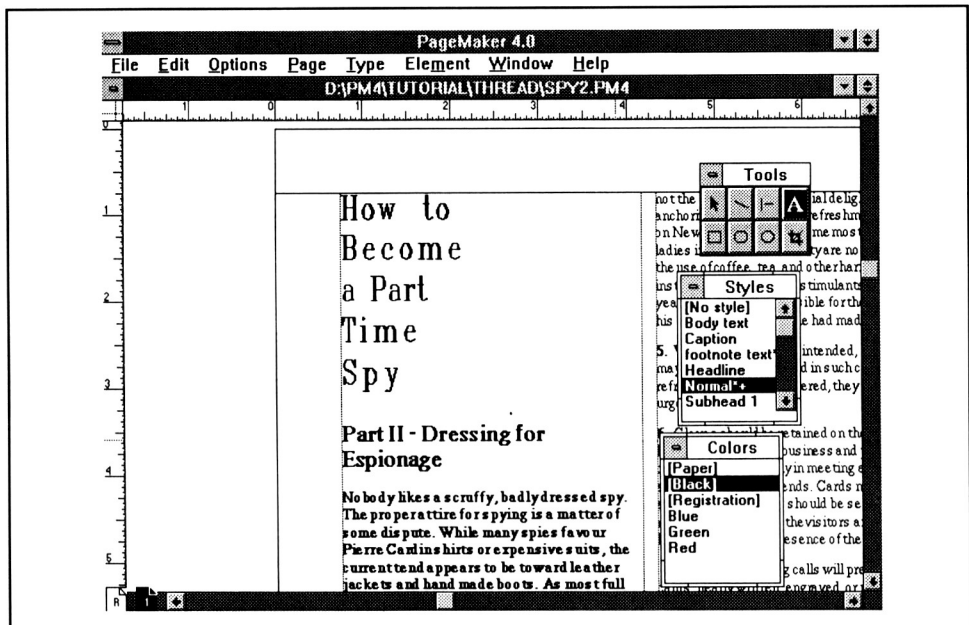

Figure 6.3: A screen from PageMaker

differing numbers of columns on different pages is a labor under Ventura but relatively simple under PageMaker. Publishing a four hundred page directory generated by a database manager is a trivial task for Ventura; it would be a serious undertaking for PageMaker.

PageMaker offers more text import facilities than Ventura. You can place text of the following types into a PageMaker document:

> ASCII files
>
> DCA files
>
> IBM DisplayWrite
>
> Microsoft Word
>
> MultiMate
>
> PC Write
>
> Samna Word
>
> XyWrite
>
> Windows Write
>
> WordPerfect
>
> WordStar

PageMaker accepts far fewer picture file formats than does Ventura. This probably won't matter to you at the moment, but being able to integrate graphics with a desktop publishing document is both one of the more interesting aspects of the art of electronic page design and one of the more powerful tools for creating interest in what might otherwise be dry text.

As with Ventura, PageMaker allows its documents to consist of a number of external text and picture files, which are included in the document when you open it under PageMaker. The PageMaker documentation refers to this as "linking." It's not handled quite as transparently under PageMaker as it is under Ventura, but the differences probably won't become apparent unless you work with both packages for a long while.

PageMaker has two features that Ventura lacks that will prove very useful for someone using desktop publishing without a background in design or page creation. They're particularly valuable when you're trying to get things done under tight time constraints. The first is very simple—the PageMaker "undo" feature. You can take back or negate your most recent action in most cases by selecting the *Undo* item of PageMaker's File menu. By contrast, Ventura forces you to undo changes by manually returning your document to its former state. This is little trouble once you've mastered Ventura, but it can be a bit traumatic while you're learning the package.

The other desirable feature of PageMaker is its built-in word processor, what it calls its "story editor." The story editor isn't as powerful as a stand-alone word processor, but it's a lot better than the rudimentary text-editing facilities that are typical of desktop publishing. It includes among other things a spelling checker and search-and-replace functions. This means, first of all, that you can make changes to a document from within PageMaker and then check the spelling of what you've done without leaving the application. It also means that you can make global changes quickly.

Once again, a solid tutorial on PageMaker would require a pretty extensive volume. Here are its primary attributes, however, to help you select a desktop publishing package:

— PageMaker is easier to learn than Ventura—while there are just as many specialized terms to become familiar with, you can get productive work out of it sooner.

— PageMaker offers a number of tools to make producing small documents easier and quicker than the same work under Ventura.

— Although PageMaker and Ventura run under Windows at about the same speed, they're both slower to use than the GEM version of Ventura.

— PageMaker is less adept at producing long, complex documents than Ventura, especially when it comes to documents with extensive formatting or pre-coding.

— PageMaker makes it easier to deal with the intricacies of typography, but ultimately gives you less control over them.

As may be apparent by now, the distinctions between Ventura and PageMaker are not all that extensive. If you read the next section, dealing with Ready-Set-Go for the Macintosh, you'll find that the issues are a bit easier to spot. In a sense, Ready-Set-Go is what PageMaker started out as.

You can regard the current implementation of PageMaker—dripping with features—in one of two ways. It's unquestionably powerful. However, in attempting to annex some of the desktop publishing users who started out with Ventura, a lot of its original identity—that of a fast, simple way for inexperienced users to build small documents—has become lost in a wash of additional facilities. Regrettably, as of this writing there isn't really a PC desktop publishing package that offers the simplicity of the original Page-Maker on the Macintosh, though it's worth noting that Manhattan Graphics was rumored to be about to release a PC-based version of Ready-Set-Go, probably to run under Windows.

READY-SET-GO

Whereas PC users might have a hard time choosing between the rapidly converging facilities of Ventura and PageMaker, you should be able to identify the respective facilities of Ventura and Ready-Set-Go which best suit your needs with only moderate consideration. The two applications are extremely different in the areas of desktop publishing they address.

Ready-Set-Go is among the best examples of desktop publishing software explicitly designed to produce pages rather than books. It's almost wholly interactive— it doesn't support pretagging its text, it doesn't "link" external files, and it doesn't really support reusable style sheets. Every document it generates is designed essentially from scratch, although as you get into using Ready-Set-Go you'll find ways to cheat on this a bit.

None of these things should be regarded as deficiencies, however. They're indicative of the substantially different approach it offers for desktop publishing.

To begin with, Ready-Set-Go is nowhere near as complex as Ventura. While it offers a surprising amount of control over the design and typography of the documents it creates, it's a bit like a Macintosh word processor, in that it lets you work with default values until you get used to its functions. As such, you can learn enough of Ready-Set-Go to get useful— if unexciting— results from it in a couple of hours.

Figure 6.4 is the main screen of Ready-Set-Go. You'll notice that it, too, is displaying the newsletter in Figure 6.1. In fact, this is not the same newsletter at all. I had to take the original elements of the newsletter, port them to a Macintosh, and recreate the newsletter from scratch as a Ready-Set-Go document.

In order to create a document under Ready-Set-Go, you define areas of each page to hold text or pictures. This involves, literally, drawing boxes with the tools provided and telling the software things like "put the picture of the unicorn here," "start the text in this box," "run the text into this box if there's too much in the first one," and so on. There are a number of things to assist you in making this process come out looking fairly professional. For example, you can switch on a grid to make the boxes you draw "snap" to predefined alignment marks.

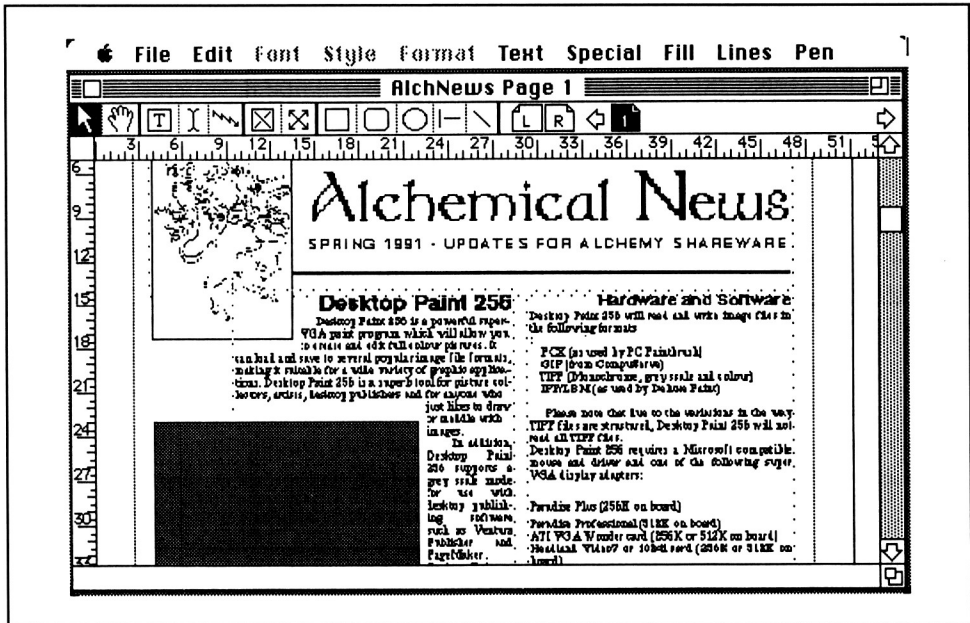

Figure 6.4: The main screen of Ready-Set-Go

Ready-Set-Go accepts text from MacWrite, among other sources, and pictures in the form of MacPaint and TIFF files. The latter two entities are standard forms for picture files on a Macintosh. It can also accept more complex graphics as EPS files, another commonly used format.

While Ready-Set-Go does not allow for the pretagging of text documents in the way that Ventura does, it will preserve the text attributes of a MacWrite file as it comes into a Ready-Set-Go document. Thus, you can set font changes and such within MacWrite and they'll remain as you've placed them when you bring your text into Ready-Set-Go. However, you can't change the characteristics of, say, all your subheads at once.

Ready-Set-Go includes a better than average spelling checker—it's certainly better than the one in MacWrite, for example. It allows you to edit text as a word processor would. You can actually create a document from scratch with nothing but Ready-Set-Go, although this isn't usually all that effective unless you're building an advertisement or a flyer with relatively little text. It can also do global text search and replace, which is handy.

There are a number of fairly advanced features in Ready-Set-Go as well. The one which seems to get used the most is its ability to wrap text around an irregular graphic. Figure 6.5 illustrates this effect.

You can, in fact, do this in Ventura and PageMaker as well. It's just a lot more elegant in Ready-Set-Go. (It's also something to be used sparingly, as its appeal vanishes if it turns up on every other page.)

There are a number of things to keep in mind if you consider Ready-Set-Go for your desktop publishing applications:

— It's very quick to learn and easy to get workable results out of within the first few hours.

— It has very strong page design tools, and is well thought out to allow inexperienced designers to create workable pages.

— It has very poor facilities for producing large documents, or ones which include complex formatting.

— It has much less control over typography and type effects than does Ventura or PageMaker, although what it does offer is arguably more than enough for most small desktop publishing applications.

— It's heavily weighted toward producing short documents.

— It comes with a short, lucid manual which is easy to understand and use, even if you have no background in graphic arts.

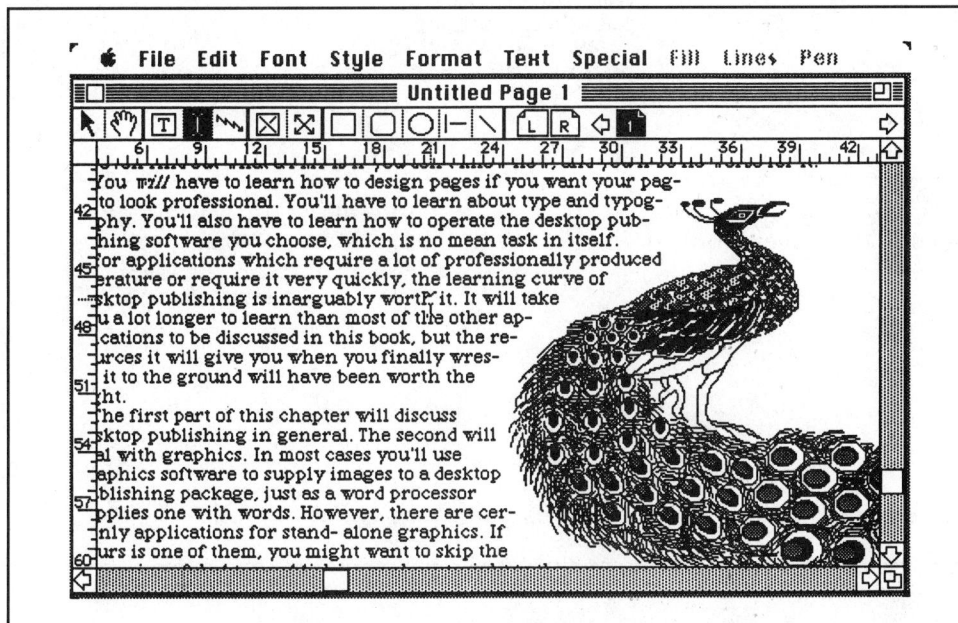

Figure 6.5: Running text around an irregular graphic in Ready-Set-Go

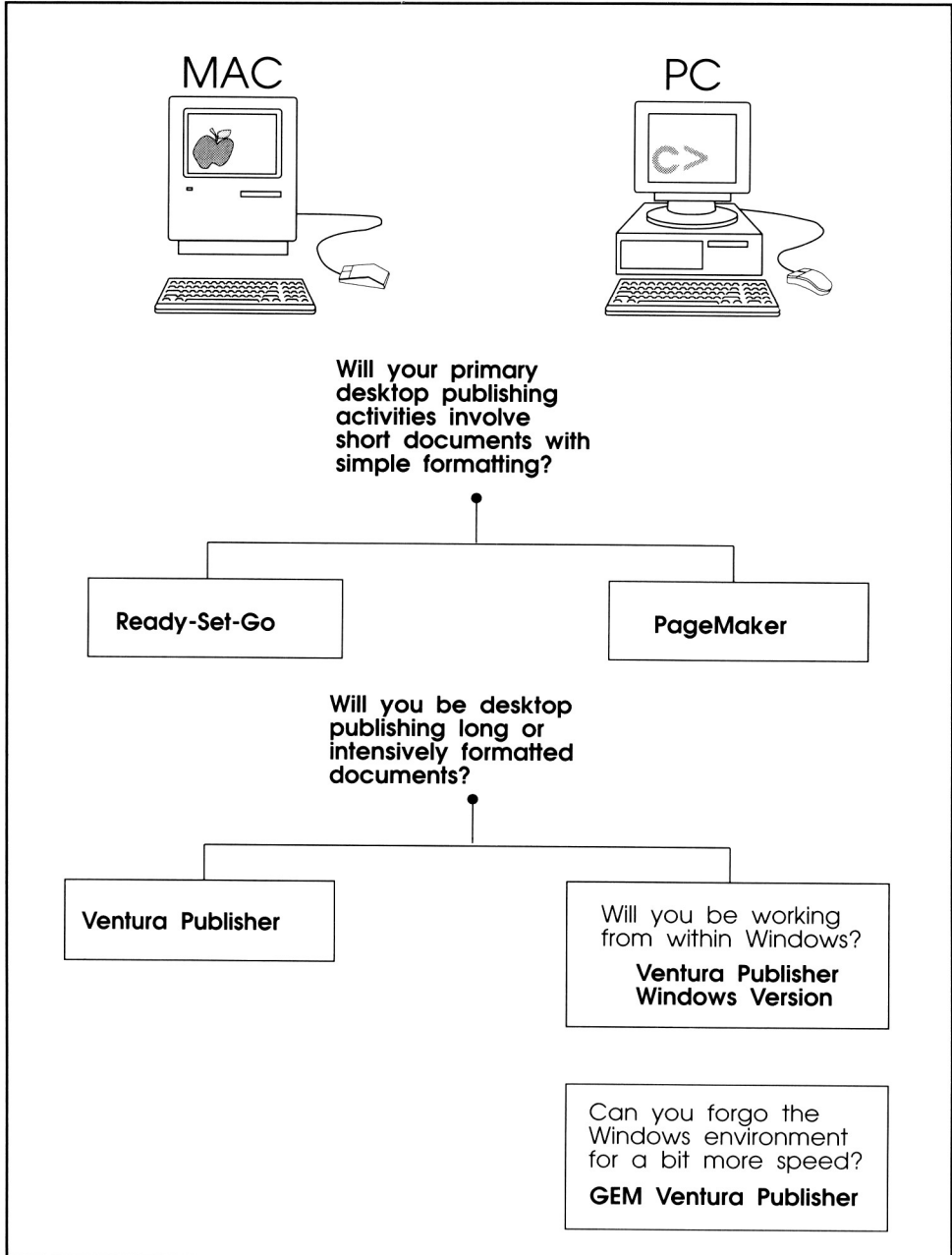

MAC

PC

Will your primary desktop publishing activities involve short documents with simple formatting?

Ready-Set-Go

PageMaker

Will you be desktop publishing long or intensively formatted documents?

Ventura Publisher

Will you be working from within Windows?

Ventura Publisher Windows Version

Can you forgo the Windows environment for a bit more speed?

GEM Ventura Publisher

AUTHOR'S CHOICE

I use Ventura for just about everything I do with desktop publishing. In almost all cases this is not because of a conscious affirmation that it's better than all the other choices. It's simply no worse, and having chosen it a long time ago and become familiar with it, it's a workable tool.

There are, however, a number of things that might still lead me to choose Ventura over PageMaker. For one thing, its GEM implementation is very fast. And though it's not very attractive visually, things like the three-dimensional buttons offered by the Windows version cease to be interesting after a few days. I'll live with a considerable degree of ugliness if doing so will help me survive a deadline.

Ventura is very transparent once you get familiar with it—that is, it keeps very little of what it does secret. As such, it allows me to pre-code text files far more than PageMaker would—once you become versed in the language of Ventura's coding you can use it to save enormous amounts of time.

If it's given a machine with some expanded memory to run on, Ventura does not seem to have an upper limit as to the size of document it will work on. I'm told you could use it to typeset a phone book.

Ventura handles graphics in ways that make more sense than the comparable facilities of PageMaker, and I'm very fond of desktop publishing which includes graphics.

I've had a long association with typesetting and graphic arts, and as such I find that Ventura communicates with me in a way which is intuitive and easy to deal with. It imposes the least amount of translation—and hence wasted time—in what it wants me to specify. Of course, this also serves to make it quite impenetrable at first to anyone with a different background.

The biggest drawback to Ventura at the moment is arguably its technical support. When Xerox acquired Ventura, the technical support situation became very corporate—and very expensive for home office users. As of this writing, you can only call to ask questions for sixty days after you buy Ventura without paying for the call. After that, there's a 900 number to call for technical support. It costs about fifteen dollars per call to use it.

In fairness, Aldus offers the same arrangement for Page-Maker, and at the same price. Both companies also offer dial-in support for a yearly fee.

I use both the GEM and Windows versions of Ventura, although most of what I do involves the former. You can, in fact, run the GEM version under Windows— the program won't look any different, but it will provide you with a fast version of Ventura that you can pop in and out of through Windows.

If you ask other users of desktop publishing packages for their opinions, you should bear in mind that it takes a very long time to get proficient in the use of one of these things. Therefore, it's not a very good idea to abandon one for something that is only slightly or ostensibly better. Should someone tell you that Page-Maker, for example, is preferable to Ventura, and that they have three years of experience to prove it, be sure to investigate how much time they've actually used Ventura during those three years. They may well be using PageMaker for much the same reason that I use Ventura— it's what they started with and they've found no irresistible reason to switch. When you really have to get something done with the software you use, sloth usually wins out over reason.

GRAPHICS

Adding images to a desktop published document can do a lot to make it readable, even if the images are only tangentially related to the contents of your text. A page with nothing but text on it looks impenetrable.

There are, of course, situations in which graphics also serve genuinely supporting functions in desktop publishing. Being able to include pictures in your pages will let you add company logos, photographs, charts, and other useful elements to your designs.

Computer graphics can be grouped into two distinct types— "bitmaps" and "vectors." A bitmapped graphic consists entirely of dots. If you scan a photograph, the result will be a bitmap. The screen of a computer is also a bitmap. Vector drawings— also called object drawings or line drawings— consist of lines, rectangles, ellipses, arcs, curves, filled areas, and complex objects made out of these simple elements. Examples of vector drawings include architectural plans, mechanical drawings, and commercial line art.

Figure 6.6 illustrates examples of bitmapped and vector art.

Each of these classes of art has distinctive characteristics. Bitmapped pictures can represent true photographic images. A bitmapped picture is produced by a finite number of dots in a fixed matrix. Because each dot will occupy a finite amount of space on a printed page, there is a natural size at which a bitmapped image will print with optimum quality. If you discover that the bitmapped picture you wish to use and the space in your desktop publishing document are significantly different, you can "scale" the image, but the resulting printed picture may exhibit a marked loss in quality.

The advantage of using bitmapped art—essentially photographic reproduction—is offset by the somewhat inflexible nature of bitmapped graphics. It's also offset by the large size of bitmapped graphic files. A relatively small scanned color photograph can occupy half a megabyte of hard drive space.

Obviously, if you wish to include scanned photographs in a document you'll have to live with these restrictions. In practice, scaling problems can be averted with a bit of forethought, and the size of graphics can be dealt with by simply having a large hard drive.

Vector art doesn't look photographic, but it can look very sophisticated. Because of their nature, vector files can be scaled as much as you like without losing any quality. As a rule, vector art files are much smaller than bitmapped ones.

As you become more familiar with concepts of page design, you'll begin to get a feel for the sort of art which best supports a particular page or document.

Graphic Sources

Obtaining graphics to include in your desktop publishing documents is perhaps more a logistical problem than a technical one. There are several ways to go about it, depending on what you're after.

The most obvious way to come by graphics is to draw them using a drawing or painting package—we'll discuss these applications in just a moment. This assumes that you're a reasonably good artist to begin with.

In fact, very few people in need of graphics create them from scratch. If you thumb through a newsletter or neighborhood flyer, you might notice that some of them share some strikingly similar graphics, and that many of these images aren't really part of the articles they adorn. They're often window dressing—something to break up pages that would

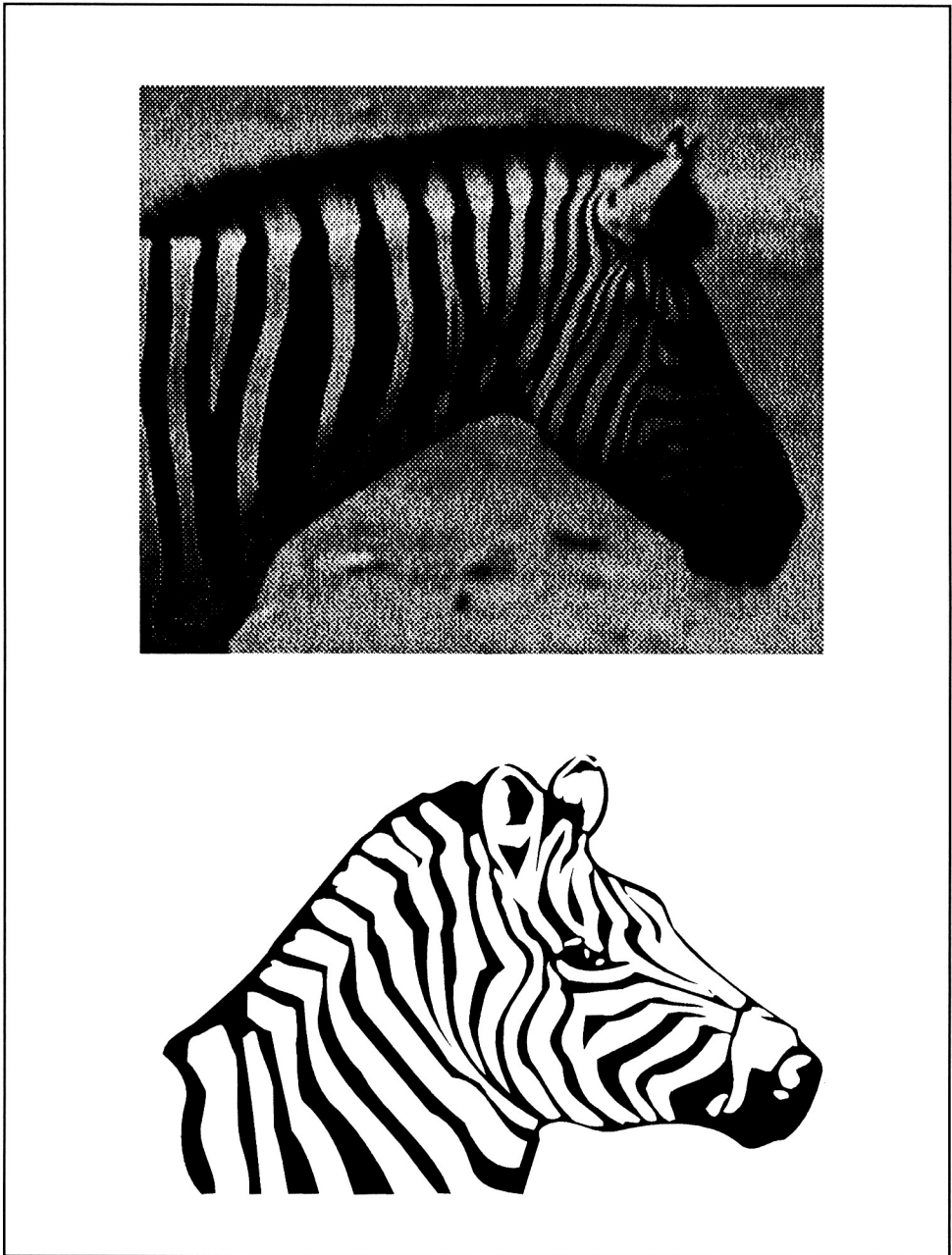

Figure 6.6: A bitmapped picture and an example of vector art

otherwise be nothing but type. These sorts of graphics are referred to as "clip art." Back in the days when publications were all pasted up by hand, there were companies that produced large sheets of generic graphics which could be cut up and stuck down to fill space. In fact, many of these companies now produce the electronic equivalent to this resource—disks full of graphic files.

You can buy disks of electronic clip art all ready to import into your publications. Most of the companies that supply these collections offer subscription services—for an annual fee, you'll be sent a disk every month if you like. Alternatively, you can usually buy collections that reflect a particular theme—a disk of images that deals with fast food, iguana ranching, gas stations, or whatever your area of interest happens to be.

While you can buy both bitmapped and vector clip art, the majority of it is supplied as vector drawings.

If your application for graphics involves using a lot of photographic art, you might want to look into buying a scanner. This is a complex subject, and one that is beyond the scope of this book to discuss in detail. In general scanners will allow you to create bitmapped images from any photograph or other piece of flat art, to be subsequently imported into a desktop publishing document. They range from simple hand scanners for scanning fairly small images—a few inches square—to elaborate, expensive flatbed scanners that will do a letter-size page in one pass.

In discussing scanners and the bitmapped art they create, it's worth mentioning that there are three distinct classes of bitmapped images—one of which may be less than obvious. When one speaks of a black and white bitmapped image—also called a two-color image—this refers to one that has only black and white in it. Such a picture does not include any grey levels, as would a black and white photograph. Some very low-cost scanners will create the illusion of grey by using alternating black and white dots, a process called "dithering," but the results are never as realistic as true grey levels.

Grey-scale images—bitmaps which have true grey levels—are structured differently than black and white images. In effect, they're color pictures in which all the colors are grey. Such a bitmapped image can really look like the photograph it was originally scanned from.

The third class of bitmapped images is color images. Of course, color images aren't all that much use if your printer can't actually print in color.

A final source of graphics that might be applicable to your desktop publishing projects is the type of art your computer might generate on its own. For example, you can export spreadsheet graphs from Lotus 1-2-3 or Microsoft Excel and import these into a desktop publishing package. This is, of course, based on the assumption that your document requires the sorts of charts or graphs that typically come from a spreadsheet package. Lotus graphs can hardly be said to be decorative.

Graphic Software

Graphics packages are a large area of application software, and one which could easily occupy the rest of this book. We'll only have a quick look at the available resources in this section—you will want to investigate the programs discussed herein in greater detail if you plan to implement graphics in your desktop published documents.

Bitmapped graphics are traditionally created and manipulated in what are called "paint" programs, and vector images are handled by "draw" programs. Paint programs can be further divided into two types—packages designed for general painting and those intended primarily for fine-tuning images from scanners—electronic retouching software. Examples of the former are SuperPaint on the Macintosh and Deluxe Paint on the PC. Examples of the latter are Digital Darkroom and Adobe Photoshop on the Macintosh and ImageIn and Grey F/X on the PC.

A retouching package can prove to be an exceedingly useful tool if you make extensive use of a scanner. This type of software allows you to adjust the contrast of a photograph, edit out imperfections, crop images, and even place part of one image into another. You can, for example, excise a group of people from one picture and place them against the background of a second one, adjusting the contrast of both so that the result really looks like a single photograph. A less exotic application of this technology might be used to clean up the photographs used by real estate agents—you can quickly compensate for cloudy days, a poorly kept lawn, or the "for sale" sign in the front yard.

Vector drawing packages have reached a high level of sophistication in the past few years. The most popular one for the Macintosh remains the Adobe Illustrator program. Illustrator is also available to run under Windows in a PC environment, but it has been largely overshadowed by CorelDRAW. The CorelDRAW software also runs under Windows—it has been fine tuned to support desktop publishing packages. The vector drawing in Figure 6.6 was created with CorelDRAW. In addition to the CorelDRAW software itself, CorelDRAW also provides you with an impressive collection of vector clip art to use in your publications and over a hundred fonts which can be used both in CorelDRAW and as downloadable fonts with many desktop publishing packages.

SUMMARY

Perhaps the real power of desktop publishing is that it gives you almost complete control over those elements of your communication with others that will most affect their impression of you. If your home office applications involve dealing with other businesses, this can make a decided difference in how effective your communication tools really are.

The negative aspect of desktop publishing is that it places the sole responsibility for your publications on you, and if you have no experience in design you'll be amazed at how ugly pages can get until you get a sense of how to structure them.

There are a number of very good books on page design in general and on desktop published page design specifically. If you decide to use desktop publishing, use some of these books as well.

CHAPTER

7

7

TELECOMMUNICATIONS

Aside from providing you with the tools to be productive in a home office, your computer can also allow you to stay in touch with a real office—or anywhere that lets you—in ways beyond mere voice communications. Specifically, through the use of telecommunications hardware and software, your computer will let you move files over phone lines with a modem and it will let you do things with FAX that a simple FAX machine could never aspire to. (FAX will be dealt with in detail in the next chapter.)

As with so many other areas of microcomputer applications, you only need to understand a fraction of the total body of information about the subject to use it effectively. If you approach telecommunications by simply buying a modem and trying to figure it all out for yourself, however, you'll probably have to get pretty deeply into the whole before you know which bits you could have safely ignored.

There is one exceedingly important thing to keep in mind in the discussion of modems, and especially of files transfers (moving files over a modem). When you use your computer, you see all the files on your disk as having distinct characteristics. A Microsoft Word document and an Excel worksheet file, for example, are hardly interchangeable. Telecommunications software doesn't make these distinctions. All the files on your disk are just files to a modem—meaningless strings of bytes. As such, absolutely anything on your disk can be transferred over a modem. If it's a Word document on your machine it will be a Word document when it gets where it's going. This also includes actual executable programs—EXE and COM files—although there are not many instances when you'd want to send these by modem.

Finally, it's worth noting that PC and Macintosh systems both use the same modems. The software that drives your modem will, of course, be specific to your computer.

AN INTRODUCTION TO MODEMS

To begin with, the word "modem" is an acronym. It means "modulator demodulator." You needn't remember this, as it will never come up again. The technical functions of a modem are irrelevant to this discussion, as the state of the art in modem design completely insulates you from them.

In its simplest sense, a modem is a box that connects your computer to a telephone line. Telephone lines deal in sound and computers deal in bytes; the function of a modem is to translate the bytes coming from your computer into sounds so they can pass over a phone line, and to translate the sounds on a phone line—originating from another modem—into bytes for your computer.

The sounds a modem produces are called "tones." In translating a stream of bytes into tones, a modem actually switches rapidly between two audible tones.

Most contemporary personal computers have "serial" ports. A serial port is simply a connector that is, by agreement, set up in the same way as the one on the computer end of a modem. Contemporary modems use RJ-11 phone jacks to connect to a telephone line. In the very early days of computers modems were available with rubber cups into which one would place the handset of a telephone, rather than actually connecting to the phone line directly. These things are no longer used for a number of reasons, not the least of which is the fascinating diversity of telephone designs of late.

Translating bytes to sound and back again is a bit of a high wire act. There are numerous variables—we'll discuss some of them in a moment—and all sorts of things that can go wrong. If the two modems in a conversation don't agree about everything they're doing, the data that emerges from the conversation will be salad. The agreement between two modems is called a "protocol." If both modems in a conversation are properly set up with a common protocol, they can communicate without error.

Data moves through a modem at a defined speed. The speed is represented by the number of "bits" the modem can transmit in one second. In other situations a bit is one eighth of a byte (the computer code for a single character), but as we'll see in a moment, a byte that moves through a modem typically involves ten bits rather than eight, two of which are used by the modem. The number of bytes that pass through a modem will therefore be one tenth the bit rate. The proper technical term for the number of bits that a modem will transmit in a second is "baud."

The slowest modems in use today run at 300 baud, or 30 bytes per second. The screen of a PC in text mode holds 2000 characters—a 300-baud modem would require just over a minute to transfer enough characters to fill one screen.

Most of the modems in use today run at 1200 or 2400 baud. As modems have evolved toward higher speeds over the past few years, they have retained "backward compatibility." In fact, they have retained it quite transparently. If you attempt to establish communications with another modem, the two modems will "negotiate" the highest common speed they can deal with. If you have a 2400-baud modem and the system you call has a 1200-baud modem, the two modems will beep and squawk at each other for a few seconds until they establish communications at 1200 baud.

As the baud rate of a modem increases, its demands for telephone line quality and "bandwidth" increase as well. The bandwidth of a telephone line specifies its ability to pass higher frequency tones reliably. Because telephone lines are extremely variable in their quality, modems have become very sophisticated about using them. For example, if a high-speed modem finds itself confronted by a really bad phone line, it will automatically "fall back" to a lower baud rate to maintain reliable communications. While most phone lines are adequate for higher speed telecommunications, you'll occasionally find some that are sufficiently degraded to make it impossible, or that get degraded at certain times during the day. This is especially true if you attempt to telecommunicate with other parts of the world.

A modem that is actually running at 2400 baud can still take an awfully long time to transfer large files, and this can be expensive if you're transferring them by long-distance. There are faster modems, but they come with a few catches.

A number of manufacturers have developed modems that run at 9600 baud or better over conventional phone lines. The most commonly used ones are the US Robotics HST modems and the Hayes V series modems, more or less in this order. The first important catch in these modems is that they're incompatible. An HST modem will not communicate with a V series modem, even though both of them may be running at 9600 baud. There are several lesser-known high-speed modem manufacturers, and none of these will communicate with modems from other manufacturers, either.

There is an emerging high-speed modem standard called V.42bis. As high-speed modem manufacturers begin to adopt it, the incompatibilities will dissolve; at the moment, however, if you want to communicate at speeds of 9600 baud or better, you must make sure that all the modems you'll be dealing with come from the same source.

Fortunately, 9600-baud modems are also capable of speeds of 2400, 1200 and 300 baud, and these lower speeds *are* compatible with modems of other manufacturers. If you find your 9600-baud modem confronted with an alien modem one day you will be able to deal with it—the dealings will just be a lot slower.

Communicating at 9600 baud over conventional voice phone lines requires some pretty exotic technology. In fact, 9600-baud modems cheat in all sorts of ways to manage what they do, as the bandwidth of a phone line is nowhere near adequate to handle 9600-baud communications in the same way that 2400-baud is done. Whereas a 2400-baud modem actually lets you send data at this speed in both directions simultaneously, a 9600-baud modem consists of one 9600-baud channel and one 300-baud channel. It assigns the 9600-baud channel to whichever side of a conversation is sending the most data, switching between them as needs be. When you send a file over a modem, almost all the data goes in one direction, and hence this cheat is extremely effective.

Bits and Other Protocols

The sorts of modems that are used with microcomputers are "asynchronous." This means that bytes of data can appear at the modem at any time, and the modem is expected to be able to handle them without losing anything. This doesn't seem as if it should be all that difficult, but in fact it's a bit tricky, especially at higher speeds.

One squawk of modem tones sounds pretty much like another. Therefore, data that is sent over a modem is handled using a protocol that allows a receiving modem to make sense of each byte that appears and to recover quickly should a byte be mangled in transmission by a hiccup on the phone line.

In order for two modems to communicate, they must agree on four parameters. The first is the baud rate of the conversation, which has been discussed. The second is the number of bits in a byte (character). This can range from five through eight—you'll want eight in most cases. The third is the "parity." Parity is a way for modems to check each byte sent. If parity checking is used, a receiving modem will receive the bits in a byte plus an extra parity bit for each byte sent. It will then count up the bits and see if the count is even or odd, comparing this to the parity bit. If the two don't compare, the receiving modem will know that the byte has been corrupted somehow.

This is a fairly rudimentary check—if *two* bits get mangled the byte may well pass its parity check even though it has been corrupted. As we'll see, much more reliable ways exist to ensure the accuracy of data which is sent over a modem. As a result, most of the time you'll use no parity checking.

Finally, every byte sent over a modem has one or two "stop" bits. These are bits that, by sounding different to a receiving modem, allow the modem to know when all the bits in a byte have been received. If a bit goes missing, the modem will know when to stop looking for it, declare the current byte a total loss, and start working on the next byte. There can be one or two stop bits—the usual setting is one.

A basic telecommunication protocol will usually be expressed like this:

2400,8,N,1

This means that communications will take place at 2400 baud with eight data bits, no parity checking and one stop bit. While the baud rate may vary, the latter three parameters are the ones you'll normally use.

Essential Operations

A contemporary external modem looks something like the box in Figure 7.1. While every modem manufacturer styles their modems a bit differently, they all look like low, flat boxes with lights.

You can, in fact, buy modems that plug directly into a PC, eliminating the external box. These internal modems are powered by your PC and appear as an extra serial port to the software that will drive them. However, they have several drawbacks. To begin with, they tie up a slot and consume power inside your computer—both of which are things to be avoided if you can do so. They also bring the 48-volt phone line directly into your computer case. It's easy to get a shock from this when you're changing cards inside your system, even with the power to the computer disconnected. It's hardly fatal, but you'll know when you've found it.

Finally, being inside the case of your system, there are no status lights on an internal modem. As will be discussed presently, the status lights

Figure 7.1: A modem. (Photo courtesy of US Robotics)

are extremely helpful in knowing what your modem is doing and in finding out what's wrong with it if it doesn't behave itself.

For all these reasons you'll probably find that an external modem is preferable.

In order to make using a modem as easy as possible—and also in order to have more features to advertise—modem manufacturers have added things beyond the basic function of moving data around. Most of these things have to do with managing the phone line. While you'll be able to ignore almost all of them, three of these things will prove essential. Specifically, a modem can

— Dial a number

— Hang up the phone

— Answer an incoming call

Virtually all contemporary modems can do these things. In effect, a modem behaves just like a conventional telephone, save that your computer does the talking. It also handles the dial and the receiver hook in a manner more suitable to a computer. A modem does not have a physical dial or a hook.

Your computer can communicate with your modem through a set of commands that are common to all modems designed for use with microcomputers, no matter who manufactured your particular modem. This is called the AT command set, or occasionally the Hayes command set. The Hayes company actually created the AT command set, but at present everyone uses it. (This AT has nothing to do with the AT designation of PC/AT computers. It actually stands for "attention.")

You will not have to know how to send AT commands in order to use your modem. Because the AT command set is universal, telecommunications software comes preconfigured to employ it. If you tell your telecommunications package to dial a number, for example, it will send the correct AT command to your modem to make this happen.

Occasionally AT commands will appear on your screen when you're using a modem. You can safely ignore them, as they're actually a conversation between your computer and your modem. Should you wish to understand them, an AT command consists of one second or more of no data, three plus signs, another one-second pause, and then a command that starts with AT. Here are a few that correspond to the preceding list:

+++ATDT555-1212 Dial the number 555-1212 using tone dialing.

+++ATDP555-1212 Dial the number 555-1212 using pulse dialing.

+++ATH Hang up the phone.

+++ATS0=1 Await an incoming call and answer it when it arrives.

If you consult the manual for a state-of-the-art modem, you'll find that there are pages of AT commands. Most of them deal with rather exotic circumstances. Therefore, while it's a good idea to look at the manual for your modem, you needn't look at it very long.

Setting Up a Modem

A modem is a very easy thing to get going. Once you pry apart the packing material you should have something like the machine in Figure 7.1 and an external power transformer. The power transformer plugs into the modem, and the modem connects to the serial port of your computer through a serial cable.

If you're using a Macintosh, your modem will plug into a connector indicated with a phone icon at the back of your computer. Depending on the Mac you have, you might require a DIN-to-serial-port adapter cable, available from your Apple dealer. On a PC the serial port may have either 9 or 25 pins. Most computers will have the serial port marked as either "serial port" or "COM1," "COM2," and so on.

The Macintosh actually has two serial ports— your printer or Appletalk cable is probably connected to the other one. If you aren't using a printer or Appletalk you can connect your modem to either port, as Macintosh telecommunications software allows you to choose the one you'll be talking to.

PC-compatible computers usually have at least one serial port. This is called COM1 by default. It's not uncommon to have a second, called COM2, and there may be as many as four. It doesn't matter which one you use in most cases, as long as you remember which you've chosen when it comes time to configure your software. If you have a serial mouse on your PC system you might have to keep this in mind when you're allocating COM ports.

Most communications software will allow you to use any COM port you like. The package we'll be discussing in this chapter, Qmodem, will actually allow for your choice of up to eight COM ports if they're present. The drivers for serial mice are usually limited to COM1 and COM2, and sometimes insist on using COM1. If your mouse driver is less flexible than your telecommunications software your modem may have to defer to your mouse.

Note that, aside from mice and modems, serial ports can be used to drive printers. While this is no longer a common situation on a PC, you can still buy serial printer cables. These look exactly like serial modem cables, but they're wired differently inside. A serial printer cable used to connect a modem to your computer will not allow the modem to function, so make sure you get the right sort of cable.

Serial port connections on a PC can be confusing. Whereas on the majority of contemporary systems the serial ports will be 9-pin male D-shell connectors, and nothing else on the back of your computer will look anything like them, on a few systems—and especially on older PC-compatible computers—serial ports may be 25-pin male D-shell connectors. (You will probably also find at least one 25-pin female D-shell connector on your computer—this is the parallel printer port.)

Modems come with 25-pin female D-shell connectors to interface to your computer. Therefore you may be faced with connecting a 25-pin piece of hardware to a 9-pin one. You will need to ascertain the type of connector your specific model of computer needs and buy the right cable when you get your modem. It's preferable to get a single cable to connect your modem directly to your computer, rather than a cable and an adapter or two. Adapters are one more thing to go wrong, or to get pulled out of their sockets and subsequently take an hour and half to locate.

When you have your modem connected up and plugged in, turn it on. Two or more of its front panel lights should come on. Your modem is now ready to reach out and touch someone—or some thing.

Reading the Lights on a Modem

Aside from being a useful indicator that your modem is plugged in, the status indicator lights on the front panel of a modem will often help you to understand what it's doing. This is particularly handy if you're trying to figure out why it's not doing what you want it to do.

The number and function of the indicator lights on modems vary between manufacturers, but there are some lights that are common to almost all modems. The following are the ones you'll find useful. It will only take a moment to familiarize yourself with them.

CD The carrier detect indicator. This will light when your modem makes contact with another modem. If it goes out while you're using your modem, the connection has been lost.

SD The send data light. Every time a byte of data passes through the modem to the phone line, this light will flash on for an instant. You can check the connection between your computer and your modem by putting your telecommunications package in terminal mode, typing something, and seeing if this light flashes. Note that at 9600 baud or faster the flashes of the SD light will be very brief and easy to miss.

RD The receive data light. It will flash on when a byte of data comes from the phone line to your computer. If you're transferring files to your computer it will stay on during most of the transfer.

AA Indicates that the modem has been told to answer the phone automatically should it ring. When this light is lit the modem is awaiting a call.

HS This light is used by high-speed modems capable of 9600 baud or better to indicate that the modem is communicating at high speed.

OH Indicates that the modem has taken its internal phone off the hook. This usually happens when it's preparing to dial a number. This light will stay on until the modem hangs up the phone again.

TELECOMMUNICATIONS SOFTWARE—A QUICK OVERVIEW

The use of modems with personal computers dates back to the late seventies. Personal computers in the late seventies were a rather underground phenomenon, and it's not surprising that the modem technology that emerged from this era was written by programmers for programmers. It was wholly inscrutable to everyone else.

The usefulness of telecommunications did not become apparent to most of the rest of civilization nearly as quickly as the usefulness of computers in general did. It has only been recently that modems stopped being almost exclusively toys for programmers. The software that drives modems reflects this heritage.

The commercial telecommunications packages that have appeared in the past few years have not been particularly impressive. By comparison, the telecommunications software that has grown out of the original modem applications has turned into some very sophisticated, user-friendly software. Much of it has been evolving for over a decade.

The packages we'll discuss in this chapter will be White Knight for the Macintosh and Qmodem for the PC. White Knight began life as Red Ryder, a shareware package, and eventually became a commercial program. Qmodem started out as shareware and remains so to this day. (If you're unfamiliar with the concept of shareware you might want to have a look at Chapter 12 of this book.) Both packages can be mail-ordered from their respective companies just like any other sort of software.

Both White Knight and Qmodem are just dripping with features, most of which you'll never have cause to use. There are probably only a few functions you'll really want to perform with your modem, to wit:

— Dialing out

— Emulating a terminal

— Uploading and downloading files

— Being a host

These will probably require a bit of explanation.

Dialing from a telecommunications package is a lot like dialing with an expensive telephone. Rather than having you key in the number you want to dial, the software can maintain a dialing directory from which you can select frequently called numbers. Having selected a number, the software will dial it for you, listen for a modem at the other end, make the connection, and return control of the computer to you when all the negotiations are complete.

Alternatively, it will tell you that the number you've called is busy or didn't answer. The software can be instructed to perform other dialing functions, such as redialing a busy number at regular intervals until it answers, or dialing a series of numbers.

Emulating a terminal sounds very sophisticated. It's actually the simplest thing a telecommunications package can handle. The "terminal mode" of a package like White Knight or Qmodem allows you to communicate with a remote computer by typing things. Everything you type will be sent to the computer your modem has called. Everything it sends back will appear on your screen.

Uploading and downloading files is a sufficiently complex subject to require its own section— we'll discuss it momentarily. These terms may be a bit confusing at first. *Uploading* a file involves sending it from your computer to a remote computer. *Downloading* a file involves having a remote computer send it to your computer.

Being a host is one of the most useful functions a computer can perform with a modem, especially if you're using your computer to communicate from your home to your office. It allows a computer to exchange files and messages without human supervision. If the computer at your office is set up to be a host, your computer can call it and its modem will answer the phone. It will ask you for your name and a prearranged password, the latter to make sure that other people with modems can't get access to your office system without your permission. It will then allow you to send files to your office computer and to download files from it to your home system. Depending upon the host you're using, you might also be able to actually operate your office computer over the phone lines through your home system. We'll discuss the capabilities of the host modes of specific packages later in this chapter.

By the way, it's worth noting that just as modems don't know what sort of computers they're talking to, the data that flows through them is pretty well system-independent. As such, you can transfer files between PC and Macintosh computers using modems. While the resulting data may or may not be useful—Mac applications will not run on a PC, for example—this does let you exchange simple types of files.

FILE TRANSFERS

In theory, you can get a file from one computer to another over a phone line by simply sending it through one modem and collecting it when it comes out of the receiving modem. In practice this is a bit questionable, and rarely works. Every time the phone line clicks, pops, burps, or beeps to indicate a waiting call—or does one of the countless other things phone lines are heir to—some of the data being transferred this way will be corrupted. If the file being transferred is a program, attempting to run the resulting program will probably crash your computer.

Because phone lines are a bit unreliable, the early programmers who got into using modems devised what are called "block transfer protocols." The most common of these is called XMODEM. A block transfer protocol is very easy to understand, and it largely overcomes the limitations of phone lines as a medium of reliable data transmission.

Consider sending a 16-kilobyte document over a phone line. This would take something over a minute to send at 2400 baud if you just stuffed it into the modem and hoped for the best. What appears at the other end might be what you sent—or it might be slightly mangled.

Using a block transfer protocol, the 16 kilobytes would be divided up into blocks. Under XMODEM, each block is 128 bytes long. Each block to be sent down the line is accompanied by several extra bytes identifying the block and its "checksum": a number derived by adding all the bytes in the block together.

When the receiving computer has the entire block, it calculates the checksum independently and compares it with the one that came with the block. If the checksums match, the receiving computer knows that the block arrived safely. It is written to the file being received and the receiving computer signals the sending computer to begin transmitting the next block.

If a block is corrupted by line noise—resulting in bad checksums—the receiving computer tells the sending computer to send the block again. This is called a "retry." Under XMODEM, bad blocks are retried ten times, after which the software decides that the lines are just too noisy and gives up.

Block transfer protocols all but eliminate the possibility of data corruption in transfer—if the phone line conditions are bad enough to make it impossible to send a file without its being corrupted, nothing will be sent at all. As such, you'll never get bad data from a file transfer.

The drawback to the XMODEM protocol is that its fairly small block size makes it slow. It was written back when 300-baud modems were common and 16 kilobytes was a big file. Every time a block has been transferred, both sides of the conversation must pause, meditate on their checksums, and decide what to do next. XMODEM was superseded to some extent by YMODEM, which uses larger 1024-byte blocks.

The YMODEM protocol was in turn superseded by the ZMODEM protocol, which uses even larger blocks and "windowing." This has nothing to do with screen windows. It means that incoming blocks are stored in memory for a while, such that the checksum for one block can be calculated while the next block is arriving and that bad blocks can be retried out of order if needs be. All other things being equal, ZMODEM can transfer files considerably faster and with more reliability than the original XMODEM protocol could.

YMODEM and ZMODEM are "batch protocols." This means that you can use them to transfer multiple files at one time. Along with sending down the data for each file, the protocol will tell the receiving computer what to name each file as it's sent. The XMODEM protocol only allows one file to be sent at a time.

There are quite a few other protocols. The foregoing are the ones you'll probably use in home office applications. All three of them are still very much in use. XMODEM is handy because it deals with bad phone lines most effectively. YMODEM is frequently used because not all software supports ZMODEM, a fairly new innovation.

There are a few rather Martian terms you'll probably encounter in dealing with file transfers. The first of these are ACK and NAK, which are codes to indicate the status of a received block. When the receiving computer wants to tell the sending computer that a block has been received correctly, it sends down ACK—acknowledge. If the block came across damaged, it will send NAK—not acknowledged—and the sending computer will send it again. By waiting for an initial NAK, the sending computer can get in sync with the receiving computer.

You will also encounter mentions of CRC. This stands for "cyclical redundancy check." Early on, the process of calculating checksums for transferred blocks was replaced with CRC checking, which is more reliable. Of the two surviving versions of the XMODEM protocol, one uses CRCs and the other uses checksums. If you transfer a file using XMODEM, the software will use CRCs if both computers know how to calculate them or checksums if they don't.

While file transfers were a bit hairy in years gone by, they're effortless now. All you have to do is tell your computer what you'd like to send or receive and wait for your software's on-screen status box to tell you that the transfer is complete.

ARCHIVAL COMPRESSION

Almost all data files exhibit what computer science types call "redundancy." For example, the beginning of this paragraph, as I typed it, began with five identical space characters for an indent. Computer science types regard this sort of thing as being dreadfully wasteful.

More to the point, each one of those characters would take time to transfer over a modem. It would be better—at least in terms of transfer time—to come up with a way to indicate that strings of identical bytes in a file are identical, such that a code or "token" could be used to replace them. Of course the token should take up less space than the original data.

The process of replacing redundant data with tokens to make the data smaller is called archival compression. Text files, such as the one containing this chapter, typically can be compressed to about half their normal size. Database files often compress down to a tenth of their original sizes—they consist almost entirely of redundant data. Other types of data show differing affinities for compression—some sorts of image data hardly compress at all.

A compression program allows you to squeeze your files into the smallest possible size, transfer the compressed files, and then expand the data back into its original form when it has made the trip. The resulting file will be identical to the one it was originally compressed from, but the file transfer will have taken much less time.

"Archival" compression programs combine a secondary feature with the basic file compression. They allow you to compress multiple files into a single archive file and then automatically separate them into their original files when the archive is decompressed.

Archival compression programs have uses other than in telecommunications—for example, they're handy for getting lots of data you won't need for a while onto a small number of floppy disks—but they were originally created to get the most out of modem connect time, and this remains a large part of their application.

The most popular archival compression program for the Mac is called StuffIt. The most popular PC package is called ZIP or PKZIP. Both use roughly the same principles; however, the resulting files aren't compatible. Both programs are available as shareware.

You may encounter an older archive standard for PC systems called ARC. The ARC package was originally written by a company called SEAware. It worked, but very slowly. It was improved by a company called PKWARE, whose PKARC program became much more popular than the SEAware ARC program. SEAware sued PKWARE, as of this writing the only lawsuit ever undertaken between shareware companies. As a result of this, PKWARE stopped making ARC programs, and renamed its package to ZIP. The ARC format has largely fallen into disuse.

If you'll be using a modem for anything but the most trivial of file transfers you should get the appropriate archive program for your system. Using one serves to keep related files together and saves a lot of time.

USING QMODEM

Qmodem is a very easy program to set up. Once you've copied it into its own subdirectory, you type QMODEM to start it. Pressing *Alt-N* allows you to initially configure it. The configuration procedure, which is menu driven, offers a "quick configuration" for pretty well every modem on the planet. Figure 7.2 illustrates part of the list of modems in Qmodem's quick configuration list.

Setting up Qmodem involves selecting your modem from this list, selecting Save from the rightmost menu, and getting down to work.

The only thing you have to remember about using Qmodem is to hit the Home key should you ever find yourself lost. This will pop up a help screen that details all of Qmodem's commands.

As with most telecommunications software, Qmodem has a lot of features that are designed to make it well suited to calling computer bulletin boards and dial-up databases. A computer bulletin board is essentially a very large computer—or more often a network of computers—running in host mode.

In its default state, Qmodem will be in terminal mode. If you type something into it, the SD light on your modem should flash.

The dialing directory of Qmodem, as seen in Figure 7.3, is accessed by hitting *Alt-D.* You can add names to it as you need to, and each entry can specify a different baud rate and protocol if you like. Dialing a number involves moving the selector bar down to the number in question, hitting Enter, and sitting back until your modem has completed the call.

```
════════════════════════ Setup Menu ════════════════════════
  Video    │Modem│   Dirs    Host    Protocols    Files    Options    Exit

          ┌─────────────────────────────────┐
You a     │ Communication Parameters ↓      │
─────     │ Modem Commands ↓                │──────────────────
          │ Port Addresses ↓                │
ATZ    ┌──│Quick Modem Config! ↓│─ to install ─────────────┐
OK     │ Practical Peripherals PM2400SA MNP                │
       │ Racal Vadic Auto Dial VA212                       │
       │ Sysdyne MDM 24H                                   │
       │ Telebit T2000 & Trailblazer Plus                  │
       │ Telebit T2500                                     │
       │ UDS 2440                                          │
       │ UDS V.3224/V.3225 (V.32)                          │
       │ USRobotics Direct 1200PC Internal                 │
       │ USRobotics Password 1200 Internal                 │
       │ USRobotics Direct 2400PC / Sportster 2400         │
       │ USRobotics MicroLink 2400                         │
       │ USRobotics VARmodem 2400                          │
       │ USRobotics Courier 2400e and 2400PC w/MNP         │
       │ USRobotics HST (96x ROM)                          │
       │ USRobotics HST (144x ROM)                         │
       └─────────────── ↑↓ for more ───────────────────────┘
  Pick a modem from the list for Quick Installation
```

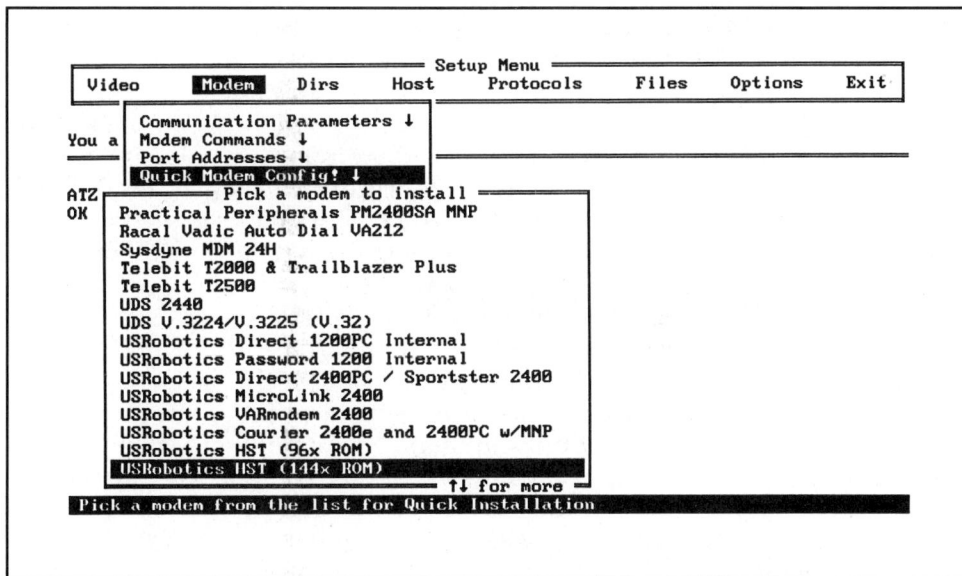

Figure 7.2: Some of the modems in Qmodem's quick configuration list

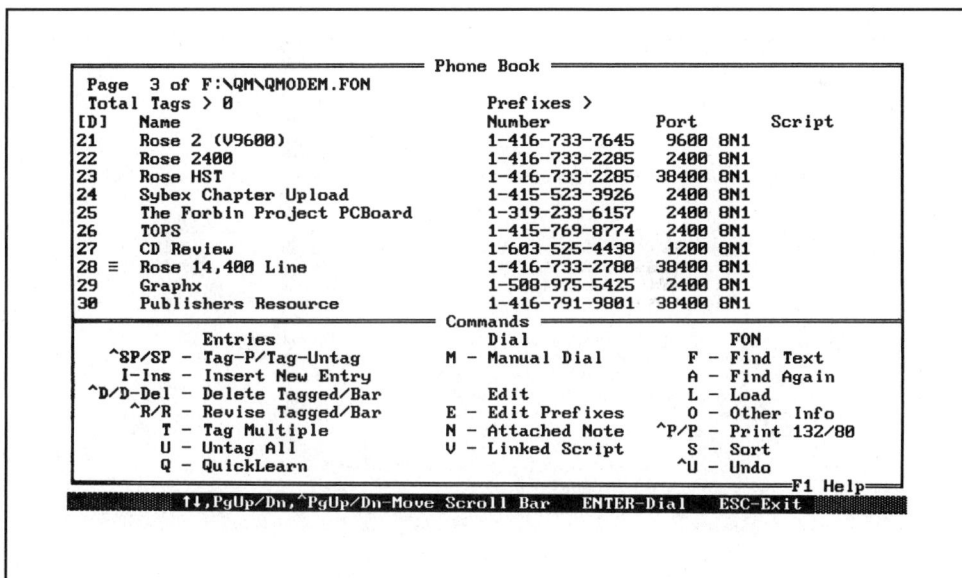

```
═══════════════════════════ Phone Book ═══════════════════════════
  Page  3 of F:\QM\QMODEM.FON
  Total Tags > 0              Prefixes >
  [D]    Name                 Number          Port      Script
  21     Rose 2 (V9600)       1-416-733-7645  9600 8N1
  22     Rose 2400            1-416-733-2285  2400 8N1
  23     Rose HST             1-416-733-2285  38400 8N1
  24     Sybex Chapter Upload 1-415-523-3926  2400 8N1
  25     The Forbin Project PCBoard 1-319-233-6157 2400 8N1
  26     TOPS                 1-415-769-8774  2400 8N1
  27     CD Review            1-603-525-4438  1200 8N1
  28  ≡  Rose 14,400 Line     1-416-733-2780  38400 8N1
  29     Graphx               1-508-975-5425  2400 8N1
  30     Publishers Resource  1-416-791-9801  38400 8N1
  ════════════════════════ Commands ════════════════════════
           Entries                 Dial              FON
   ^SP/SP - Tag-P/Tag-Untag    M - Manual Dial    F - Find Text
   I-Ins - Insert New Entry                       A - Find Again
  ^D/D-Del - Delete Tagged/Bar      Edit          L - Load
   ^R/R - Revise Tagged/Bar    E - Edit Prefixes  O - Other Info
      T - Tag Multiple         N - Attached Note  ^P/P - Print 132/80
      U - Untag All            V - Linked Script  S - Sort
      Q - QuickLearn                              ^U - Undo
  ═════════════════════════════════════════════════════ F1 Help ═
   ↑↓,PgUp/Dn,^PgUp/Dn-Move Scroll Bar   ENTER-Dial   ESC-Exit
```

Figure 7.3: Qmodem's dialing directory screen

When the call has been completed and your modem is connected to a remote modem, the dialing screen will disappear, returning you to terminal mode so you can communicate with the remote computer.

Uploading and downloading files with Qmodem is extremely easy. It's initiated from terminal mode. Hitting the PgUp key uploads and hitting the PgDn key downloads. The only important thing to keep in mind is that you must select the same block transfer protocol for Qmodem as the remote computer will be using. In most cases, the remote computer will allow you to select among XMODEM, YMODEM, ZMODEM, and others. Just make sure you select the same choice when Qmodem's transfer box comes up.

The Qmodem file transfer status box, as seen in Figure 7.4, will tell you how things are proceeding during a file transfer. If you use YMODEM or ZMODEM to transfer files, each file will be preceded by a header that tells Qmodem not only the name of the file, but also what its size will be when all of it has been transferred. Qmodem will use this information to tell you how much time remains in the current transfer, updating this number with each block received. This number doesn't take into account any time that might be lost if blocks are corrupted and must be resent.

The Qmodem host mode is also accessed from its terminal mode. Hit *Alt-5* and Qmodem will automatically send the correct AT commands to

```
   (1 Used, 80 Left) IBM (2) Conference - Your Command Steve? d

   Download Flagged Files? (Y)

                          ══ Download Status ══
     File  WHRIS44B.ZIP      Protocol ZMODEM CRC32
     Path  H:\

     Bytes Total 47354       Blocks Total 47      Time Elapsed 00:00:07
     Bytes Rcvd  7168        Blocks Rcvd  7       ++ Remaining 00:00:43
     Error Count 0           Block Size   1024    Efficiency   96.46%
                                                  Chars/Second 926
     Status Msgs
     Completion  14%   ████████▐■■■■■■■■■■■■■■■■■■■■■■■■■■■■■■■■■■■■■
   Batch Download Time:  0.8 minutes (approximate)
   Batch Download Size:  47354 bytes (47 blocks)
   Batch Protocol Type:  Zmodem       (Batch U/L and D/L)
   (Ready to Send in Batch Mode)

   (G)oodbye after Batch, (A)bort or (E)dit Batch, (Enter)=continue? ( )
   Sending File(s) - Start your download ...

   ████████▌  Download In Progress    ESC-Cancel Transfer  ████
```

Figure 7.4: Qmodem's file transfer status box

your modem to tell it to answer the phone automatically when it rings and then to be a host. You can configure the host mode to provide whatever level of password security you want.

Calling Qmodem when it's in its host mode is pretty painless, as it presents you with menus for everything you might want it to do. If you hang up on it unexpectedly it simply resets itself and awaits another call.

Once you've logged into Qmodem's host mode, you can shell out to DOS on the remote machine. This means that you can actually get to a DOS prompt on your office computer when you're at home. You can perform most simple DOS tasks this way—this includes copying files, changing directories, and so on. If you have a fairly simple word processor and a high-speed modem, you can even type a letter this way.

Shelling to DOS from a remote machine is less than instantaneous, but it's an extremely useful feature if you want to hunt around your hard drive for a file and your hard drive is fifty miles away.

Qmodem is a very easy package to use, especially for the simple telecommunications you're likely to need in a home office. While it has all sorts of features that haven't been discussed here, few of them will get in your way if you don't need them.

USING WHITE KNIGHT

When you first boot up White Knight it will be in terminal mode. Whatever you type will be sent to your modem. You can customize it using its menus—you might have to set things such as the baud rate and other protocol items to get it going.

Figure 7.5 illustrates White Knight at work.

The thing that makes White Knight well suited for use in a home office is that it's so easy to operate. It has quite a few advanced features, but you can safely ignore them if they don't pertain to you. Everything can be found in a menu.

Dialing from within White Knight is pretty effortless. The package stores phone numbers in "phone books." If you open the phone book and select a number, it will be dialed automatically. White Knight will handle all the initial dialog between your modem and the remote one, eventually either presenting you with a connected call or telling you that the other modem didn't answer or was busy.

If a number is busy, White Knight can retry it at intervals until it answers. You can select multiple entries in the phone book and have each of them tried in sequence until one of them deigns to answer.

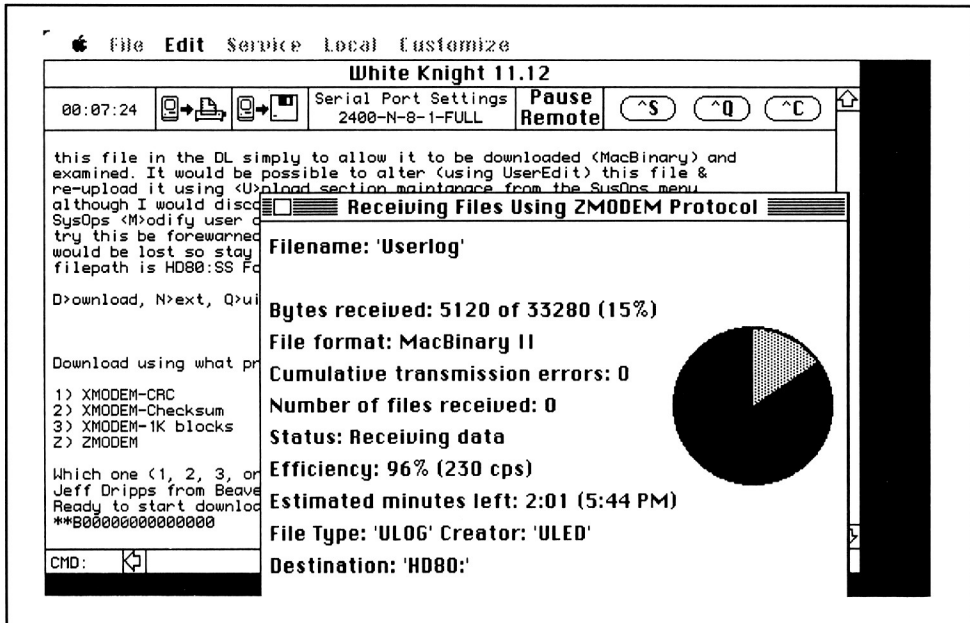

Figure 7.5: White Knight downloading a file

White Knight supports all of the file transfer protocols we've discussed in this chapter, as well as several more that you'll probably never need to know about. It will also do batch transfers: given multiple files to send or receive, it will handle them all without any further human intervention.

The White Knight host mode is initiated by selecting *Host Mode* from the Local menu. When it's active, your Mac will answer incoming calls and allow callers to upload and download files without you being around. The password structure of the White Knight host mode is a bit different from that of Qmodem: you can provide different people with different passwords. Thus, if a number of people will be using the host computer at your office, you can control which ones have full access to the host, which ones have access to upload files only, and which ones have access to download files only.

The White Knight host mode is arguably a bit more complicated to use than the one in Qmodem, as it's based on commands rather than menus. This means that it will take you longer to learn, but it's quicker to work with once you do, as you won't have to watch a menu print to your screen every time you have the host perform a function.

The White Knight host doesn't have an equivalent to Qmodem's doorway function; that is, you can't actually run your Mac over the phone as you can a DOS system.

AUTHOR'S CHOICE: TELECOMMUNICATIONS

Somewhere in my back room there's a box that contains nothing but old modems. Some of these are quite old—their rubber cups designed to hold phone receivers have become brittle with age.

Modem technology has advanced very quickly, and modems become obsolete almost before you get to know them well. This used to be tolerable—modems were among the least expensive computer gadgets available. Today's high-speed modems, however, are no longer inexpensive.

My current modem is a US Robotics HST, which has more lights and a higher maximum useful baud rate than any of the other popular modems available at the moment. We live way out in the sticks—where everything is long distance—and a fast modem is therefore essential.

If there is an existing standard in the current tangle of competing 9600-baud modems, it's probably HST. The Hayes V series modems haven't caught on nearly as well. If your application for telecommunications will involve your calling a lot of different modems, you'll have a better chance of being able to use 9600 baud or better if you have an HST modem.

The HST modem I use has proved to be very reliable. The popularity of HST modems has brought with it a lot of discounts and deals—they currently cost a lot less than most other 9600-baud modems.

It's worth noting that there are quite a few different HST modems. The original version supported only 9600 baud. This was superseded by the "dual standard" HST, which supported speeds up to 14,400 baud. The most recent release also supports V.42bis, which will be nice to have in the event that it actually becomes an accepted standard. US Robotics used to be pretty liberal about upgrading older HST modems, but this appears to have changed. The last time I looked into it, the price for an upgrade and the price of a new modem were nearly indistinguishable. If you buy one of these things, make sure it's one of the recent models and not the original 9600-baud-only version.

I use Qmodem for almost all the telecommunications I do. Modem software is a really hot issue among people who are on a first-name basis with their modems. Everyone I've met knows of a better package than Qmodem, although no two of them seem to know of the same one. Perhaps the best thing to say about Qmodem is that it's easy to use and has been around long enough to have had most of its bugs fixed.

Finally, one of the marketing things that phone companies occasionally do when the cash flow is slipping is to avail their customers of free "call waiting" for a while— presumably in the hope that some of them will pay for it when the free period has expired. This feature allows you to put your current conversation on hold to answer a second call.

Call waiting confuses modems to no small end. When you use a modem, first make sure you have disabled call waiting. You may have to phone your telephone company to figure this out.

Modems are quite an issue with some phone companies. A few of them are of the opinion that only businesses use modems, and hence that anyone who has one should be paying business rates for their phones. The logic of this is beyond the scope of this book to fathom.

CHAPTER

8

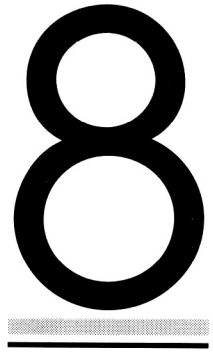

8

FAX

 F AX machines have existed since about the turn of the century, although they've gotten considerably easier to use in the ensuing years. Early FAX machines printed the documents they received by burning lines into a drum covered with wet paper.

In a sense, a modern FAX machine is a combination of several of the technologies that have been discussed in this book. Specifically, it scans outgoing documents, turning visual information into computer data, then uses a modem to transmit the scanned data to a remote FAX machine, which finally prints it out using a variation on the dot matrix printer technology discussed early in this book. Because a contemporary FAX system has all its disparate components combined into a single box, you never need to worry about the baud rate of its modem, for example, or what to do about bad blocks of data. The FAX machine does everything.

The important part about the foregoing discussion of FAX is that between sliding your original document into your machine and having it unroll itself from the receiving machine, all the information is handled as computer data. This means that in theory a computer could stand in for either one of the FAX machines. In fact, using a microcomputer as a FAX system, or as an adjunct to one, offers tremendous advantages over a conventional FAX machine. Such an application offers all sorts of features that simply can't be performed by a paper FAX machine.

CONVENTIONAL VERSUS COMPUTER FAX

This chapter will present both types of FAX: the conventional FAX, which requires paper at each end of the transmission, and computer-based FAX, which relieves you of having to print out your documents in order to send them or read them.

Conventional FAX

The easiest way to understand how a FAX machine works—and hence to visualize what you can potentially do with FAX—is to think of it as very, very slow television. A television transmission works by breaking the original image into a series of lines, or a "raster," and transmitting one line at a time. The lines are reassembled in their original order on the screen of your television. Because this happens very quickly, the image on your television appears to be a complete image, rather than a single line at a time.

A sending FAX machine scans your original documents one line at a time too. The result of each scan is a line of black and white dots, or "pixels," that represent the visual information on one line of your page. A line will be either 1/100th or 1/200th of an inch deep, depending on whether your FAX machine is in normal or fine mode. The width of a FAX document is 1728 pixels.

Having scanned a line of image data, a FAX machine compresses it for transmission using a process something like the one used by the archival compression programs discussed in the last chapter. It then sends the line through its internal modem. The current generation of FAX machines use 9600-baud modems which are capable of falling back to lower speeds if the line conditions don't permit transmission at high speed.

It's important to note that conventional FAX machine modems are not compatible with the types of computer modems discussed in the previous chapter. You need a special FAX board and driver to use a computer to send data to a remote FAX machine.

Received FAX data is usually printed one line at a time as it's received and decompressed. In order to operate faster, some FAX machines actually save up eight or more lines and print them all in a single pass.

Computer FAX

Figure 8.1 illustrates the same text sent as three FAX transmissions. The first one is a conventional FAX; that is, it was printed out and

Dreadlord & Leech
Parrot Mongers
1511 East Igneous Court
Coppertown, CA 94716

Preston Brett Hatbox
612 Silicon Road
Coppertown, CA 94720

2 May 1991

Dear Mr. Hatbox,

    Let me begin by thanking you most superficially for your recent order.
I should like at this time to offer you a reply to your various questions
regarding the care and maintenance of parrots.

    1. Oven temperature: We do not recommend keeping parrots in an oven, as
such a habitat would be dark and not conducive to the well-being of the bird.

Dreadlord & Leech
Parrot Mongers
1511 East Igneous Court
Coppertown, CA 94716

Preston Brett Hatbox
612 Silicon Road
Coppertown, CA 94720

2 May 1991

Dear Mr. Hatbox,

    Let me begin by thanking you most superficially for your
recent order. I should like at this time to offer you a reply to
your various questions regarding the care and maintenance of
parrots.

    1. Oven temperature: We do not recommend keeping parrots in
an oven, as such a habitat would be dark and not conducive to the
well-being of the bird.

Dreadlord & Leech
Parrot Mongers
1511 East Igneous Court
Coppertown, CA 94716

Preston Brett Hatbox
612 Silicon Road
Coppertown, CA 94720

2 May 1991

Dear Mr. Hatbox,

    Let me begin by thanking you most superficially for your recent order. I should like at this time to offer
you a reply to your various questions regarding the care and maintenance of parrots.

    1. Oven temperature: We do not recommend keeping parrots in an oven, as such a habitat would be dark
and not conducive to the well-being of the bird.

Figure 8.1: Three versions of the same FAX

sent through a paper FAX machine. The second two were computer-generated. They never existed on paper until they rolled out of the FAX machine that received them.

There are a number of important things to note about the three FAX documents in Figure 8.1. To begin with, all of them travelled about 3000 miles from central Ontario to northern California. The first one took about a minute to send. The second took less than half as long. The third was a bit slower than the second, but only by a few seconds.

The first FAX was sent by a Canon Faxphone FAX machine. The second two were sent using an Intel Connection Coprocessor FAX board in a 386-based computer. The latter of these was sent directly from Windows Write.

The computer-generated FAX transmissions in Figure 8.1 both look a lot nicer and took less time to get that way. They also took a lot less time to prepare—it wasn't necessary to wait for them to be printed out before they could be sent.

The data compression process used by FAX machines is called "Huffman encoding." Its effectiveness depends on the sort of image data it's given by the scanner of your FAX machine. If the data is of a regular, predictable sort, Huffman encoding will manage to squeeze it down to next to nothing. As it becomes a bit erratic, however, the effectiveness of Huffman encoding diminishes very rapidly.

When a computer generates text—as was the case in the computer-generated FAX transmissions in Figure 8.1—the black dots from which the text is formed will always appear in regular, predictable places on the page. By comparison, if you take a document and stuff it into the scanner of a FAX machine, the location of the dots as seen by the scanner will be determined by how well the page is aligned in the scanner feed slot, how clean the scanner happens to be, how well-formed the dots are, and so on. In most cases, the results will be, as far as the Huffman encoding process is concerned, a random line of pixels. As such, the resulting compressed lines won't be all that small, and they'll take a lot longer to transmit.

The computer-generated FAX documents in Figure 8.1 were generated by a board and some software that a computer thinks is a printer, and that a FAX machine thinks is another FAX machine. It handles all the dialing and negotiations required to initiate a call to a remote FAX machine. It then makes the remote FAX behave like a printer and the entire intervening phone line a sort of extensive printer cable.

Although sending a FAX over noisy phone lines may result in pages with stray black dots and other unwanted effects, most of the aberrations introduced into a FAX happen when you are using a conventional

FAX machine. These aberrations are a result of scanner error caused by dust and misaligned paper. Inasmuch as a computer-based FAX system lacks a scanner, it can't introduce scanner errors.

Advantages of Computer FAX

It used to be true that whereas busy people didn't always read their mail, they always read their FAX transmissions. FAX implied a sense of urgency. This was before the advent of junk FAX. When half the FAX transmissions waiting for you in the morning are advertisements from health clubs and BMW dealerships, the urgency of FAX may begin to elude you.

Computer-generated FAX is still fairly new. It's also eye-catching: it's so much more readable than conventional FAX that people are a lot more likely to look at it. A computer-generated FAX document can include graphics and text effects—you can print desktop publishing chapters to a FAX board with the right software. The results are impressive.

If you will be communicating frequently through FAX, there's a lot that a computer-based system can do to make the medium more effective. The specific benefits of sending FAX transmissions from your computer include

— Faster transmissions

— Lower long-distance costs

— Better quality on the receiving end

— The ability to send mass FAX documents more effectively

— Less paper and printer time used

— Delayed FAX transmission—you can create a FAX during the day but have it sent automatically at night when the long-distance rates drop.

It's worth noting that while most of the discussion of computer-based FAX in this chapter will involve sending FAX documents, computer FAX systems can receive FAX transmissions as well. For reasons that will become apparent when we look at this facility in detail, you will probably not want to use the receive feature of a FAX board if you anticipate receiving many FAX documents. If you have a conventional FAX machine, you can connect both it and a FAX board to the same phone line such that incoming FAXes can be handled by your FAX machine and outgoing ones by whichever FAX device is appropriate.

USING COMPUTER-BASED FAX

Computer based FAX is unusually easy to set up and use—if you're using a PC and if you choose the right hardware and software. For reasons that are not easy to fathom, the early history of computer FAX systems is littered with very dubious engineering. A lot of the FAX systems that emerged from this period—a few of which linger on today—are exceedingly unreliable and likely to send you scuttling back to your paper FAX machine, cursing under your breath.

Of the really workable FAX systems, the Intel FAX boards are the most flexible, the most reliable, and the best-supported by third-party software. The current version of the Intel FAX system is called the SatisFAXion board—an earlier system, called Connection Coprocessor, also exists. The differences between them are largely marketing concerns. We'll be discussing the SatisFAXion board in this chapter.

Using an Intel FAX Board

The thing that separates the Intel SatisFAXion system from other FAX systems is that the Intel boards are intelligent: the SatisFAXion card has its own microprocessor on board to manage its FAX facilities. It doesn't have to steal time from the processor of your computer, nor will it get confused if it requires processor time and your computer has none to spare, a major failing of earlier FAX systems.

Before it's compressed, a single page of FAX information can entail almost half a megabyte of data. A FAX board has to be able to handle a lot of information in a fairly short time, which is why a dedicated processor just to run the FAX is all but essential.

The SatisFAXion system works as a background task in your computer. This means that it will send and receive FAX transmissions while you're using your computer for other things. In fact, if you have some expanded memory in your system, the SatisFAXion system won't even take up a meaningful amount of DOS memory. Virtually all PC applications will run with a SatisFAXion card FAXing away behind them. As we'll discuss in a moment, many of the applications can be made to deal with the SatisFAXion board directly.

The SatisFAXion system consists of a card that plugs into your PC—it's quite large as peripheral cards go—and a set of disks that will install the software which supports the card on your hard drive. The installation procedure is all menu driven. The card connects to your phone line through a standard RJ-11 jack. If you'll be using it on the same line as your voice phone or with a conventional FAX machine, you can plug a second telephone device into the card, obviating the need for a Y adapter.

As part of the SatisFAXion card's installation procedure, it will automatically FAX your warranty information back to Intel.

The SatisFAXion card includes a built-in modem. It runs at speeds up to 9600 baud, but, as with the Macintosh FAX boxes, its 9600 baud speed isn't compatible with any of the popular 9600 baud data modems currently in use. You can use it at speeds of 2400 baud and below to call other modems.

The basis of the SatisFAXion card system is a driver that loads into your system when your computer boots up. The driver manages the FAX board. Software which sends FAX transmissions does so by negotiating with the driver.

One of the reasons the SatisFAXion system is so useful has nothing to do with the software that accompanies it. Anyone who wants to write software to communicate with the board can obtain the details of its inner workings from Intel just by asking for them. You'll probably never want to do this, but because the "architecture" of the board is easy to come by, a growing number of very clever third-party FAX packages have grown up around it. The most clever of these is a package called FaxIt, from Alien Software. In fact, it's so clever that as of this writing it was being bundled with the SatisFAXion card. We'll discuss FaxIt later in this chapter.

The SatisFAXion driver hides in the background. It watches the clock in your computer, listens for incoming calls on the phone line connected to the SatisFAXion card, and waits for FAXes to be "posted." Software that wishes to send a FAX through the SatisFAXion system doesn't actually send it directly—it simply tells the driver to send it.

Posting versus Transmitting

A FAX document may take several minutes to transmit. By comparison, posting a FAX is instantaneous—all that it really involves is telling the driver where the contents of the FAX are, where it's to go, and when it's to be sent. Once a FAX has been posted, the software that actually did the posting can go on to other things, or it can terminate and you can run another program. The FAX itself may not be transmitted for hours.

When you post a FAX to the SatisFAXion driver, you're really adding it to the current queue of outgoing FAX transmissions. As such, you can post a few dozen FAX documents at one time if you like and then get on with other work. Over the next hour or so—or as long as it takes—the SatisFAXion card will send your FAXes out for you. It will retry busy numbers—FAXes which can't be sent immediately will be returned to the queue for another try later on. It will also keep a log of each call so you'll be able to check for FAX documents that didn't get sent.

If you post a FAX with a later time or date associated with it, it will remain dormant in the queue until the time of its transmission arrives, at which point the SatisFAXion board will begin trying to send it.

The SatisFAXion board comes with DOS-based software that will handle the posting of simple FAX transmissions for you. It maintains a dialing directory and allows you to add a graphic cover page to your FAXes if you like. You might want to include your company logo in the graphic, for example. There's a rudimentary paint program included with the card to help you create graphics, should you have no other way of coming by them.

The SatisFAXion card's posting software is menu driven and very nearly foolproof to use. It allows for multiple postings, delayed FAXes, and long FAX documents. It isn't as flexible as it might be for including graphics with your transmissions, and everything it sends is in the same rather pedestrian font seen in the middle document in Figure 8.1. This makes for the most efficient use of long-distance connect charges, but it's not as impressive as it might be.

Using FaxIt

The FaxIt FAX manager for Windows comes with the SatisFAXion card. It includes an installation program to make it extremely painless to get going.

FaxIt makes the SatisFAXion card look like a printer to any software which runs under Microsoft Windows. If you attempt to print to the FaxIt device from Windows Write, Ventura for Windows, Excel, Windows Paint, Corel Draw, or any other Windows applications, a box will appear prompting you for a phone number. It includes a dialing directory so you can store frequently used phone numbers and avoid retyping them. Having been told whom you want to send a FAX to, FaxIt will place the call and transmit your document more or less as it would have looked had it been sent to a printer.

Figure 8.2 illustrates the FaxIt window that pops up when you try to print to the SatisFAXion board.

It's worth noting that installing the FaxIt package doesn't interfere with printing to whatever printer you would normally use to produce hard copy from Windows applications. It simply adds an extra printer device to your system. In order to print to a regular printer, you need only open the printer section of the Windows control panel and select the printer you want to use.

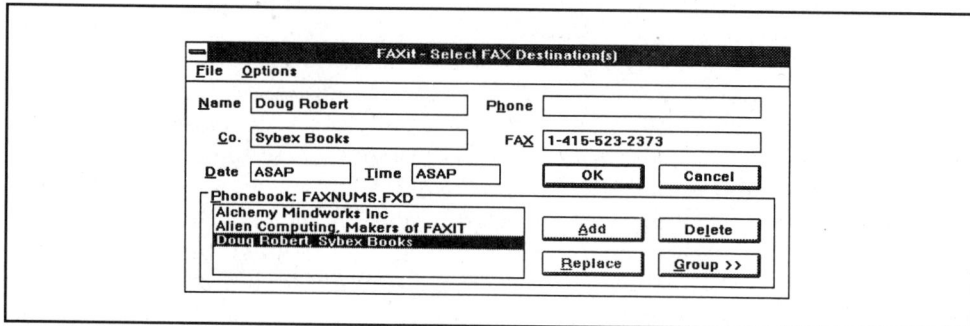

Figure 8.2: The FaxIt window

There isn't a lot you can't do with FaxIt. It will FAX desktop publishing chapters, word processing files, spreadsheets, drawings—its capabilities are limited only by what you can run under Windows. Perhaps more to the point, however, is that it allows you to combine the quality and speed of a computer-generated FAX system with the attractive typography and graphics associated with laser printed output sent by conventional FAX.

Figure 8.3 illustrates a couple of cropped examples from complex pages sent by FAX through FaxIt.

FAX for the MAC

FAX has never really become as popular in Macintosh circles as it has with PC users. This might be due to the fact that Macs with slots are only a recent phenomenon—prior to being able to plug a FAX board into one's Mac, an external FAX device had to occupy one of its two serial ports, very likely displacing some other useful peripheral.

As of this writing almost all of the workable Macintosh FAX systems consist of external FAX boxes that connect to one of the Mac's ports. Among the most popular are the ProModem 24/96, which is both a 2400-baud modem and a 9600-baud FAX system, and OrchidFax, which offers modem speeds up to 9600 baud as well as 9600-baud FAX. It's worth noting that the 9600-baud modem used by OrchidFax isn't actually compatible with any of the popular stand-alone 9600-baud modems—its 9600-baud FAX section will, however, deal with all other FAX machines.

Whereas internal FAX cards for PC systems have been around a while and seem to have had their bugs ironed out, this technology is still quite new for higher-end Macintosh systems. The Datalink/Mac system, for the Macintosh II, for example, is an internal FAX card that provides send-only FAX capabilities. Unfortunately, the cards released to date also crash a lot.

III. SHAFT AND BEARING SELECTION

Since the design of the shafts and the choice of the bearings are close both shall be dealt with in this section.

The magnitude of the load applied at the sprocket is dependent upon A smaller sprocket will require a larger chain tension, hence, a larger load to torque. Link belt catalog 1050 lists the smallest sprocket for this horsepowe approximately 5.5 inches in diameter. (See Figure 1.) Assuming the tension concentrated on one side of the sprocket, the force (F) required to transmit tl pounds. This force can be applied in any arbitrary direction.

Figure 1 - Sprocket #PL 7034

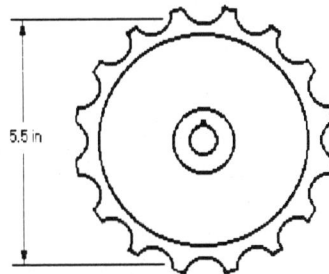

5.5 in

WEST COAST SALES				
	Jan	Feb	Mar	
Mike Jones				
Greenville	$7,128	$8,135	$12,200	
Hempton	$5,675	$5,919	$6,295	
S. Minton	$7,750	$13,982	$17,055	
Mike's Totals	$20,553	$28,036	$35,550	
Pam Coburn				
Metro Area	$7,005	$8,106	$7,877	
East End	$2,172	$2,124	$2,103	
Pam's Totals	$9,177	$10,230	$9,980	
Janis Kincaid				
Clear Spring	$7,328	$13,054	$13,981	
Lakewater	$13,175	$21,075	$22,092	
Riverton	$3,285	$3,165	$3,385	
Janis's Totals	$23,788	$37,294	$39,458	
TOTALS	$53,518	$75,560	$84,988	

Figure 8.3: Details from FaxIt transmissions from Microsoft Word and Excel

Because they're in the early part of their development, Macintosh FAX systems will probably change a lot and get significantly better over the next year or so. Quite a lot may happen in this area between now and the time you read this book. If the facilities discussed in this chapter appeal to you and you'll be using Macintosh hardware, you should discuss the state of the art in Macintosh FAX systems with an Apple dealer.

RECEIVING FAX TRANSMISSIONS BY COMPUTER

The SatisFAXion system will receive incoming FAX transmissions. You should probably shut this feature off if you don't need it, or if your incoming FAXes will be handled by a conventional paper FAX machine. Some of the Macintosh FAX boxes handle incoming FAXes as well, although many are only capable of sending them. This isn't as much of an omission as it seems. Receiving FAXes by computer isn't nearly as useful as sending them can be.

A FAX transmission page is essentially a large scanned picture of a sheet of paper. The data is image data, not text data, and there is no easy way to translate the words in a FAX into text of the sort which a word processor can inhale. Incoming FAX transmissions are stored as picture files, not text files, and must be viewed as such.

A FAX document is 1728 dots wide. By comparison, the screen of a super-VGA card will usually manage no more than 800 pixels across— the really high-end ones get up to 1024 pixels across, but the difference in price between a standard multisync VGA monitor and one that can handle 1024 pixels would pretty well cover the cost of a paper FAX machine.

In order to read a FAX that has been received by a FAX board, you must either print it out or view it with a lot of panning around. While this isn't impossible, it won't have you looking forward to reading your FAX mail. If you do wind up getting a lot of junk FAX for health clubs and BMW dealerships this might not be all bad, of course.

In addition to being cumbersome to read, FAX documents take up quite a bit of disk space. Because they're received automatically, they can accumulate on your disk without your really noticing them. As a rule, having your FAX board receive FAXes for you requires that you be fairly scrupulous about killing off your FAX files once you've read them.

If your FAX board is the only thing you have to receive FAXes, it will entail having your computer on all the time if it's to be able to deal with FAXes around the clock.

There *are* several positive points to receiving FAX transmissions with a FAX board rather than with a FAX machine—they're just not all that pertinent to a home office. The first of them is unquestionably security. Unlike a FAX machine, which leaves its incoming mail where anyone can peruse it, a FAX board can put your FAX documents somewhere safe until you're ready to look at them. If you lock the keyboard of your computer when you're not around it should be pretty difficult for someone to get at your FAX mail.

It might well be argued that if security is a problem in your home office you may need a new home. The only FAX security problem I've encountered to date is that Jones the dog seems to like the taste of FAX paper, and has chewed a few important documents.

Another advantage of using a FAX board for incoming transmissions is that it allows you to print out only those FAX documents that you really want hard copies of—assuming that you're prepared to read the rest by panning around with an image viewer. This probably won't appeal to you unless your home office is the recipient of a substantial volume of FAX mail.

It's worth noting that the image files which a SatisFAXion board produces when an incoming FAX is received are actually standard PC Paintbrush PCX files. Once received, they can be used with anything that accepts image files in this format. You can, for example, include a FAX as a picture in a desktop publishing chapter this way.

FAX OF THE FUTURE

Though it's not quite workable as I write this, a still better way to use FAX with your computer will probably be available by the time this book is printed. A growing number of manufacturers of conventional FAX machines are fitting them with serial ports so they can be interfaced to personal computers. Among the machines so equipped are models from Canon and Ricoh. This allows you to have a dedicated paper FAX machine and to be able to send FAX transmissions through it directly from your computer. In most cases you can also use the FAX machine as a printer—albeit to print on shiny chemical FAX paper—and as a fair to middling black and white page scanner.

While these FAX machines certainly exist now, I've yet to see software for either Macintosh or PC systems that would drive them in anything like a user-friendly way. I've heard of several companies working on the development of suitable drivers for these systems. If computer-based FAX has applications in your home office—and if you have yet to spring for a conventional FAX machine—you might want to look into the possibilities of a combination FAX machine and computer FAX system.

CHAPTER

9

9

SPREADSHEETS

Despite their decidedly digital character, spreadsheets can be among the most useful of microcomputer applications. They can save you hours of calculation and, perhaps more to the point, they'll allow you to experiment with versions of your financial future— to ask "what if" questions— and see the results in real time.

In many respects, spreadsheets allow you to replace a lot of time-honored numerical models and approximations with real, authentic numbers calculated to the last penny or decimal place. A spreadsheet will allow you to know the cash flow of a business down to the last paper clip and memo pad, or to prognosticate about the future using differing scenarios. If you maintain a spreadsheet model of your business, you can adjust those figures that represent the present state of your finances and the spreadsheet will update its version of the future.

HOW SPREADSHEETS WORK

Figure 9.1 illustrates a spreadsheet program. In order to differentiate between the spreadsheet program itself and the data it works with, the actual information in a spreadsheet program is referred to as a "worksheet." All worksheets start off as a matrix of empty boxes. Each box is called a "cell."

Each cell on a worksheet has a unique address, as specified by its row and column number. The rows are numbered and the columns are

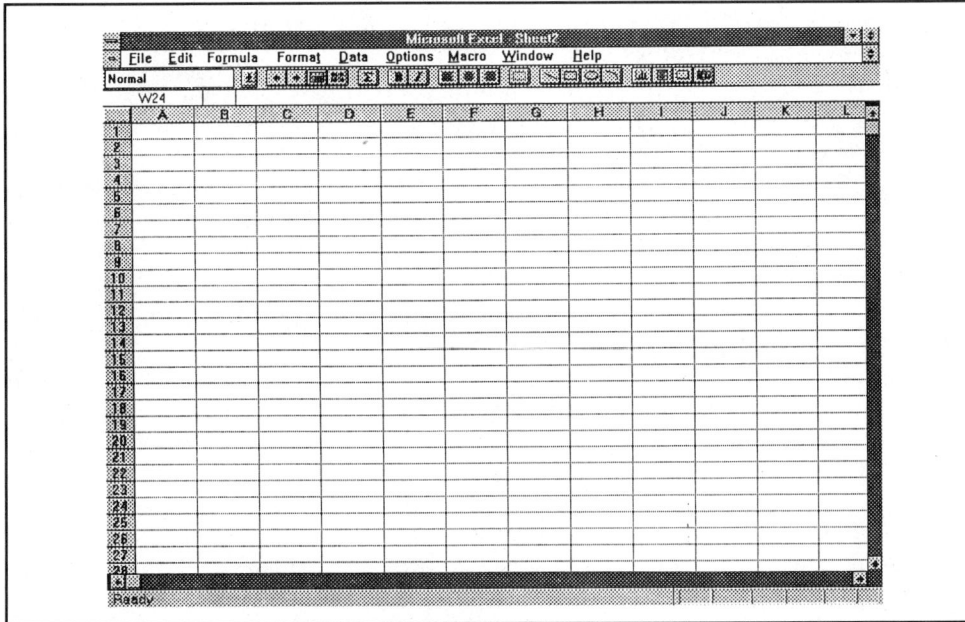

Figure 9.1: A blank worksheet

lettered. The cell in the upper left corner of the spreadsheet is referred to as cell A1; the one next to it and down one is cell B2; the next one across and down is C3; ... etc.

In theory, a worksheet begins in the upper left corner and extends out in both dimensions to infinity. The row numbers can increase indefinitely. When you move rightward past column 26, the letter designations double. Hence, the column to the right of column Z is column AA, followed by AB and so on.

In fact, the maximum dimensions of a worksheet are limited by the design of the spreadsheet program and by the amount of memory available to put the worksheet in. This will be discussed in a bit more detail later in this chapter.

For the purposes of this basic discussion of spreadsheets, a worksheet cell can contain one of three things, to wit:

— Text

— A number

— A formula

Text in a worksheet cell is used to label things. For example, if you'll be working with a column of numbers that represents the cash flow for your business in January, you might want to put "January" in the cell at the top of the column to help you keep track of what the column contains. This is especially helpful as your worksheet becomes more complex.

The numbers that you put in worksheet cells represent the data you'll be working with. All worksheet numbers are "floating point" values—"real" numbers—by default, although as we'll see you can specify how they'll be displayed to suit the sort of data you're working with.

Worksheet cell formulas are what make spreadsheets so powerful. Any cell in a worksheet can contain a formula that performs arithmetic calculations using the values to be found in other cells in the worksheet. If the values of those cells change, the formula can automatically recalculate. You can elect to view a cell's formula or the result (the value) of its calculation. In Figure 9.2 the worksheet shows only values.

The worksheet in Figure 9.2 calculates the total cost of the premises of a laudably uncomplicated company for the first quarter of the year. In this worksheet, the rent is a fixed cost each month, as are the maintenance and parking fees. The other expenses vary with use.

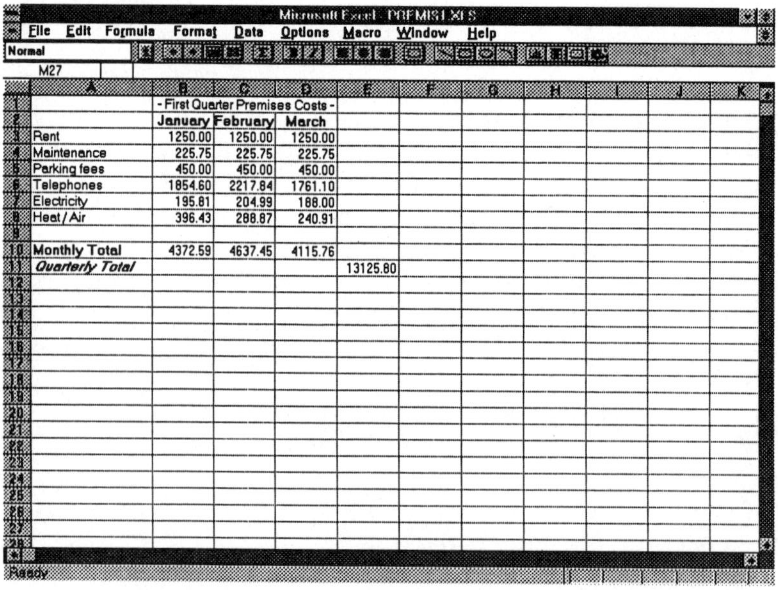

Figure 9.2: A simple worksheet to calculate premises costs

Cells B10, C10, and D10 have automatically calculated the monthly totals for these figures, and cell E11 has calculated the quarterly total. For example, the monthly total for January is calculated by cell B10. The formula I originally typed into cell B10 was

=SUM(B3:B8)

This means that the contents of this cell equals the sum of all the values from B3 through B8. In this example these cells contain fixed numbers—I simply typed the values into their respective cells—but some of them could just as easily contain formulas.

In fact, because the rent in this worksheet is fixed, I didn't have to enter it in cells C3 or D3. Instead, in cell C3 I typed a very simple formula:

=B3

This means that the rent for February will be the same as the rent for January. Likewise, cell D3 contains the formula

=C3

The rent for March will thus be the same as the rent for February.

This arrangement is very powerful, and makes keeping the spreadsheet up to date a lot easier. It also allows you to speculate. For example, if the rent were to increase in February by $250.00, I could change the formula in cell C3 to

=B3+250.00

The value displayed in cell D3—the rent for March—would change automatically, as would any subsequent dependent months.

Here's another way you might employ formulas in this spreadsheet. The parking costs are based on the number of employees in the company who bring cars to work, with each space costing $45.00. There are presently ten parking spaces involved. You could enter this data in each of the three cells for parking costs. Alternately, you could modify the spreadsheet a bit, as seen in Figure 9.3.

The worksheet in Figure 9.3 makes it easier to allow for changes in the number of cars to be parked and the cost of each parking space. The

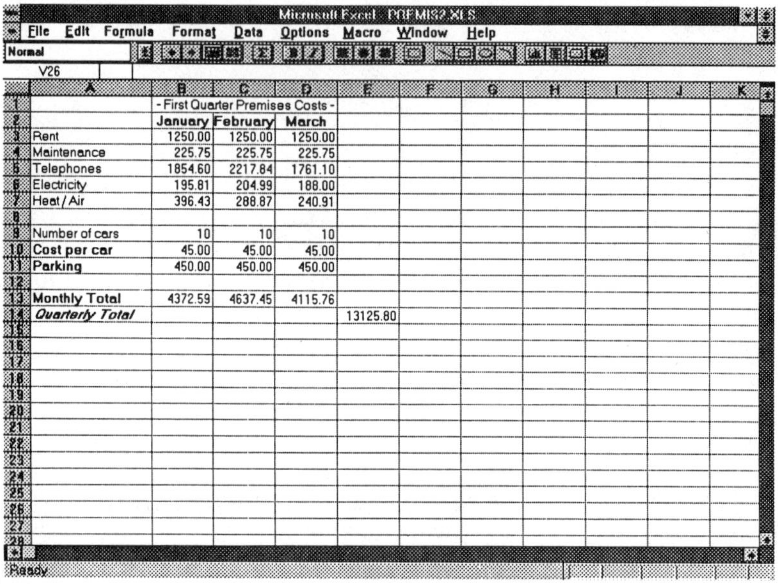

	A	B	C	D	E
1		- First Quarter Premises Costs -			
2		January	February	March	
3	Rent	1250.00	1250.00	1250.00	
4	Maintenance	225.75	225.75	225.75	
5	Telephones	1854.60	2217.84	1761.10	
6	Electricity	195.81	204.99	188.00	
7	Heat/Air	396.43	288.87	240.91	
8					
9	Number of cars	10	10	10	
10	Cost per car	45.00	45.00	45.00	
11	Parking	450.00	450.00	450.00	
12					
13	Monthly Total	4372.59	4637.45	4115.76	
14	*Quarterly Total*				13125.80

Figure 9.3: Using variables to handle changes in parking costs

contents of cells B9 and B10 are the number and cost of the parking spaces respectively. Cell B11 contains the formula

=B9*B10

Obviously, cells B9 and B10 shouldn't be included as part of the summation for the monthly total in cell B13. They simply represent data that is used to derive the value in B11. The value in B11 should be included. The formula in cell B13, then, is

=SUM(B3:B7)+B11

Now, let's consider the prospect of this company moving its offices to take advantage of a lease that looks like a better deal, at least on the surface. The monthly rent is lower but the parking spaces cost more. Specifically, the rent is $1050.00 per month instead of $1250.00, but the parking spaces cost $65.00 each. You can see the resulting cost by changing the values in cells B3 and B10 respectively. The rents for February and March will reflect whatever the rent for January is; likewise, the cost per parking space for January will be reflected for February and March as well. In both cases, I entered numbers in the January cells and formulas in the February and March cells referring to the value for the preceding month.

The results can be seen in Figure 9.4. They don't look too good. Moving to the new office would save $25.00 per quarter—hardly enough to keep the executive vice-president's Lincoln in gas for a week.

It might turn out, however, that fewer of the employees who presently drive to work would need to do so in the new location. You could change the value in cell B9 to reflect this, and the quarterly total would again recalculate. It might also be the case that the prospective new premises have been vacant for a while, and that the landlord would be willing to negotiate the rent when confronted with a worksheet that points out why there would be very little point in moving as things stand.

A Non-Financial Worksheet

It's worth pointing out that while spreadsheets are used primarily for financial calculations, they can have other functions. For example, Figure 9.5

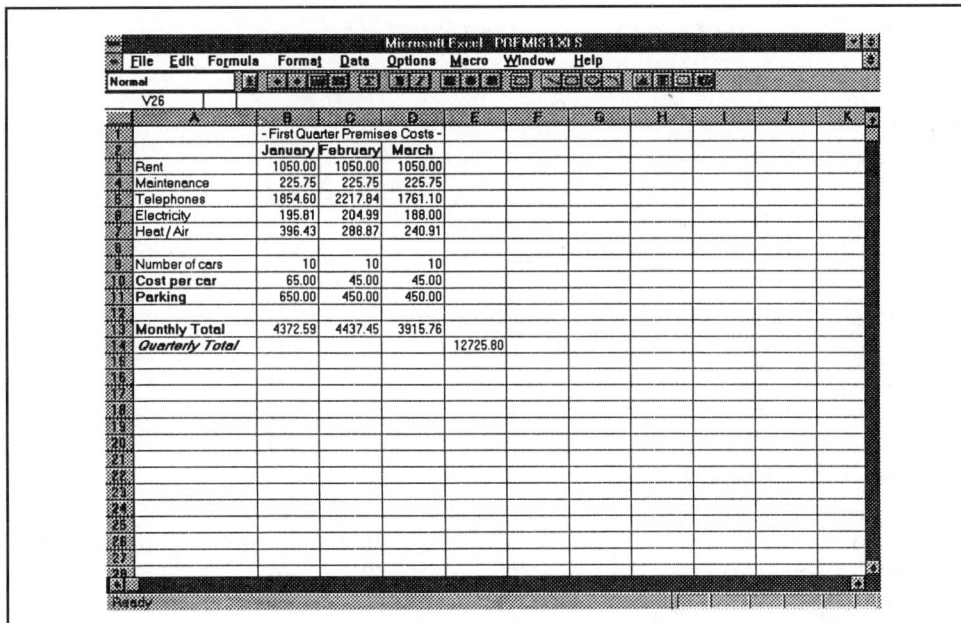

Figure 9.4: The results of changing premises

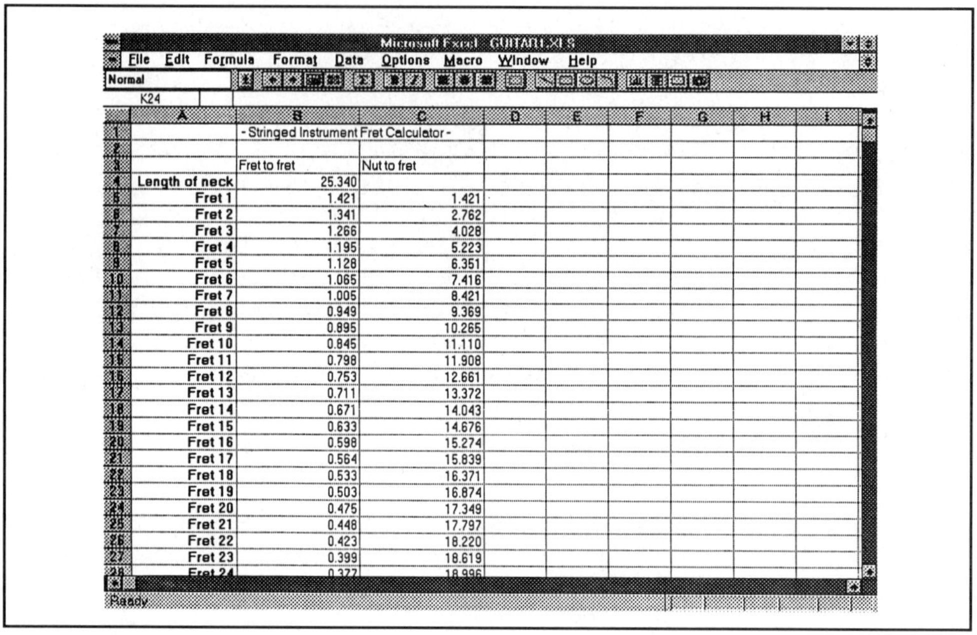

	A	B	C
1		- Stringed Instrument Fret Calculator -	
2			
3		Fret to fret	Nut to fret
4	Length of neck	25.340	
5	Fret 1	1.421	1.421
6	Fret 2	1.341	2.762
7	Fret 3	1.266	4.028
8	Fret 4	1.195	5.223
9	Fret 5	1.128	6.351
10	Fret 6	1.065	7.416
11	Fret 7	1.005	8.421
12	Fret 8	0.949	9.369
13	Fret 9	0.895	10.265
14	Fret 10	0.845	11.110
15	Fret 11	0.798	11.908
16	Fret 12	0.753	12.661
17	Fret 13	0.711	13.372
18	Fret 14	0.671	14.043
19	Fret 15	0.633	14.676
20	Fret 16	0.598	15.274
21	Fret 17	0.564	15.839
22	Fret 18	0.533	16.371
23	Fret 19	0.503	16.874
24	Fret 20	0.475	17.349
25	Fret 21	0.448	17.797
26	Fret 22	0.423	18.220
27	Fret 23	0.399	18.619
28	Fret 24	0.377	18.996

Figure 9.5: My rule-of-eighteen spreadsheet

illustrates one of the spreadsheets I use from time to time. It has nothing to do with money.

The spreadsheet in Figure 9.5 implements the "rule of eighteen," a set of calculations that is used to work out the position of the frets on the neck of a guitar or other stringed instrument. While not impossible to work out with a calculator and a sheet of paper, the rule of eighteen is rather nasty because it involves a lot of successive calculations, each based on the one before it. If you get one of them wrong, all the subsequent ones will be wrong as well. If you don't notice the error you'll find up with a fifty dollar slab of ebony that only has applications as a paint stirring stick.

The rule of eighteen is, to begin with, actually the rule of 17.835. To work out the position of the first fret on a guitar neck, you would measure the distance between the bridge and the nut of the guitar and divide this value by 17.835. The resulting number would be the distance between the nut and the first fret. You would then measure the remaining distance and divide this by 17.835. This would be the distance from the first fret to the second fret, and so on.

Column B of the worksheet represents the distances from one fret to the next. The actual distance from the nut to the bridge of the guitar in question is entered into cell B4. Cell B5, then, contains the formula:

=B4/17.835

Cell B6 contains the formula:

=B5-(B5/17.835)

and so on.

Column C offers the measurements from the nut to each fret, rather than from one fret to the next, which is actually a lot more useful than the measurements in column B. This isn't very complicated to set up. The first cell, C5, contains the formula:

=B5

The next cell, C6, contains the formula:

=C5+B6

This is the previous value plus the current fret-to-fret distance. The formula in cell C7 would be the same arrangement:

=C6+B7

In this way, the cumulative distance down the fretboard will work itself out down column C.

The only drawback to the values in column C is that they're all in decimal values. The rulers used to measure fretboards are typically measured out in sixty-fourths of an inch. As such, it's worth making an additional modification to the worksheet, as shown in Figure 9.6.

Column D in the revised worksheet figures the distances from the nut to each fret in sixty-fourths of an inch. There's absolutely nothing complicated about this column. All the cells in column D have been instructed to display their values as fractions rather than decimals. Spreadsheet programs can do things like this rather easily. Each separate cell in column D thus simply contains a formula that refers to the adjacent cell in column C. Hence, cell D3 merely contains the formula:

=C3

Subsequent columns could be duplicated in the same way.

Microsoft Excel - GUITAR2.XLS

File   Edit   Formula   Format   Data   Options   Macro   Window   Help

Normal

H39

A	B	C	D	E	F	G	H
	- Stringed Instrument Fret Calculator -						
	Fret to fret	Nut to fret	Nut to fret in 64ths				
Length of neck	25.340						
Fret 1	1.421	1.421	1 27/64				
Fret 2	1.341	2.762	2 49/64				
Fret 3	1.266	4.028	4 2/64				
Fret 4	1.195	5.223	5 14/64				
Fret 5	1.128	6.351	6 22/64				
Fret 6	1.065	7.416	7 27/64				
Fret 7	1.005	8.421	8 27/64				
Fret 8	0.949	9.369	9 24/64				
Fret 9	0.895	10.265	10 17/64				
Fret 10	0.845	11.110	11 7/64				
Fret 11	0.798	11.908	11 58/64				
Fret 12	0.753	12.661	12 42/64				
Fret 13	0.711	13.372	13 24/64				
Fret 14	0.671	14.043	14 3/64				
Fret 15	0.633	14.676	14 43/64				
Fret 16	0.598	15.274	15 18/64				
Fret 17	0.564	15.839	15 54/64				
Fret 18	0.533	16.371	16 24/64				
Fret 19	0.503	16.874	16 56/64				
Fret 20	0.475	17.349	17 22/64				
Fret 21	0.448	17.797	17 51/64				
Fret 22	0.423	18.220	18 14/64				
Fret 23	0.399	18.619	18 40/64				
Fret 24	0.377	18.996	19				

Ready

Figure 9.6: Making the worksheet adjust its calculations into fractions

CHOOSING A SPREADSHEET

Spreadsheets have done more to make the people who run companies like computers than almost any other type of software. They're among the most popular business applications in use. Not surprisingly, there are a lot of competing spreadsheet packages.

The most popular spreadsheet application at the moment is one called Lotus 1-2-3. Lotus was the first really powerful spreadsheet for PC systems, and it has continued to grow and develop as larger and more powerful computers have evolved to run it.

Unfortunately, Lotus has evolved a bit more than it probably should have of late. In the interest of being able to claim that it has all the features of all the other spreadsheets available, it has gotten a bit unwieldy. Its user interface is blindingly fast if you're a Lotus guru, but it's quite inscrutable for the rest of us. In fact, many of the things that endear Lotus to Lotus gurus will confound you as you try to learn the rudiments of spreadsheet operation.

The most practical spreadsheet for use in a home office environment is arguably Microsoft Excel. Excel comes in both a Macintosh version and one that runs under Windows 3. Both packages have similar capabilities; while the examples in this chapter have been drawn from the Windows version, all of them could have just as easily been created on a Macintosh.

If you don't want to use Windows on your PC but you do want the power of a large spreadsheet package, you can use Lotus—all of the techniques and examples in this chapter can be handled by Lotus with only nominal changes. Alternatively, you might want to have a look at a package called As Easy As. This refers to its being as easy as Lotus. In fact, it's a lot easier, and a lot cheaper. As Easy As is a spreadsheet package that works just like Lotus and will read and write Lotus worksheet files. It's distributed as shareware. As Easy As will be discussed in Chapter 12.

It's worth noting that the worksheet files that a spreadsheet program saves are formatted in a way that is specific to the software that created them. The most commonly used PC worksheet file format is the one generated by Lotus. These files are usually given the extension WK1. Excel stores its worksheet files, by default, as XLS files, which are in a different format. However, it will read Lotus worksheets and quite a few other flavors of worksheets if you ask it to. This won't matter if you're working exclusively with Excel, but it's a handy facility if some of your colleagues use Lotus or if you want to use commercial worksheets that are provided in the Lotus format. The most common instance of the latter case is income tax worksheets. Toward the end of the year you'll usually find quite a few worksheets that will not only let you prepare your taxes as spreadsheets, but will also allow you to see what happens if you change some of the parameters.

Hardware Considerations

There are two things that may impair the performance of Excel if you use it to manage particularly large or complex worksheets. The first is the available memory in your system. The second is the processor speed.

Memory has always been the largest limitation for spreadsheets—every cell in a worksheet has to live somewhere, and when you create a worksheet that starts to really reflect the financial dynamics of a real-world business you'll find that your numbers and formulas occupy an enormous number of cells. Unless your worksheets will all be of pretty modest dimensions, a system with four to eight megabytes worth of memory will not go to waste. Windows offers better memory management than the Macintosh as of this writing—the fact that it has virtual memory, as discussed in Chapter 3, gives it the ability to free up memory when confronted by a huge worksheet. At such time as the Macintosh System 7 operating system is easily available and debugged, the Mac may have much the same capabilities in this respect.

The speed of the processor in your computer won't specifically affect the size of the worksheets you can work with, but it may limit the ones that can really be used effectively. The process of recalculating all the values in a complex worksheet can be pretty time-consuming. Bear in mind that many formulas contain values that are dependent upon other values, which may in turn may be dependent upon still other values, and so on.

The worksheets that have appeared in this chapter have been decidedly trivial. They all recalculate instantly. If you plan to create really huge models on a spreadsheet package, you should plan on using a fairly high-end computer—an 80386-based PC or a Macintosh II.

It wasn't uncommon for first-generation neolithic PC systems to require half an hour to recalculate a large worksheet. While this isn't likely to occur using the hardware discussed in this book, having to wait for a minute or two for your worksheet to settle down is probably more delay than you'll want to put up with. It's the sort of thing that can keep you from trying additional permutations of a worksheet, for example. Being able to play with numbers quickly and effortlessly is what makes using a spreadsheet so powerful.

TEN MINUTES WITH EXCEL

It would probably be a bit adventurous to say that Excel is *the* most powerful spreadsheet package available, but it's certain up there with the best. It seethes with features—we won't be discussing a tenth of what you can do with it here. You can get a lot done with Excel and never learn to operate its macros, linking facilities, goal seeking, and so on.

The following overview of Excel's operation is merely intended to help you to understand what's involved in using it. You'll still want to have a look at Excel's manual to get a proper start in working with the package.

The worksheet in Figure 9.2, back at the beginning of this chapter, was entered from scratch. To create one like it— presumably to solve a problem that is closer to the reality of your own work—you would begin by booting up Excel and opening a new worksheet from the File menu.

As we'll see in a moment, you can move things around a worksheet after you start creating it. If you discover that you need an extra row or column somewhere to add a previously unthought-of item, Excel enables you to simply open up some space and shift everything below it or to the right of it. However, a bit of forethought concerning where the items in your worksheet will go can save considerable shuffling later on.

There are a number of useful rules for typing things into cells. To begin with, Excel will decide whether you're typing text, numbers, or formulas based on the first character in the cell. Numbers start with digits or with a plus or minus sign. Formulas start with equal signs. Everything else is text. If you want to start a text field with a dash—as was the case for the title of the worksheet in Figure 9.2—precede it with a space so Excel won't think it has a number with bad characters in it.

Excel normally tries to show you as much of your text cells as it can. If you enter text that would extend past the right margin of the cell, Excel will allow it to overflow into adjacent cells to the right if there's nothing in them. This allows you to create titles and other long text strings that span multiple cells.

Each column and row in a worksheet can be of any width you like. Back in Figure 9.2, column A was wider than the other columns, as it contained fairly verbose text legends. To widen a column, simply place the cursor in the space where the column letter designations are and grab the line you want to move. The cursor will change from the standard Excel cross cursor to a vertical bar with two arrowheads. Drag the line to where you want the column's new right margin to be. All the columns to the right of it will shift appropriately.

You can likewise enlarge the area occupied by a row by grabbing the end of its line in the space where the row number designations are and dragging it to a new position.

If you click on a cell, its contents will appear in a field at the top of the Excel window. This is the cell editing field. Note that if you select a cell that has a formula in it, the cell will display the result of the formula, but the editing field will display the actual text of the formula. If you click in the editing field you can change the contents of the selected cell.

If you double-click on a cell with a formula in it, all the cells that the formula takes into account when it recalculates will be highlighted.

Excel is very clever about allowing you to duplicate cells and their contents. For example, consider the worksheet in Figure 9.2. Having entered the data for January in column B and the formulas and data for February in column C, it might occur to you that column D, the March entry, is really just a copy of the formulas in column C with some new data. You can replicate the contents of column C by placing the cursor on cell C3 and holding down the mouse button while you drag it to cell D10. This will highlight all the pertinent parts of column C and the corresponding cells in column D where the replicated data and formulas are to go. Now select *Fill Right* from the Edit menu.

By using the Fill Right (or Fill Down) features of Excel to replicate cells this way, Excel will automatically change the cell formulas to match their new locations. Thus, when Excel replicated the formula in C3 that looked like this:

=B3

it wound up in D3 looking like this:

=C3

This saves a lot of manual adjustments.

You can also highlight cells and cut and paste their contents using the appropriate items of the Edit menu.

If you want to insert one or more blank rows or columns in a worksheet—such as to make room for some additional items you didn't think of at first—hold and drag the cursor over the area where the blank cells are to go. Select *Insert* from the Edit menu. A dialog box will pop up asking you whether you want the adjacent cells to shift down or to shift to the right.

By default Excel presents you with numbers to seven decimal places. In the guitar fretboard worksheet, having measurements displayed to seven decimal places was a bit pointless, as I have nothing that can measure distance anywhere near that accurately. Having the decimal numbers in columns B and C displayed to three places was more than adequate. To have Excel do this, I selected all the cells in columns B and C that contained numbers or formulas—cells B4 through C28—and then selected the *Number* item from the Format menu. A list of prearranged formats appeared, but this format was so simple as to make hunting for it in the list a bit pointless. You can create your own by entering a format into the edit field at the bottom of the box.

You can specify a number with three decimal places using this format:

0.000

The format for the numbers in column D is a bit more obtuse. These values are to be displayed as fractions. To use fractions with the lowest possible denominators, you would use this format:

 # ??/??

In the case of the fretboard it was a lot more convenient to have all the fractions with the same denominator: 64, the smallest division on the ruler

I was using to measure fret distances. The format for fixed-denominator fractions with denominators of 64 is, as you might expect,

 # ??/64

You might want to consult the Excel manual for a more complete discussion of how to use some of the more obtuse formats.

Small worksheets such as the ones discussed in this chapter don't take any time at all to recalculate, even on a fairly slow computer. The most arithmetically intensive one, the guitar fret calculator, will recalculate in well under a second even on a 10-megahertz AT. As you get into much larger worksheets, however, you might find that Excel's thinking gets a bit ponderous. Because Excel abhors an out-of-balance worksheet, every time you change the contents of a cell that contains a number or a formula, Excel wants to recalculate the entire worksheet so that everything that depends upon this cell will reflect the changes. This can be very tedious even if the recalculations only take ten or fifteen seconds. By default, Excel will want to perform them every time you edit a cell.

You can force Excel to accept an out-of-balance worksheet and recalculate it only when you ask it to. Select the *Calculate* item from the Options menu and select *Manual* from the ensuing dialog box, and no more automatic recalculations will take place. You can request a recalculation any time you like by selecting *Calculate Now* from the Options menu or by using the keyboard shortcut, *Alt-O* and then *N*.

As a final note, you should keep in mind that Excel is capable of keeping multiple worksheets in memory at once, each one in its own window. You can resize worksheet windows just as you would any other windows. This will allow you to have multiple permutations of the same financial model available at the same time, for example. In the case of the premises cost model discussed at the beginning of this chapter, you could open the worksheets in both Figure 9.3 and Figure 9.4 at the same time to compare the bottom lines in both.

BECOMING A SPREADSHEET GURU

Spreadsheets can be almost addictive if your work involves a lot of financial planning, cash flow management, or other applications where you have to juggle a lot of dependent numbers. You'll find that Excel is a fabulously creative tool—in a fiscal sense—as it lets you see answers to your questions almost as fast as you can think up the questions.

In any real-world model—whether it's based in finance, engineering, or any other analytical discipline—there is invariably more data available than you need to come to a conclusion. The real art of using a spreadsheet program well is not in learning how to replicate cells and do clever things with macros. It's in knowing what to include in your worksheets and what to omit. The first step in learning this art is in realizing that not everything should be included even if you have enough memory to make doing so possible.

As with any art, there are no rules to help you decide whether something belongs in your spreadsheet models. Your own understanding of your business should help you decide this, but a bit of experience with Excel will be an asset too. It can be very educational to spend a few hours working up a spreadsheet that takes into account absolutely everything in your business—right down to the paper clips—only to find out that the effect of half of it is so small as to be incapable of actually affecting the result of the total calculation.

CHAPTER

10

10

DATABASE MANAGEMENT

For a great many business applications, database management—or at least, the concept thereof—seems like the most powerful and productive use of a microcomputer. If you understand the basic concepts of what a database package can do for you, you will appreciate its potential uses. A database manager can, for example, take care of maintaining a mailing list, keep track of inventory, do your company's payroll—the potential uses for databases seem limitless.

The most commonly mentioned database management program is dBASE IV, by Ashton Tate. In fact, this will be one of the few times it will be mentioned in this chapter. While it is a genuinely powerful application and the continuing delight of dBASE gurus, dBASE has a protracted learning curve, which makes it more work to use than most home office applications can justify. In addition, many of the features which make it so powerful—and so hard to learn—aren't really needed for basic database management. There are other, albeit lesser-known solutions to database handling.

The thing that makes dBASE and applications like it so powerful is that they aren't applications at all. They're programming languages that have been designed specifically for writing programs to handle databases. Because they're genuine programming languages, you can do virtually anything you can imagine to your data, with no restrictions imposed on you by what the authors of dBASE had in mind. Of course, you have to become a really proficient programmer to accomplish this.

There are a number of database packages that aren't nearly as powerful as dBASE, but which offer significantly shorter learning curves. Among the most popular of these are Q&A for the PC and FileMaker Pro for the Mac. This chapter will discuss Q&A, but Mac users should read it as well, since Q&A's capabilities are more or less translatable to those of File-Maker Pro.

The power of Q&A is that it lets you set up a database and subsequently "query" it— that is, get it to return the selected information you're after— in a very non-technical way. You needn't ever actually write a program. Perhaps the most remarkable aspect of Q&A is its "natural language" interface, what it calls its Intelligent Assistant. You can type in a command in English and the Intelligent Assistant will push all the right buttons of Q&A.

THE ART OF DATABASES

Unlike spreadsheets, databases are very easy to visualize in real-world terms. In fact, the analogy you use to explain one to yourself will probably vary with the sort of database you want to conceptualize. We'll work with a fairly simple one here.

Figure 10.1 illustrates one entry in a database. As you can probably see, Figure 10.1 does not show an entry in a computerized database. It's a card from a Rolodex®. A Rolodex is a mechanical database manager with relatively few data management functions. Each entry in this database contains one name and address— and a bit of other useful information. Each entry is physically represented by words on a piece of cardboard.

In electronic database terms, each card in a Rolodex would be regarded as a "record." A record can contain any number of "fields." Each field is assigned the characteristic of containing a specific sort of data. The Rolodex card in Figure 10.1 has a field for the name of the person listed on the card, a field for the address, a field for the phone number, and so on.

In order to find things in an organized Rolodex, you would look through the cards in alphabetical order until you located the name you were after. I don't use a Rolodex anymore because I could never be bothered to add cards to it in alphabetical order, and as a result finding things in it was a bit like sorting mosquitoes.

As database managers go, a Rolodex is pretty helpless. All it can do is allow you to find single entries by a fairly rudimentary— and time-consuming— search process. It can't, for example, present you with a list, or "report," of all its entries that are located in the state of Wyoming, nor can it generate mailing labels sorted in post code order for the Canadian Post Office, nor can it allow you to browse quickly through only those

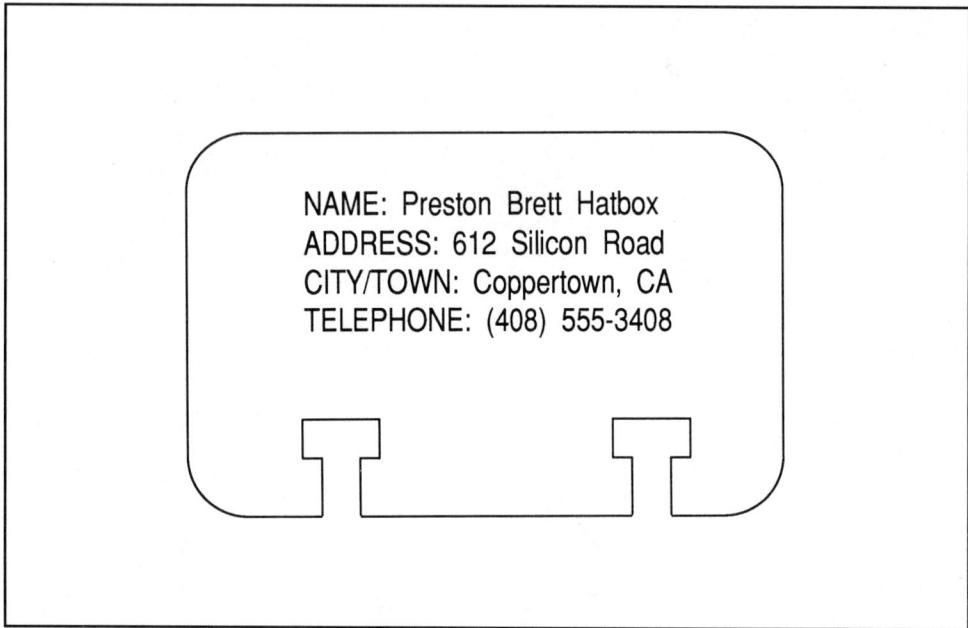

Figure 10.1: An entry in a database of addresses

entries that have a 415 area code. You can do all these things with Q&A, and considerably more.

The simplest sort of computerized database is what's called a "flat file" database. A computerized Rolodex could be implemented as a flat file database. Technically, Q&A is a flat file database, but it's an enormously sophisticated one.

By comparison, you'll hear dBASE referred to as a "relational" database. It's beyond the scope of this chapter to discuss the distinction between these two terms. Unless your ultimate use of databases eventually expands to outstrip the considerable resources of Q&A, you may never need to know what makes dBASE relational.

In order to create a flat file database to hold Rolodex entries, you would first define what each record in the database should look like. Here's how we might define one record to hold the information in Figure 10.1:

NAME: 24 characters

ADDRESS1:   24 characters

ADDRESS2:	24 characters
CITY/TOWN:	16 characters
STATE/PROVINCE:	2 characters
ZIP/POST CODE:	12 characters
PHONE NUMBER:	13 characters, digits and dashes only
FAX NUMBER:	13 characters, digits and dashes only
TYPE OF BUSINESS:	24 characters

If you added up all these characters, you'd find that one record of the Rolodex database occupies 152 bytes. If a disk file existed with lots of these records stored one after the other, the first record would be the 152 bytes at the beginning of the file, the second record would be the 152 bytes starting 152 bytes into the file, the third would be the 152 bytes starting 304 bytes into the file, and so on. Computer programmers express this as

Record position = size of record * record number

(It's worth noting that computer programmers invariably start sequences of things—such as record numbers—with zero rather than one, so this formula does actually work.)

In order to display this information on your screen, to search through it for all the entries located in the state of Wyoming, or whatever you want to do with your collected information, a program which manages this file of records must know the structure of the data. It must know that a record is 152 bytes long, of which the first 24 are the name, the next 48 are two lines of an address, and so on.

In a simple flat file database, this is handled by writing the database manager with the structure of a record hard-wired into it. You might do this, for example, if you were a programmer writing a program which would manage a list of names and addresses in the above format exclusively—a dedicated computerized Rolodex, in effect.

In the real world of database management, however, hard-wired programs like this don't exist—for two reasons. The first is that the usefulness of database management in general is that *you* get to decide what data to manage and how to manage it, rather than the programmer who wrote your database software. The second is a bit more complex. Considering the aforementioned database record, imagine the problem of having two thousand such records in a file and suddenly realizing that you must add an extra field to allow for the number of employees at each location. As there's no room to put it in the existing record structure, you'd have to find a way to make each record larger and shuffle the existing data accordingly. This is called "swabbing," and it's definitely a task you would prefer to have a computer help you with.

Because the very nature of a database manager is to let you deal with your data flexibly— and not to confine you to your initial notion of the nature of your data for the rest of eternity— a system that forced you to swab your data every time you wanted to change some aspect of its structure would be very nearly unthinkable.

There are a few other things which the foregoing model of a database would make difficult or awkward. For example, consider sorting a large database of name and address entries. The simplest form of sorting is what's called a "bubble" sort. It works by repeatedly scanning through all the objects to be sorted two at a time, reversing the order of any pairs that are out of order. This continues until a pass through the data can be made with no pairs requiring repositioning.

The speed at which data can be sorted is inversely proportional to the amount of data to be dealt with, all other things being equal. If you wanted to sort the name and address database into alphabetical order by name, your sorting function would have to move relatively large 152-character records around even though only 24 characters of each record are really involved in the sort.

Contemporary database management packages, such as Q&A, deal with these issues by approaching databases in a somewhat different way from the model we've just looked at. Specifically, each database file contains not only its data but also a "header" which tells Q&A how the data in each record is structured and, hence, how big each record is. This allows Q&A to change the details of a record structure long after it has been created and is in use. When you change the nature of a database file's record structure, Q&A in effect performs all the internal swabbing for you.

Manipulative functions performed on large databases under Q&A— things like sorting a database or merging two databases while eliminating duplicate records— are handled under Q&A through the use of "indexes." If the database of Rolodex cards were handled as a Q&A file and you asked Q&A to sort it for you alphabetically by name, Q&A would begin by indexing the file: it would create a sort of "mini-database" of the pertinent fields of each record. In this case the only pertinent field is the name field. It would then sort the *index*, which involves moving a great deal less data around than sorting the complete records. When the index was sorted, it would rearrange the order of the records in the database file to correspond to that of the index.

USING A DATABASE

The Q&A package is probably among the most user-friendly packages you're likely to work with on a PC. It's also among the largest database managers available, running to well over three megabytes of hard drive space. It's fairly easy to install, though, and all menu-driven once you run it. It uses a mouse if one is present and there is "context-sensitive" help available all over the program. Context-sensitive help is the type of help facility that will provide you with assistance that is specific to the area of the program you happen to be using when you ask for help.

A database manager must allow you to design the record structure of your database, and thus the entry screen that will appear when you want to add a record or change the data in an existing record. In fact, Q&A handles this process in the reverse order: it has you create an entry screen and derives the definition of the record structure for your database from this. We'll discuss the process of creating a screen in the next section.

Figure 10.2 illustrates a Q&A database screen. This screen is from an inventory database.

The aspects of database management that you'll probably spend the most time using are fortunately also the simplest. Entering data into the

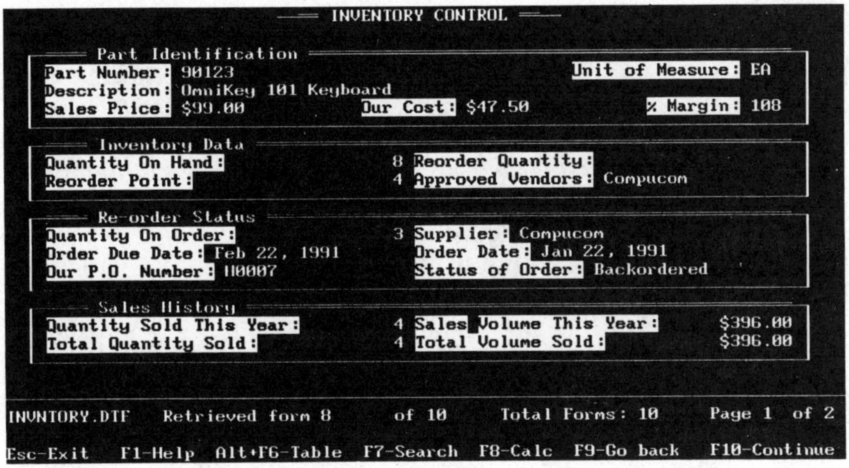

Figure 10.2: The record screen of an inventory management system setup running in Q&A

database and subsequently looking at or modifying individual records are almost like using a particularly single-minded word processor under Q&A. You can call up specific records in a number of ways, and edit the contents of their fields by simply cursoring to them and typing.

The most complex aspect of using a database manager is having it generate reports. Reports can be anything you like. For example, in a hypothetical database of names and addresses you might want the database manager to generate a report of everyone in the database with a last name beginning with R who is male, lives in Wyoming, and has a FAX machine, sorted by the names of their streets in ascending order—with the results printed on Avery mailing labels, if it's not too much trouble. Clearly, there is no obvious way to create a database manager that could anticipate all your complex selection criteria with menu options or some other elementary user interface.

It's in generating reports that Q&A really gets to apply its Intelligent Assistant. In larger "professional" database management packages such as dBASE you would have to write a program to inspect each field of each record in the database and decide whether each record being considered met all the criteria of the report. Under Q&A, you would type in your request in very much the same way it was phrased in the preceding paragraph. In a sense, Q&A would write the requisite program for you and run it without your really being aware of it.

Each database file you create under Q&A will consist of a screen definition—which, in turn, will specify a record structure, as we've discussed. It will also include whatever data you add to the file. It will furthermore include what you teach Q&A about that particular database.

Initially, Q&A can recognize several dozen words. The words tend to be generic database terms, but you can tell it to learn words that are specific to a particular database. For example, you might instruct it that when you refer to "EMPLOYEE" in a database of people's names and addresses, you really mean one record of the database. Likewise, each field in a record can be given a reasonable English pseudonym by which you can describe it to Q&A, such as "PHONE NUMBER," "SALARY," and so on.

When you initially set up a database, you'll find that there's a fair amount of teaching required to make Q&A able to interpret your English requests reliably. Fortunately, it's smart enough to query you about words it doesn't understand. If you ask it to do something with a phrase that contains a new word, it will pause and request that you define the word in terms it currently understands. Figure 10.3 illustrates it doing so.

As you work with a new database you'll find that Q&A will begin to learn the terms you tend to use to describe your data, and its queries will become less frequent.

```
┌──────────────────────────────────────────────────────────────┐
│ ┌────────────────────────────────────────────────────────┐  │
│ │LIST ALL THE ENTRIES IN WYOMING                         │  │
│ │                                                         │  │
│ └────────────────────────────────────────────────────────┘  │
│ ┌────────────────────────────────────────────────────────┐  │
│ │   I don't know the word highlighted above.  What would you like │
│ │   to do?                                                │  │
│ │                                                         │  │
│ │            E - Edit the highlighted word                │  │
│ │            T - Teach me a new word                      │  │
│ │            S - See or change my vocabulary              │  │
│ │            G - Go ahead (the word doesn't matter)       │  │
│ │                                                         │  │
│ └────────────────────────────────────────────────────────┘  │
│                                                              │
│ MAILLIST.DTF                                                 │
│ Esc-Exit                                          ↵ Continue │
└──────────────────────────────────────────────────────────────┘
```

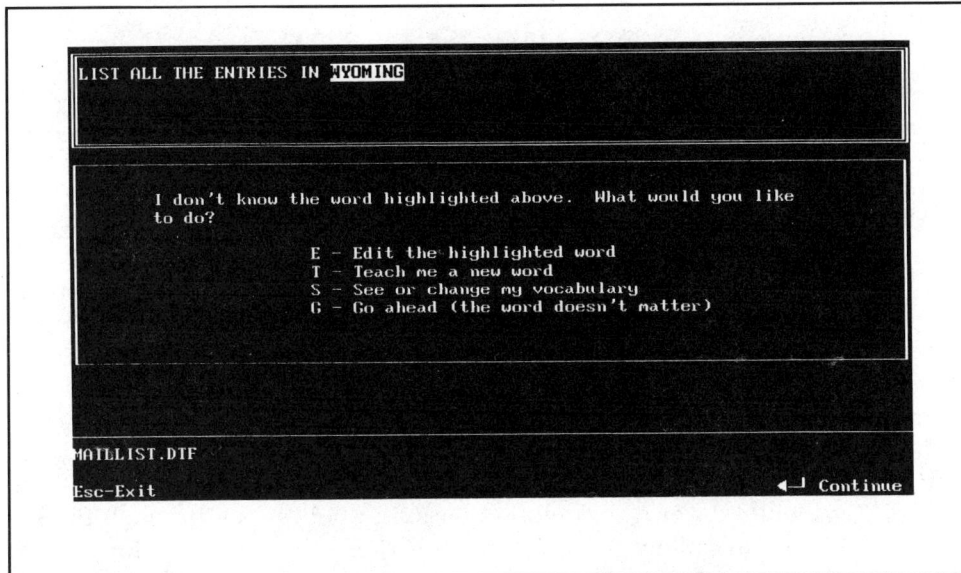

Figure 10.3: Q&A dealing with an unknown word

It's important to note that Q&A gives you recourse to its Intelligent Assistant facility for all aspects of using the software. You can use it to modify your data and your database, as well as having it manage complex reporting tasks. In this way, you can tell it things like

INCREASE ALL PRICES BY 15 PERCENT

or

ADD A NEW FIELD

and in reality, the Intelligent Assistant will use the various Q&A functions that correspond to the words you are using.

The Q&A Intelligent Assistant is, in effect, a very sophisticated shell program, in much the same way that a DOS shell is. Just as with a DOS shell, in time you'll get comfortable enough with the actual workings of Q&A to handle the functions yourself. If you don't invoke the Intelligent Assistant, it won't interpose itself between you and Q&A and you'll be able to use the database functions directly.

Creating Screens

The first thing to do in creating a new database is to arrange its data entry and editing screen, which is, in effect, the process of defining its record structure. For the sake of this discussion, we'll deal with each screenful of data as representing a single record in the database. However, it's worth noting that Q&A doesn't actually restrict you to records that will fit on a single screen.

Figure 10.4 illustrates the screen for a database of names and addresses. This has grown considerably more complex than the initial example of a database record at the beginning of this chapter.

In order to create a screen like the one in Figure 10.4 under Q&A, you would begin with a blank screen and move your cursor to each location where you want to have a data field. Type in the name of each field, ending each name with a colon. You can define the length of each field by placing an angle bracket at the end of the field. When you finish setting out the screen, Q&A will go over it with you, assigning "field types" to each field.

Field types allow Q&A to do a bit of quick data pre-checking when you enter data into your database. For example, you can specify that a field intended to hold phone numbers hold only numeric information. Q&A will then refuse to allow letters to be entered into such a field.

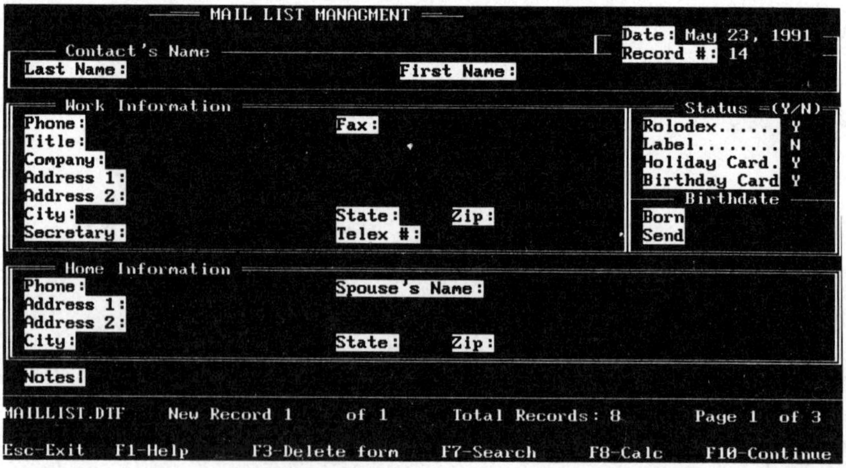

Figure 10.4: Creating a screen for a database of names and addresses

In defining a screen, Q&A will allow you to add, resize, and delete fields and move elements of the screen around even after you have created and begun using your database. It will handle any attendant data swabbing for you. This means that you can alter your original record structure later on. However, if your database gets fairly large before you decide to add a field or otherwise modify the structure of a record, Q&A may require a significant amount of time to swab your data. Forethought, while not essential, is desirable when you anticipate working with lots of data. For this reason, it is helpful to limit the size of each of your fields to no more than a reasonable maximum. Most types of database fields occupy their specified maximum size no matter how much data is in them. For example, if you create a record with a 48-character field called "NAME" and never enter more than seven characters into it, every record in the database will still tie up 48 characters, 41 of which won't be doing anything but taking up space. If such a database encompassed 2000 records, about 80 kilobytes worth of disk space would be wasted by this record structure.

Entering and Finding Data

Entering data into any database manager is a bit tedious, as it invariably involves a lot of typing. In this respect, Q&A is about average. Entering data for a new record really involves adding a blank record to the database and then editing its fields. Q&A handles the mechanics of this for you.

To add a new record to a database you've created, you would tell Q&A

ADD A NEW RECORD

Your data entry screen would appear and you would be able to enter data into each of the fields.

Figure 10.5 illustrates entering data into a database of names and addresses. Using this screen points up some of the more sophisticated aspects of Q&A. For example, upon attempting to assign Mr. Hatbox a February 30 birthday, Q&A noted that this was an impossible date. It allowed me to use it upon my insisting that I wanted it there, but it knew it was having its leg pulled.

You can move around the screen, changing things as you like in the data entry screen. Once entered, the data in a field can be changed whenever you wish. Hitting F10 will then update the database file with your new record. If you originally got to the data entry screen by telling Q&A

ADD A NEW RECORD

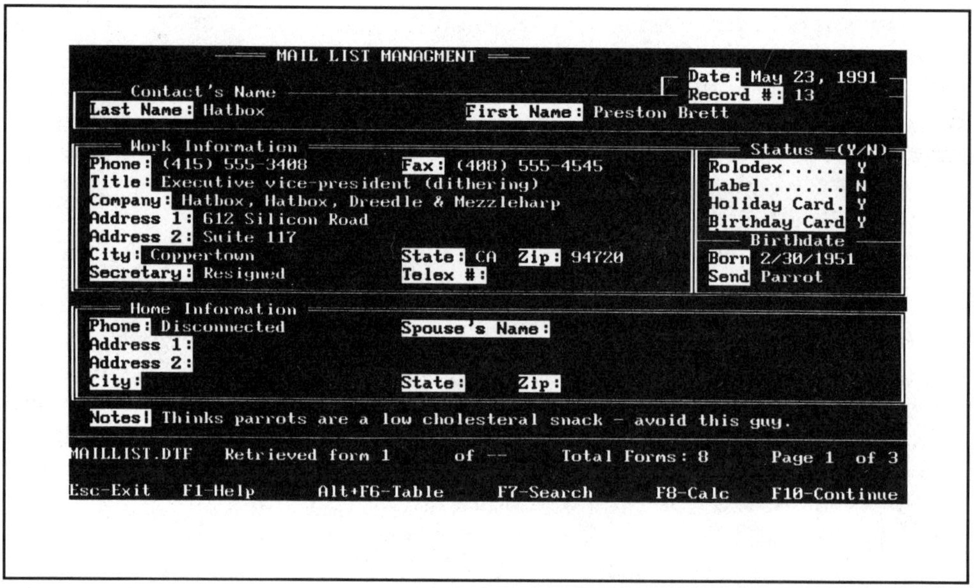

Figure 10.5: The data entry screen for the database of names and addresses

it will save your record and then present you with another blank screen should you in fact wish to enter several new records. You can hit Esc if you don't want to.

Finding a record in the database is just as easy as adding one. For example, I could locate the record in Figure 10.5 by telling Q&A

FIND HATBOX

I could also turn up that record by saying

FIND PARROT

In this latter case, Q&A would create a list— in essence, a report printed to the screen— of all the records in the database which contain the word "PARROT."

The searching facilities of Q&A are very sophisticated. You could tell it to

FIND PARROT BUT NOT HATBOX

which would cause Q&A to find all the records in your database which involved mention of parrots but to exclude any of those in which Mr. Hatbox was also mentioned.

In many cases Q&A will query you in attempting to narrow down your searches a bit. For example, if you tell it

FIND CA

in a name-and address-database, it might ask you if you had in mind that it regard CA as being the abbreviation for the state of California.

Having located a record you're interested in, you can edit its contents and replace it in the database if you like. In this way, you could fix the anomaly concerning Mr. Hatbox's date of birth, for example, update the prices in an inventory database, and so on.

Reporting

Your use of a database management application might never entail any formal, printed, reporting. For example, you might never need to print out all the names in a database of names and addresses— many offices' databases exist only for infrequent searches. However, you may occasionally have cause to produce a hard copy arrangement of some or all of the information in your database.

A report generated by Q&A can be as simple or as sophisticated as you like. It can also be formatted in all sorts of ways. Assuming that you know how to arrange the fields in your database for printing, you can have a mailing list generate mailing labels, an inventory database print out invoice forms, and so on.

Generating complex reports under Q&A involves two distinct tasks. The first is telling Q&A how to identify the records you want to be included in the report. The second involves telling it how to present the information in the records.

You will probably already have a pretty good idea of how to go about telling Q&A how to select records to include in a report. Using the Intelligent Assistant, you can specify selection criteria in English for just about any logical database report you can imagine. Such a selection criterion can be as complicated as you like.

When Q&A goes to actually print something, it does so one field at a time. You can specify which fields it will print— for example, in printing mailing labels you would want to omit those fields that contain the addressee's FAX number, birth date, and so on. You can also specify the order in which fields are printed. You can tell Q&A how to arrange the fields it prints— with a little forethought and patience, you can have it fill out preprinted forms by telling it to print so that its fields fall in the form spaces.

As an aside, one of the early database projects a lot of people learning Q&A and similar applications undertake is creating a database to fill out Federal Express airbills. This is a pretty good exercise in making the software do most of what a database manager should be able to do. If you use couriers a lot it's also a great timesaver once you get it working.

The combination of the search criteria and printing definition of a report can be saved along with the corresponding database file. Thus, if you set up a reporting procedure to print mailing lists or fill out Federal Express forms or whatever, you can subsequently call up everything you need to create your hard copy at one time.

It's also worth noting that Q&A allows you to print a report to the screen without necessarily sending it to your printer. Thus, having designed a report you can see what it looks like without actually having to create hard copy until you're certain it's the way you want it.

SUMMARY: MANAGING YOUR DATA

A few years ago, database managers were sufficiently complex to make them unapproachable by anyone not prepared to immerse themselves in the lore and complexities of low-level database programming.

Natural-language interfaces such as the one in Q&A have now made database management a realistic prospect for use in a home office. Professional database management users— species of the aforementioned dBASE gurus— will laugh at Q&A. It's not as powerful as dBASE, it's slower, it takes up more hard drive space, and it's less efficient in the way it handles its files. These things are important if you'll be managing a 50,000-record mailing list. They're less important if you'll be keeping track of a few hundred inventory items.

What especially recommends Q&A and database managers like it is that in giving up the "leading edge" of database power and flexibility, they've made what's left accessible to anyone with two or three hours to learn the package.

11

DISK UTILITIES

In an ideal world a hard drive would be something exclusively to store data on— perhaps in the way that bookshelves store books— and nothing more would ever need to be done with it. In practice, this isn't the case. Unlike bookshelves, a hard drive is a very complex system which gets more complex still when it's confronted with advanced software that uses it in unusual ways. While in many cases you can ignore your hard drive and not deal with any of the things to be discussed in this chapter, knowing about these things will frequently allow you to improve the performance of your system and occasionally save you from disasters.

Disk utilities are small programs that perform low-level disk maintenance and disaster recovery functions. Because selling a single utility program is a pretty hopeless marketing effort, the disk utilities to be discussed in this chapter usually come in collections. The PC utilities have been drawn from Norton Utilities and PC Tools and a few others. The Macintosh ones come largely from the Symantec Utilities. All of these are store-bought packages.

The determination of which companies' utilities I should present in this chapter was made according to a single important criterion: these are the utilities I use. I have found them to be reliable, effective, and generally available. It may very well be that there are other packages that are equally reliable, effective, and available; your understanding of how the various types of utilities approach their tasks will presumably not be limited by my choosing specific products.

While most of the functions to be discussed in this chapter are applicable to both Macintosh and PC systems, you'll find that a few of the PC utilities don't have Macintosh counterparts. In most cases this is because the Mac's operating system comes with many functions built in which the PC requires separate utilities to manage. (Real die-hard Macintosh proponents love reading sentences like that.)

A Note on DOS 5's Disk Utilities

By the time this book is available, the newest version of DOS will also be available, offering a number of the disk utilities discussed in this chapter. As most of these utilities were originally invented by third-party software companies specifically to overcome deficiencies of the previous versions of DOS, you will find those deficiencies referred to in the course of the following discussions. In many cases the deficiencies still exist in DOS 5 (one exception being that DOS 5 includes a disk caching facility that will allow you to use extended or expanded memory); the major difference in regard to disk utilities is that now you can overcome the deficiencies with DOS's own utilities instead of having to buy a third-party package.

DISK CACHING

In the course of using your hard drive, your computer will often find itself reading the same sections of it repeatedly. For example, every time an application goes to open a file, your computer must read the area of your hard drive where the file directory is located to find out if the file exists, how big it is, and so on. Macintosh programs, which are often written so that parts of them can be loaded from the disk, used, and then thrown away, are notorious for reading the same disk areas repeatedly.

Even using a fast hard drive, disk access is relatively slow. Each time your software goes to read data from a disk—even if it's the same data it read a minute earlier—it must pause while the disk finds the data it's asked for and gets it into memory.

Eliminating the delays inherent to repeatedly accessing the same areas of your hard drive can make a startling improvement in the performance of your computer. Applications that make a lot of use of disk files may experience overall performance improvements of several hundred percent. The tool for doing this is called a "disk cache."

A disk cache uses a reserved area of memory which stores or "buffers" parts of your disk as they're read. Specifically, each time a block of data is read from a cached hard drive, it's both handed over to the program which asked for it and it's written to the memory of the cache as well. If the program asks for that block again, it can be read from the cache rather than from the disk, eliminating the delay inherent to reading from the disk. There is a slight speed penalty imposed on the first read—it takes a small but measurable amount of time to add the block of data to the cache—but all subsequent reads will be very much faster.

The memory of a disk cache keeps the most recently used blocks of disk data in memory, and throws away ones which haven't been used in a while when its memory gets full. The effectiveness of a disk cache improves with the amount of memory it's given to hold disk data in.

The Macintosh's operating system has a built-in disk cache which you can switch on or off using the control panel. This disk cache can be set to use as much memory as you can spare. You will probably have to use your system for a while, experimenting with different cache settings, until you find one that suits the hardware you have and the work you do with it.

There is an important thing to keep in mind about disk caching on the Mac. If a Macintosh application calls for some memory and the Mac can't find enough of to satisfy the request, the application will throw part of itself away to free up memory. When it needs these parts in the future, it will load them back from the disk. If you tie up a lot of the memory of your Macintosh in a disk cache, you may improve the performance of the system's disk file access as a result but slow down many of your larger applications in the process.

The PC's DOS operating system doesn't have a disk cache built in. The most flexible and powerful disk cache you can get for it at present is a package called Super PC-Kwik. Unlike on the Macintosh, where all memory is just memory, the PC's memory consists of the 640 kilobytes of DOS memory and then whatever other memory you've added to the system as extended or expanded memory. The thing that makes PC-Kwik notable—aside from its oddly spelled name—is that it only needs about ten kilobytes of DOS memory to run. All of its actual caching can be done in either extended or expanded memory, depending upon how you've set up your system.

PC-Kwik can use a disk cache of any size. A one-megabyte cache in expanded memory can shift your hard drive into light speed.

UNERASING FILES

Few things are more upsetting than erasing a file and then realizing that you wish you hadn't. The Macintosh actually forces you to erase files in a two step process—you must drag them to the trash and then explicitly empty it—but even this becomes routine after a while and one rarely thinks about what might be in the files.

The ease with which valuable data can be lost on a computer through inadvertent erasure is at least in part offset by the fact that erased files aren't really gone immediately after their deletion. They're only missing.

As you work with it, your hard drive has all its files and a pool of currently unused space from which to allocate new files if one of your applications goes to open some. When you delete a file, what really happens is that the operating system of your computer is told that all the space which the file formerly occupied can be returned to the pool of free space, ready to be re-allocated as needed at some time in the future.

If you delete a file and immediately realize that you should not have done so—that is, if you realize it before you do anything else with your computer—the whole file will still be almost exactly as it was. It will have apparently vanished from your hard drive, but its contents and most or all of its name will be just as they were before you killed them. With the right tools you can usually reincarnate a deleted file.

The most important thing about "unerasing" a file is to not allow anything to be written to your disk until you perform the unerase operation. Every time you copy a file to your hard drive or allow an application to save the contents of a file, part of the pool of free disk space of your hard drive will be allocated to the file in question. If some of the allocated space contains part of your recently deleted file, the jig's up.

One common mistake that people make in using unerase programs is to copy the unerase program into their hard drives after a file has been inadvertently deleted. The unerase program itself can wind up overwriting part of your deleted file if you do this. You should either keep your unerase program on your hard drive all the time or run it from a floppy disk if you suddenly realize you need it and haven't previously loaded it.

The Symantec Tools package provides a way to recover deleted files, although it takes a bit of forethought to make it reliable. The package includes a program called "Guardian," which must be permanently installed in your Macintosh. The Guardian keeps track of files which have been deleted, allowing the "Disk Clinic" program, another of the applications included with the Symantec package, to undelete them.

The Guardian also improves the reliability of several other disaster recovery functions of the Symantec package, such as its hard drive crash restoration program.

The most commonly used unerase program for the PC is from the Norton Utilities package. As long as the unerase program is available on your hard drive, you can bring back your just-erased files by typing Norton's special unerase command.

When DOS deletes a file, it does so by replacing the first character of the file name with an illegal one, that is, one which DOS will not allow as part of a valid file name. As such, the first character of a deleted file's name is the only part of it which really is gone for good. The unerase program will prompt you for the first character of the name of each file to be undeleted.

DISK DEFRAGMENTATION

When an application writes something to a file, the operating system of your computer finds someplace to store the data being written by allocating parts of the pool of free disk space. When files are deleted, their space is added back into the pool. Because files are created and deleted in no particular order, the operating system doesn't usually get to free up disk space in precisely the inverse order in which it was allocated. In fact, it rarely comes close.

After you've used a hard drive for a while, the pool of free disk space will be more like a lot of little puddles, with free areas trapped between the various files on the disk. If one of your applications wants to write data to the disk, the operating system will still be able to allocate all these little bits of space to a file. However, because the parts of the file will be physically displaced from each other across the surface of the disk, reading data from the file will be slower than it might be as the disk read heads will have to skip around the disk to find all the parts. This also shortens the life of your hard drive a bit, as it means that the disk head mechanism has to work more than it otherwise would.

This condition is called "fragmentation." It happens to all hard drives with use. You can defragment a disk with a utility which moves the parts of your files around on the surface of the disk until they're all contiguous and the pool of free disk space is also contiguous. You should defragment your hard drive periodically.

Hard drive defragmentation utilities have a nasty reputation. There are a lot of them which work poorly, or which won't work on some hard drives, or which will leave your hard drive in a scrambled state if they're interrupted for any reason. The Norton SD—Speed Disk—utility for PC systems—and the Symantec Hard Drive Tune Up program for the Mac *are* reliable. They both work in such a way as to never actually delete part of a file from one portion of your disk until it has been written to another. If one of them is interrupted your disk may not be totally defragmented, but it will be intact.

As a result of their conservative designs, both of these programs are pretty slow. It takes the Symantec Hard Drive Tune Up program the better part of half an hour to defragment the 40 megabyte hard drive on my

Macintosh, and SD required only slightly less time to handle one badly fragmented 33-megabyte partition on my PC. However, both disks have repeatedly survived the experience, which is not always the case with defragmentation programs.

The performance improvement you'll experience after using a hard drive defragmentation program will vary with the severity of the fragmentation of your drive before it was run. It's not uncommon to find that well over half of a hard drive consists of badly fragmented files, and that defragmenting such a drive really does make a noticeable improvement in its performance.

Obviously, you should not defragment your drive unless you have a bit of time to kill while the defragmenter gets on with its work.

As a final note about hard drive fragmentation, users of Microsoft Windows should note that defragmentation can indirectly improve the performance of Windows considerably more than it will applications running under DOS. If you defragment your hard drive, Windows will allow you to allocate a "permanent swap file." This is an area of your disk which Windows permanently reserves for use in writing temporary files. It actually bypasses most of DOS in using this file, and as a result it deals with it much more rapidly than it would with conventional temporary files. However, it can only cheat effectively with a permanent swap file if it's allocated as contiguous (non-interrupted) disk space, hence the need for a newly defragmented disk before you enable this feature.

FILE SHELLS

The Macintosh's Finder is a pretty comfortable place to work with files. You can select multiple files and move or delete them, copy them to floppies, and so on, all with no typing and very little mouse action.

For this reason, DOS file "shells" have been around almost as long as DOS has been. There are numerous commercial shells, countless shareware shells, and, if you bought DOS 4.0 or 4.01, a shell included with DOS itself.

File shells allow you to move a cursor bar through a list of files in order to "tag" the ones you want. Having tagged a batch of files, you can have the shell delete only the tagged ones or copy them to a new disk or directory. You can also rename files, view files, and usually execute programs from within a shell. This latter function should be used with some caution—as was discussed earlier in this book, running one application from within another under DOS usually leaves the second, or "child," application with greatly restricted memory.

One of the reasons for the great profusion of file shells for DOS is that they're very much an acquired taste. Your personal preferences will largely determine what you do with a shell. There are DOS users who use a shell program for everything they do, and as such use very elaborate shells.

The most popular commercial DOS shells are Norton Commander—that's the same Norton who did the utilities we've been looking at throughout this chapter—and the shell available in PC-Tools. The drawback to the current version of PC-Tools is that the complete package occupies several megabytes of hard drive space. The first thing I used the PC-Tools shell for was to delete most of the rest of the package.

Microsoft Windows is, in a sense, the DOS shell to end all DOS shells. If you'll be using Windows most of the time, a stand-alone DOS shell will probably prove superfluous.

PRINT SPOOLING

One of the things that makes experienced computer users bang on the sides of their computers in frustration—ultimately voiding the warranties of some of them in extreme cases—is the propensity of applications to put the universe on hold while they go to print something. If you use desktop publishing software, which typically prints exceedingly elaborate pages, you might find yourself staring at a brain-dead computer for twenty minutes while your system repeatedly sends fragments of data to your printer and then waits to be asked for more.

Printing is a very simple function—it uses almost none of the actual power of your computer. However, it's also a painfully slow function in many cases because even fast printers aren't fast in the way that computers are. Fast printer deal in minutes rather than nano-seconds, and a minute's a very long time when you're in a hurry.

There are two ways to deal with this problem. I have a second computer which has numerous computer games on it—if I'm not printing something particularly urgent, I play the games until the print job's finished. This isn't very productive, to be sure, and if I didn't already have the second machine in the first place it would have entailed a significant additional investment in hardware to be this unproductive. That's one approach.

The second approach is to use a print "spooler." This isn't as much fun but it does get around almost all the waiting typically associated with a print job.

When an application goes to send something to your printer, it waits until the printer's ready to receive data, sends what it thinks the printer can handle, and then waits until it's ready to receive a bit more. If there were a hypothetical very fast printer that was never busy, all the data to be printed could be sent down to it very nearly instantly and you could get back to work.

While fast printers of this magnitude don't really exist, you can fool your applications into thinking otherwise by using a print spooler. A spooler is a disk utility which intercepts the data to be sent to a printer and stores it somewhere out of the way. As long as "out of the way" is a place that can accept data much more rapidly than a real printer can, your application will be able to send its data to the spooler in almost no time at all. It will think that the print job has been completed almost as soon as it began, and it can return to its active, working state.

In the mean time, the print spooler will get to work actually printing your file. It functions as a background task, sending the stored print data to the printer at the real—very much slower—speed that the printer normally expects. It might still take twenty minutes to complete the job—you won't see your output any faster as a result of using a print spooler—but you'll be able to use your computer normally during this time.

There is a catch to print spoolers, of course. In order to be effective, a print spooler needs that out-of-the-way place that is both fast and large enough to hold a whole print job. Especially if you use desktop publishing with a PostScript printer, the place a print spooler spools to can find itself confronted with a lot of data. For example, the newsletter page back in Chapter 6 involved something on the order of a megabyte of data sent to the printer—and, of course, held temporarily by the spooler.

There are two out-of-the-way places a spooler can use to store things. The most desirable is memory. If sufficient memory isn't available the next best thing is a disk file. The drawback to a disk file—especially if you'll be spooling a lot of data—is that disks aren't always much faster than printers, so much of the advantage of a spooler can be lost if it has to spool to disk.

If you use MultiFinder on the Macintosh you can enable an internal print spooler from the Chooser. However, MultiFinder is a bit of a memory hog, and you might find that unless you have a fairly high-end Macintosh it's hungrier than you'd like. You can use a stand-alone print spooler with the Finder instead—I use SuperLaserSpool from Fifth Generation Systems. They also have SuperSpool, for use with ImageWriter dot matrix printers.

There seems to be an inordinate number of really bad print spoolers for PC systems. One of the exceptions is PrintCache from Laser-Tools. It's quite small—if you disable all of its options it only uses five kilobytes of DOS memory. It can spool to extended or expanded memory or to a disk file. In fact, you can actually spool to DOS memory with Print-Cache, but there are few cases in which you'd want to. It will spool parallel and serial printers, and has a feature to help it out when confronted with printers that have very long cables.

PrintCache is one of the few really viable PC print spoolers. It will also coexist with Windows. Windows ostensibly has a built-in print spooler—its Print Manager—but it's notable in that it hardly ever works. PrintCache makes Windows printing extremely quick.

PrintCache is most effective when it's given extended or expanded memory to spool with. The amount of memory to allocate to it will vary with the sorts of things you'll be printing. If you have to wait more than twenty or thirty seconds when you print something to a spooler, its buffer is probably full and you might want to consider enlarging it next time. I find that one and a half megabytes of expanded memory keeps PrintCache pretty happy.

I do run applications that don't print enough data to make spooling them important—but which could use the memory that PrintCache would otherwise tie up. Because of this, I load PrintCache only when it might be needed and unload it afterwards. For example, the batch file that I use to boot up Ventura invokes PrintCache just before Ventura runs and then removes it from memory as soon as Ventura returns to DOS.

FAST FORMATTING
AND DISK COPYING

Floppy disks will probably become the most tedious aspect of your computer in time. They're dreadfully slow—it's frightening to think that for years they were the only real storage medium available for microcomputers.

The most time-consuming aspects of using floppies are formatting and duplicating. Formatting is the process that cleans up a new disk and prepares it to receive data. Duplicating a disk simply creates an exact image of the disk on a second disk—this actually entails formatting the new disk first, but the duplication process handles this for you.

On a Macintosh, formatting a floppy disk is slow, but it's agreeably easy. When you put a disk that has not previously been formatted in one of the Mac's floppy drives, a dialog box will automatically appear asking if you'd like it formatted. Simply click on OK to have the process carried out. If you decline the offer, your Mac will spit the disk out and carry on with whatever it was doing before the offending disk turned up.

Duplicating disks is also equally easy on a Macintosh—but only if you have two disk drives. You simply drag the icon of the disk you want to copy over to the icon of the disk you want to copy it to. The Mac will do the rest. Unfortunately, it won't do it very quickly.

There are a number of very powerful disk duplication utilities that can copy Macintosh disks considerably faster than the Mac's internal copying function can. They can also deal with copying with a single floppy drive, in that they'll load as much of the disk's data into memory as will fit, spit out the source disk, and prompt you for the disk to copy to. Unless you actually have enough memory in your Macintosh to store the contents of a whole floppy at once, you will be asked to swap disks again a few times, because only a portion of the disk's contents will be copied with each pass. Bear in mind that some of your Mac's memory will be tied up by the Finder and the copying program itself. You cannot, for example, copy a floppy disk in one pass with only one megabyte of memory. The floppy disk may only hold 800 kilobytes, but considerably less free memory will remain in a one megabyte Mac.

The Symantec Utilities include a very snappy disk formatter and duplicator called QuickCopy.

For the PC, the FORMAT program that comes with DOS is painfully slow. It's also reprehensibly complex to use at times. In order to format some of the newer disk formats—such as 3½" microfloppies—you frequently have to include cryptic command-line switches when you run FORMAT.

The PC-Tools package includes a program called PCFORM. It can format a floppy in about half the time that the DOS FORMAT command requires. Should you have to format something peculiar, its command-line switches are easier to remember, and it has a built-in help screen should you forget what they are.

The MS-DOS disk copying utility, DISKCOPY, works well enough on 360-kilobyte floppy disks, but it's a bit limited in that it only stores the data from the disk it's copying in DOS memory. On a 640-kilobyte PC there will be enough DOS memory to handle a 360-kilobyte disk this way, but all of the other, higher density formats which DOS supports will require more memory than is available as DOS memory alone. If you ask DISKCOPY to duplicate such a disk, it will want you to swap the source and destination disks several times. This is frustrating if you have eight megabytes of memory in your computer, most of which will be ignored by DISKCOPY.

The disk duplication program I use is actually one of the functions of the PC-Tools DOS shell. It will copy a whole disk by storing it in expanded memory if there isn't enough DOS memory to handle the task. As such, it eliminates any need to swap disks.

TEN THOUSAND DISK UTILITIES

There is, in fact, an uncountable number of disk utilities, especially when you consider shareware, which will be discussed in the next chapter. Some of them are brilliant. The few that have been dealt with here will make your hard drive a safe and efficient place to work. As you grow more familiar with your system you'll probably find lots of little utility programs to make it just a bit more convenient. In most cases they don't take up a lot of disk space, and it's extremely rewarding to be able to type a few characters or click on an icon and have a previously insurmountable problem go away.

12

SHAREWARE

The appeal of commercial software is often subdued somewhat by its price. In many cases costing several hundred dollars and up per package, it's not always practical to try out several of those shrink-wrapped boxes to find one that really works for you.

Computer software is actually a very curious commodity. The real cost to the software company for the material part of it— the floppy disks— is almost nonexistent. The manuals that come with software are these days fairly well printed and bound, but even this cost represents only a fraction of the price of the package.

Some part of the price you pay actually defers the cost of developing the software, of course, but a lot of the purchase price of an application pays for a number of intangibles. It covers the overhead of the company that produces the software, the cost of advertising, distribution costs and several levels of markup, a factor built in to offset software piracy, and so on.

With the possible exception of piracy, which is an issue more or less unique to software, this situation exists for most commercial products. You'll be offsetting a lot of advertising and distribution overhead the next time you go to buy a car, too. The difference is that you can't duplicate a car for 25 cents.

There is an alternative to commercial software in some cases. It's called "shareware." The idea behind shareware may sound a bit questionable, but it exists and it works— both for software authors and a lot of people who use this alternative source of applications. You'll probably run into some shareware sooner or later.

Commercial software invariably comes with a long license agreement and several other forms of exhortation to dissuade you from passing copies of it around to your friends. Shareware is handled in quite the opposite way. It encourages you to hand around as many copies as you can. Each time one of them boots up, it will ask its user to send its author a registration fee.

Figure 12.1 illustrates such a message, what shareware users call a "beg notice."

Registering a shareware package usually entitles you to an updated version of the program—sometimes with additional features implemented—a telephone number to call for technical support, printed documentation in some cases, and sometimes other amenities.

In most cases, shareware is written by one or two people, rather than a team of programmers. If you need help with a shareware package, you can usually discuss your problems with its author, rather than a technical support person. As a rule, shareware companies are too small to have a phone system which greets you with a tape recorder telling you that "all our operators are busy."

Aside from being a lot cheaper than commercial software, shareware allows you to try out software before you actually spend any

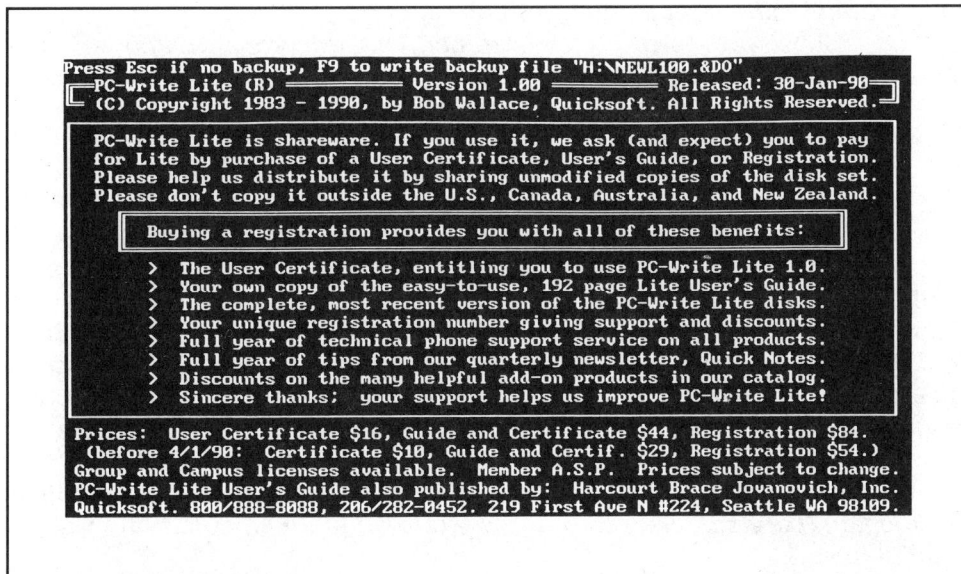

```
Press Esc if no backup, F9 to write backup file "H:\NEWL100.&DO"
┌─PC-Write Lite (R) ═══════════ Version 1.00 ═══════════ Released: 30-Jan-90═┐
└ (C) Copyright 1983 - 1990, by Bob Wallace, Quicksoft. All Rights Reserved.┘

  PC-Write Lite is shareware. If you use it, we ask (and expect) you to pay
  for Lite by purchase of a User Certificate, User's Guide, or Registration.
  Please help us distribute it by sharing unmodified copies of the disk set.
  Please don't copy it outside the U.S., Canada, Australia, and New Zealand.

    ┌──────────────────────────────────────────────────────────────────┐
    │ Buying a registration provides you with all of these benefits:    │
    └──────────────────────────────────────────────────────────────────┘

      >  The User Certificate, entitling you to use PC-Write Lite 1.0.
      >  Your own copy of the easy-to-use, 192 page Lite User's Guide.
      >  The complete, most recent version of the PC-Write Lite disks.
      >  Your unique registration number giving support and discounts.
      >  Full year of technical phone support service on all products.
      >  Full year of tips from our quarterly newsletter, Quick Notes.
      >  Discounts on the many helpful add-on products in our catalog.
      >  Sincere thanks; your support helps us improve PC-Write Lite!

  Prices:  User Certificate $16, Guide and Certificate $44, Registration $84.
   (before 4/1/90:  Certificate $10, Guide and Certif. $29, Registration $54.)
  Group and Campus licenses available.  Member A.S.P.  Prices subject to change.
  PC-Write Lite User's Guide also published by:  Harcourt Brace Jovanovich, Inc.
  Quicksoft. 800/888-8088, 206/282-0452. 219 First Ave N #224, Seattle WA 98109.
```

Figure 12.1: The beg notice from a shareware application

money on it. This is a worthwhile feature, because, after all, the fact that a commercial package arrives in a well-designed, shrink-wrapped package doesn't necessarily mean that it's free of bugs or that it will really do everything it claims to.

In fairness, shareware isn't a practical solution for everyone. As you'll see as you get further along in this chapter, the cost savings offered by shareware are often offset by the time it will take you to find shareware that is capable of doing what you want it to do. In a sense, using shareware allows you to trade some extra work on your part for a lower purchase price. However, having made this trade you could wind up with software that is more in keeping with your special or limited needs than what you might find available or affordable commercially.

WHAT'S AVAILABLE

When a commercial software house releases an application it's only after months of market research have ascertained that there's a lot of money to be made from it. Developing and marketing a single software package can represent an investment of millions of dollars. In view of the potential costs, a lot of potential applications never get written, as they simply aren't commercial enough to break even.

Shareware is rarely constrained by these considerations. While there are shareware counterparts for many commercially successful packages, there's an awful lot of shareware that could never have appeared as commercial software. Some of it's too specialized to have made a commercial release practical. Some of it's too small—a lot of handy utilities exist only as shareware. And occasionally you'll come across shareware that is just too far ahead of its time to have interested commercial distributors.

There are a number of general areas of software that you can't really find as shareware. The first is the operating system of your computer. There are no shareware counterparts to MS-DOS, Microsoft Windows, or the Macintosh Finder or MultiFinder, nor are there likely to be. Among other things, these packages were created by teams of programmers, using resources that are generally beyond the reach of shareware authors.

Really huge packages, such as a shareware counterpart to large commercial desktop publishing applications, are also not really practical. Once again, they represent too much work for a single author to realistically undertake.

Just about all of the small to medium size applications discussed in this book have shareware equivalents. The utilities discussed in the foregoing chapter all do. There are thousands of other shareware programs as well, and the list grows daily. Shareware is very dynamic, and very quick to produce applications that address new uses that crop up in working with computers.

How to Find Shareware

The obvious source of shareware is sharing, that is, getting it passed along to you by a friend. This only works if you have some friends who are into computers and who use the same sorts of applications as you do, of course.

The traditional medium of shareware distribution has been computer bulletin boards. If you have a modem and a fair amount of time, you can troll through a bulletin board's library of shareware and download whatever looks promising. Keep in mind, however, that the process can be very time-consuming, and by no means will everything you download turn out to be useful. Most bulletin boards worth bothering with require an annual user's fee.

The most practical source of shareware for home office users is a commercial shareware distributor. These are companies that acquire shareware directly from its authors, test it, and sell the better applications for a nominal distribution fee. In a sense, they do all the weeding out that you'd have to do if you were downloading shareware from a bulletin board. They also check for viruses, something we'll discuss in a moment.

Here are three of the better PC shareware distributors:

The Public Software Library
P.O. Box 35705
Houston, Texas
77235-5705

PC-SIG
1030D East Duanne Avenue
Sunnyvale, CA
94086

Public Brand Software
P.O. Box 51315
Indianapolis, IN
46251

The following company is among the largest distributors for Macintosh shareware:

Educorp
7434 Trade Street
San Diego, CA
92121

Each of these companies' programs cost less than ten dollars apiece.

A Word about Viruses

Few things relating to computers have caught the attention of the popular media more readily than the notion of computer viruses. While viruses do exist and are a threat, the paranoia over them has probably done at least as much harm as the viruses themselves. There are computer users who start looking for a virus every time a program refuses to boot or their system crashes.

A computer virus is a piece of code that attaches itself to an executable program on your disk, or in some cases to part of the operating system. If an infected program is run, the virus may look for other executable programs to copy itself to. If you copy the infected program to someone else's computer, the virus will be able to spread.

Most viruses are time delayed. Because you won't know for a while your system has been infected, the virus has a chance to spread unnoticed. After a period of dormancy it will appear and do something nasty. The nastiness varies with the virus in question. A number of fairly benign ones exist—they're irritating but not necessarily destructive. Quite a few of the more lethal ones can be very nasty indeed—they'll wipe out the data on your hard drive, for example. It's probably worth noting that a number of the ostensibly benign ones have been fairly badly written, and actually will damage data on your disk even though they do not appear to have been intended to do so.

In order to attach itself to part of your computer, a virus must disturb something. Having infected a file on your disk, the file itself will be modified. It will usually get bigger. The date stamp may change. Certainly the workings of the file will be altered to allow the virus to hook itself into the program.

Note that viruses cannot be transmitted through anything but executable code. Your computer can't be infected through word processing files, worksheets, or picture files, no matter how questionable their contents may be. Note also, however, that booting your computer from a floppy disk constitutes running executable code. If the floppy's infected, your computer's hard drive may be too.

Because viruses modify the files they infect, they can be detected. There are programs such as McAfee's Scan for the PC and Virex for the Macintosh which will allow you to check out new programs being introduced into your computer—or to check your whole hard drive from time to time if you'd like to be really careful—and be dead certain that nothing nasty is afoot. Both these packages come with tools to help you remove viruses from your system if you find you've acquired one.

The only drawback to virus scanners is that they're somewhat transitory. Once a virus scanner is publicly available to look for viruses, it's also available to potential virus authors to test their creations against. Someone writing a PC virus would certainly try to make sure that it could remain undetected by the current version of McAfee's Scan.

As a result, virus scanners are updated frequently. New versions of McAfee's Scan appear every month or two, and can trap virtually everything that's current.

The final thing to note about viruses is that while they do exist, they're anything but common. In most cases, the ones which do manage to propagate themselves do so through carelessness. The largest virus problem by far can be found in schools, where floppy disks are wont to float around pretty indiscriminately. This is unlikely to affect a home office environment.

You can protect yourself from viruses by doing the following:

— Don't accept software from unknown sources.

— Don't use shareware except from a reputable distributor.

— Get a scan program and use it on every executable program you bring onto your hard drive before you run anything.

PC SHAREWARE

The volume of new shareware released each month for PC-compatible systems makes it impossible to cover in detail most of what's available. To be sure, a very large part of it won't pertain to your use of a computer in your home office. There are games, networking utilities, patches for all sorts of application-specific problems, and a lot of very weird programs, none of which you'll probably ever want to come in contact with.

There is still a lot of first-class shareware which may prove useful to you. Some of this will be tiny little programs to make your life easier. There are a number of really superb complete applications which can be acquired as shareware, too.

The tiny programs probably deserve discussion first, as in many cases these are things that don't have equivalents in commercial software. The following list is of course highly restricted, and if you browse through a shareware catalog for a while you'll probably find many more to add to it.

Utilities

The following is a list of some of the most commonly used little shareware programs for PC systems. It's by no means exhaustive. However, if you come across the system of someone who's been using computers for a while, the odds are that you'll find at least some of these on it.

DOSEDIT

The most useful bit of shareware I can think of is one that is so common among PC users as to go wholly unnoticed. It's called DOSEDIT. The DOSEDIT program makes your DOS prompt a bit less hostile.

As DOS comes out of the box, typing something incorrect at the DOS prompt usually entails retyping it. Typing a long command and discovering that there's a mistake at the beginning of the line is enough to bring some DOS users to tears.

With DOSEDIT installed, you can move your cursor through an existing DOS command line and edit it, changing, adding, and deleting characters as you see fit. However, more than this, DOSEDIT remembers the most recent DOS commands you've typed. If you hit the up and down arrow keys on the numeric keypad of your keyboard, earlier commands will appear at the DOS prompt. You can move back and forth through a "stack" of stored commands, reusing old commands or editing them into new ones.

It should be noted that DOS 5 will include a counterpart to DOSEDIT, called DOSKEY, which will even let you string series of commands into macros.

LIST

The DOS TYPE command is another speed demon. If you TYPE a text file on a reasonably fast machine, it will typically scream past your monitor too quickly for you to know what it's about. Like DIR, the TYPE command dates back to the days when PC systems ran at about a tenth of their present speed, and there was time to pause a rapidly scrolling display.

The LIST program is a file "browser." When you invoke it with a file to list, it lets you scroll through the file one page at a time using the PgUp and PgDn keys of your keyboard. You can hit Esc to return to DOS.

Raw text files—of the sort that LIST can ingest—are fairly common on PC-compatible systems. For example, almost all commercial software and shareware comes with some on-disk documentation. Commercial programs usually include a file called READ.ME which contains last-minute update information. While you can read such files with a word processor, LIST is a lot more convenient.

Screen Blanker

Many longtime Lotus users have discovered that running out of memory isn't the only problem Lotus can cause. Because it displays much the same thing all the time, it can etch the phosphor on your monitor in the areas that are always lit up. This leaves a permanent image of Lotus on the screen after a while, even when you're actually using Lotus. I call it "Lotus Burn."

In fact, you can permanently burn the inner surface of a monitor with any application which leaves the same image on the screen all the time. If you leave your computer on most of the day, one way around this problem is to use a screen blanker.

A screen blanker is a small resident program that will keep track of the keyboard of your computer, and in some cases the mouse as well. If you don't use these devices for a predetermined time—say two or three minutes—the screen blanker will shut down the display controller of your computer and your screen will go dark. As soon as you hit a key, the screen will pop back to its original state. However, while it's dark the monitor's phosphor will be safe.

Screen blankers are a lot cheaper than picture tubes.

There are a lot of shareware screen blankers. Someone appears to have observed recently that with its screen blanked a working PC looks very much like one that has been shut down, and that once it's blanked you might well forget that your system is still powered up at the end of the day. Thus, many screen blankers will blank your screen and display a random graphic to indicate that the system is working, but idle at the moment. Because the graphic is constantly moving, it won't burn your monitor. There are screen blankers which display fireworks, snowflakes, a kaleidoscope, and so on.

There are also special screen blankers for use with Windows. The most popular of these at the moment is one called Screenpeace. If you register it, the author promises to contribute the registration fee to Greenpeace.

Pop-up Calculator

There are two ways to keep a calculator near your computer. Mine involves a length of chain. If you feel that this would spoil the finish of your desk or make the rest of your family think you don't trust them, you might want to install one of several shareware pop-up calculators in your system. By hitting an Alt key combination—usually *Alt-C*—a window will appear on your screen with a traditional calculator in it. There are pop-up calculators available to do everything from simple four-function arithmetic to scientific number crunching. There are also dedicated Windows calculators available, several of which emulate Hewlett-Packard programmable scientific calculators.

MaxiForm

If you recall the discussion of floppy disks at the beginning of this book, you'll recall that a disk is structured as a series of concentric tracks. A standard dual-density 5¼″ floppy disk has 40 tracks. As it happens, the heads of a floppy disk drive which read and write these tracks can move beyond the range of these agreed-upon tracks.

The MaxiForm program allows you to format floppy disks to use these extra tracks, and thus get more on them. A 360-kilobyte floppy disk will hold over 400 kilobytes after it has been run through MaxiForm. The remarkable thing about MaxiForm is that using it doesn't seem to diminish the reliability of the disks it works with. It offers you more disk storage with no real penalties.

Envelope Addresser

The more you think about it, the more difficult addressing envelopes gets, assuming that you aren't prepared to either do it by hand or break down and use a typewriter. You can type each address into a word processing file and then print the file to an envelope, but this is tedious and involves typing each address twice.

A resident address program lets you cheat. With one installed, you can roll an envelope into your printer, place the cursor on your screen at the beginning of the address you'd like to print on the envelope and hit a special key combination. The envelope program will copy the address from your screen and position it in the center of the envelope. Some envelope programs will also add a return address if you like.

Tree Display

A large hard drive with a lot of subdirectories can be a pretty awkward thing to find your way around in. It's not hard to forget which subdirectories contain sub-subdirectories and where specific subdirectories lie. One way to get an overview of where everything lies is to use a tree display. The most commonly found shareware tree display program is called VTREE. Run it and it will display a complete map of your hard drive.

Screen Clock

A screen clock is a small resident program that will put the time and date at the top of your screen, updating the display periodically. A screen clock will be visible over the top of pretty well any text-based PC application. Many clock programs also have reminders and programmable reminder alarms in them, making it possible to have your computer beep at you when it's time to do something.

Windows comes with a clock as one of its programs, but there are quite a few other ones available as shareware that are less obtrusive. The Windows clock takes up a lot of screen real estate because it wants to display the time with synthetic clock hands. There are shareware digital Windows clocks which take up almost no space at all but will save you hunting around for your watch just as well.

Hot Dos

Hot Dos is one of several DOS task-swapping programs. Having loaded Hot Dos and run an application, you'll be able to pop out of the application and get to a DOS prompt to run a second program. This will allow you to sneak out of your word processor without having to save your current document, for example, should you find that you have to look something up in a database.

Resident DOS prompts and task switchers of this sort seem to be a favorite project for shareware authors, possibly because they're so tricky to write and so satisfying when they're done well. It's worth noting that while they're enormously useful, they don't offer you true multitasking under DOS. Hot Dos is a handy thing when you're working with fairly small applications which run in text mode. It runs into all sorts of problems if you ask it to switch out of a really big program.

Microsoft Windows, of course, does offer true multitasking, and something like Hot Dos isn't really of much use if you'll be running most of your applications under Windows.

Larger Applications

PC Write

As was discussed in Chapter 5, the PC Write package is a great word processor for applications that call for basic text handling and little fancy document formatting. It's fast and very easy to learn.

Figure 12.2 illustrates PC Write in action.

There are actually quite a few word processors available as shareware. I'm partial to PC Write largely because it has been around for quite a while, and all its bugs and limitations have long since been stomped. It comes with support for a battery of printers and has features for pretty well everything you might want to do with a word processor of this caliber. As of this writing, PC Write costs $89 to register.

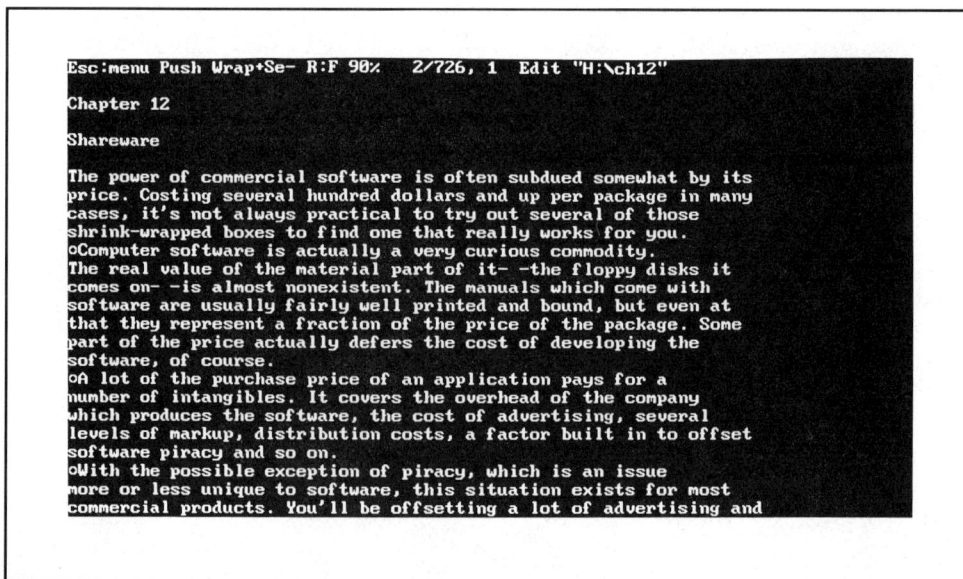

```
Esc:menu Push Wrap+Se- R:F 90%   2/726, 1  Edit "H:\ch12"

Chapter 12

Shareware

The power of commercial software is often subdued somewhat by its
price. Costing several hundred dollars and up per package in many
cases, it's not always practical to try out several of those
shrink-wrapped boxes to find one that really works for you.
oComputer software is actually a very curious commodity.
The real value of the material part of it- -the floppy disks it
comes on- -is almost nonexistent. The manuals which come with
software are usually fairly well printed and bound, but even at
that they represent a fraction of the price of the package. Some
part of the price actually defers the cost of developing the
software, of course.
oA lot of the purchase price of an application pays for a
number of intangibles. It covers the overhead of the company
which produces the software, the cost of advertising, several
levels of markup, distribution costs, a factor built in to offset
software piracy and so on.
oWith the possible exception of piracy, which is an issue
more or less unique to software, this situation exists for most
commercial products. You'll be offsetting a lot of advertising and
```

Figure 12.2: PC Write

As Easy As

As Easy As is one of the most remarkable Lotus 1-2-3 compatible spreadsheets available. While very inexpensive and easy to use, it manages to do almost everything Lotus does. In fact, in many respects the user interface of As Easy As is a lot easier to deal with than that of Lotus.

Figure 12.3 illustrates As Easy As. The worksheet it has loaded was actually written as a Lotus file.

As Easy As is one of the most vigorously maintained shareware packages, with updates as frequently as once a month at times. As with PC Write, it has been around for quite a while and it's a well debugged application. Its updates offer a lot of new features.

Wampum

Wampum is a dBASE III compatible database manager. It allows you to use existing dBASE III code—and perhaps more to the point, to learn to use a database manager with some of the many extant dBASE books. However, as with all shareware, Wampum costs a lot less to register than its commercial counterpart does to buy.

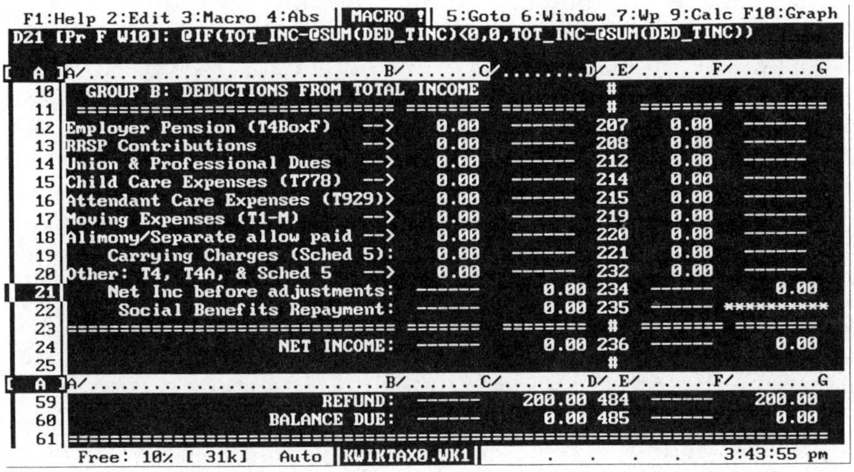

Figure 12.3: The As Easy As spreadsheet package

Wampum isn't quite up to doing everything that dBASE IV can, but you might find that you don't need those high-end facilities unless you plan to really immerse yourself in working with databases.

Despite its less complex demeanor, Wampum offers a simple menu structure to augment the dBASE command-line interface. It's not a lot easier to learn than dBASE is, but it's certainly no harder. If you aren't sure whether you really want to tackle dBASE programming, Wampum offers a way to find out without having the inevitable dusty copy of dBASE in your bookcase forevermore if it turns out that you don't.

MACINTOSH SHAREWARE

Shareware for the Mac is subtly different from that of PC systems. There is certainly as much of it, but most of it seems to be on a smaller scale. There are fewer full applications, and a lot more little gadgets.

Part of the reason for this is probably one of scale. All other things being equal, writing an application for the Mac is a much larger undertaking than writing one for a PC.

Macintosh programming is not something to be undertaken lightly. It's probably fair to say that there are far fewer really accomplished shareware authors writing for the Mac than there are writing shareware for the PC. There has also been a notable migration of applications for the Mac from shareware into commercial packages, as was the case with the White Knight telecommunications package discussed in Chapter 7.

Quite a lot of the shareware found for the Macintosh is of a fairly specialized sort. There are things like chiropractic billing packages, real estate agents' databases, and so on. There are also a lot of Hypercard "stacks."

Hypercard is an application that hasn't been discussed in this book. Although it's a powerful Macintosh data management tool, it probably doesn't belong in a discussion of home office software. Unlike Mac applications, Hypercard stacks (its data files) are pretty easy to work with. As such, there are countless shareware stacks on a variety of topics.

The most useful general-purpose Mac shareware for a home office is probably found as desk accessories. There are a lot of very clever ones, and many can be genuine timesavers.

If you don't choose to use MultiFinder, desk accessories offer the most practical approach to having something like multiple applications available on your Macintosh. You can pop open a desk accessory window in the middle of another task. There are specialized desk accessories for all sorts of purposes. The following listing is anything but exhaustive, and to some extent only reflects those desk accessories that have proved useful enough to have found a place in my Macintosh.

Because the Mac will only allow you to install a maximum of fifteen desk accessories at one time—and because a typical Mac usually already includes about half this many as it comes out of the box—you'll probably have to be a bit selective in browsing through the scores of desk accessories that are available as shareware. Alternatively, you can use one of the various desk-accessory expanders to give you access to more desk accessories than the Mac ordinarily allows for. One of these is available as shareware, and will be the first desk accessory to be discussed.

Other

Other is a desk accessory that runs other desk accessories. Specifically, it runs desk accessories that are stored on your disk as files, rather than being loaded permanently into the Apple menu of your Macintosh.

While Other is a bit inelegant in operation compared to simply selecting a desk accessory from the Apple menu, it effectively removes any limitation on the desk accessories you can use. If you find yourself immersed in desk accessories you just can't bear to part with, you can install the ones closest to your heart in the Apple menu of your Mac and get at the rest when you need them using Other.

MiniDOS

One of the fundamental tenets of the design of the Macintosh is that it must always insulate its users from the cruel world of file names, attributes, and other low-level, system things. The MiniDOS desk accessory allows you to cut through all this insulation and get right to the heart of the Mac's file system. Specifically, you can rename, delete, and modify certain aspects of files from within other applications.

No matter how large a hard drive you have in your Mac, it will be filled one day. Unless you're of a meticulous disposition—I'm certainly not—the chances are very good that you won't discover it until you go to save a file and find that there's no space left on your disk. In this situation, if you had MiniDOS installed in your Apple menu, you could open it, delete a few unimportant files, and save your work. As you get more familiar with the workings of your Mac, MiniDOS will let you do things like alter the type and creator fields of files—something the Mac *should* insulate you from doing, but frequently does not.

Figure 12.4 illustrates MiniDOS.

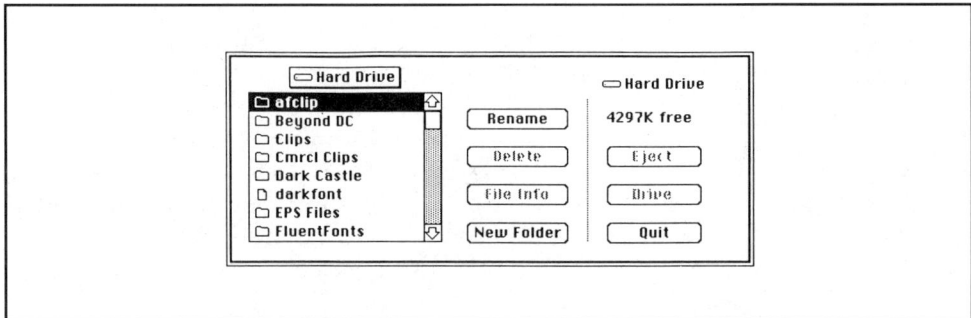

Figure 12.4: The MiniDOS desk accessory

JoliWriter/miniWriter

Two of a number of desk-accessory word processors, JoliWriter and miniWriter will allow you to pop open a window that will serve as a note pad, text file browser, and, in a pinch, a means to writing simple letters and short documents. Both lack most of the capabilities of a true word processor, such as MacWrite or Word. They're a handy place to jot down notes for later importation onto a proper word processor, however.

Figure 12.5 illustrates both these desk accessories.

Moiré

The Moiré screen blanker isn't actually a desk accessory at all. It's a CDEV and an INIT, which are the Mac's rather cryptic names for things you place in the system folder of your hard drive and which work themselves into the Mac's operating system when it boots up.

Once it has installed itself, Moiré will blank the screen of your Macintosh after a preset period of inactivity. Because of the standardized placement of things like the menu bar and the windows of some Macintosh applications, it's fairly easy to permanently etch the inside of your Mac's monitor if you leave it with the same image displayed on it all the time. Moiré will keep this from happening.

In order to indicate that your Macintosh is still powered up when it's gone to sleep under the auspices of Moiré, a moving geometric pattern will ooze across your screen. As soon as you move your mouse or touch a key, the screen will return to its previous state and your computer will be ready to work.

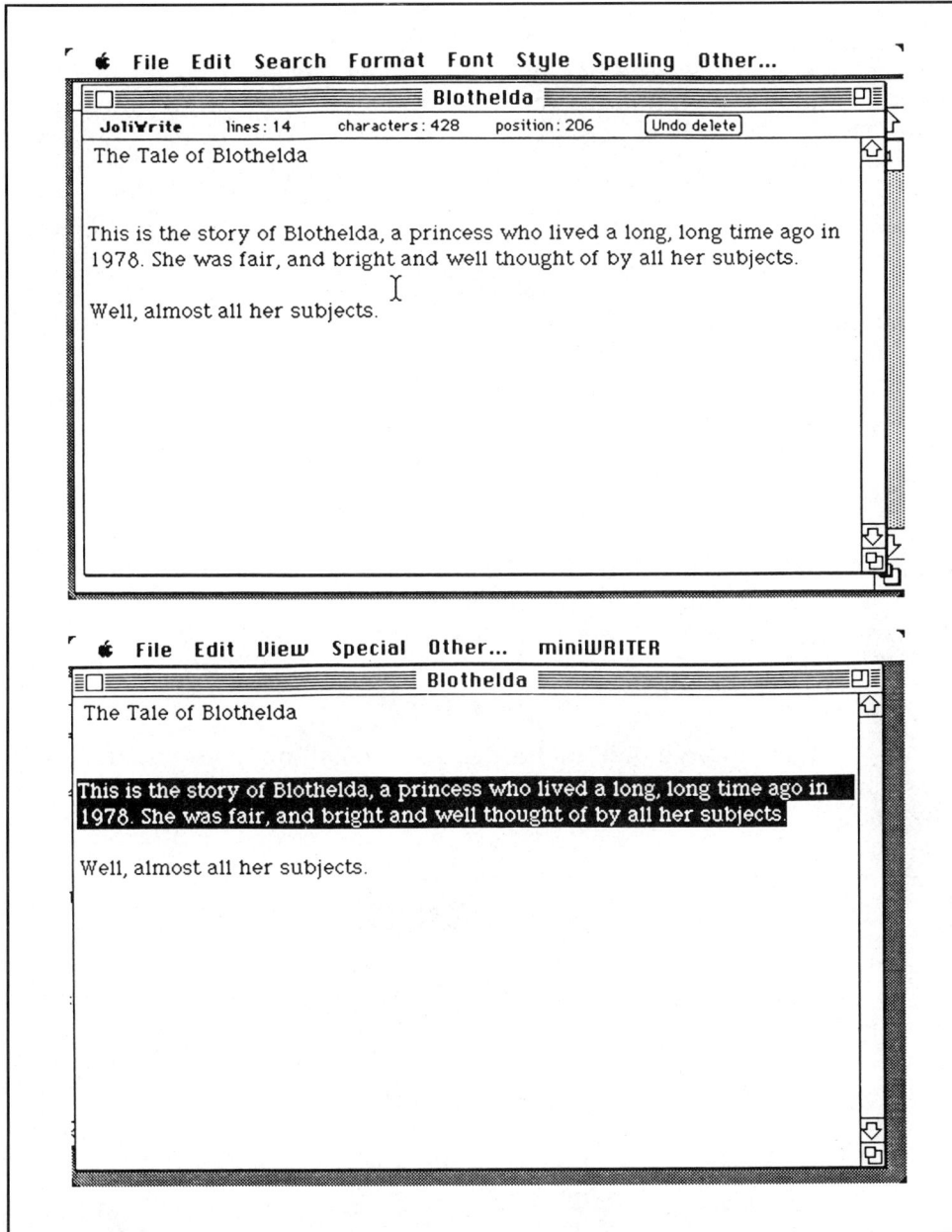

Figure 12.5: The JoliWriter and miniWriter small word processors

SciCal

The SciCal scientific calculator desk accessory is one of an almost limitless number of shareware calculators to have appeared in the last few years. This is one of the most sophisticated ones, and can be used to replace the calculator desk accessory that comes with the Mac. It can be seen in Figure 12.6.

As with a real scientific calculator, SciCal can do trigonometric functions and exponential calculations, and handle huge numbers with great precision. Unless you're really into mathematics you'll probably never use a tenth of its features.

Calendar

There are a number of Calendar desk accessories for the Macintosh, all of which will read the Macintosh's internal system clock and then pop up a window with the current month displayed in it. I use one that allows me to look at calendar pages for other months or, in fact, for any year from the late sixteenth century forward by adjusting its two scroll bars.

As with calculators, a calendar that lives in your computer is a lot less likely to be misplaced or made off with.

Area Code

There are two potential drawbacks to calling long-distance numbers when you aren't sure where the phone at the other end will ring. The first is that you may be calling Hawaii—in which case it'll cost a lot unless

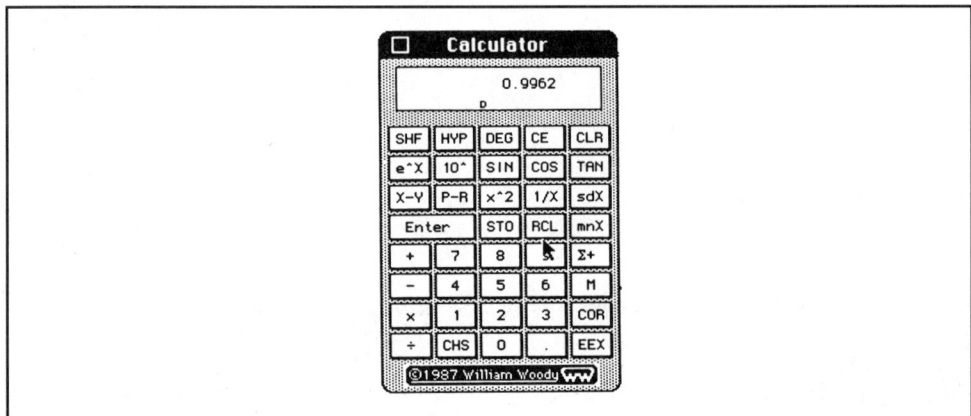

Figure 12.6: The SciCal calculator

you happen to be in Hawaii when you do it. The second is that it might well be five in the morning in Hawaii, which will not please whoever you happen to be calling.

An area code desk accessory is a very handy thing. There's one shown in Figure 12.7. Given a three digit area code, it will tell you where its local calling area is and what time zone it exists in.

This particular area code accessory keeps its area codes in a text file which you can update.

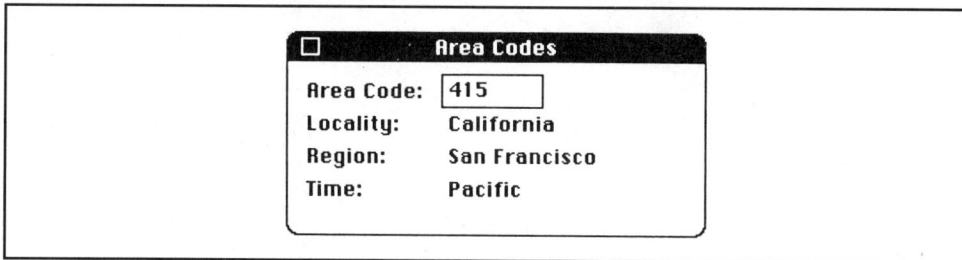

Figure 12.7: An area code desk accessory

APPENDIX

SOURCES FOR HARDWARE
AND SOFTWARE MENTIONED
IN THIS BOOK

Adobe Photoshop

Adobe Systems, Inc.
1585 Charleston Road
P.O. Box 7900
Mountain View, CA
94039
(415) 961-4400

Canon BubbleJet

Canon USA, Inc.
One Canon Plaza
Lake Success, NY
11042
(516) 488-6700

CorelDRAW

Corel Systems Corporation
1600 Carling Avenue
Ottawa, Ontario
K1Z 8R7
(613) 728-8200

Dark Castle

Silicon Beach Software
9770 Carroll Center Road
Suite J
San Diego, CA
92126
(619) 695-6956

The Datalink/Mac

Applied Engineering
P.O. Box 5100
Carrollton, TX
75011
(214) 241-6060

dBASE

Ashton Tate
20101 Hamilton Avenue
Torrance, CA
90509
(213) 329-8000

Dell Computers

Dell Computer Corporation
9505 Arboretum Boulevard
Austin, TX
78759-9860
(800) 876-1490

DeskJet

Hewlett-Packard Company
19310 Pruneridge Avenue
Cupertino, CA
95014
(800) 752-0900

Digital Darkroom

Silicon Beach Software
9770 Carroll Center Road
Suite J
San Diego, CA
92126
(619) 695-6956

Excel

Microsoft Corporation
One Microsoft Way
Redmond, WA
98052-6399
(206) 882-8080

Filemaker Pro

Claris Corporation
5201 Patrick Henry Drive
P.O. Box 58168
Santa Clara, CA
95052
(408) 727-8227

FoxBase

Fox Software, Inc.
134 West South Boundary
Perrysburg, OH
43551
(419) 874-0162

Hayes Modems

Hayes Microcomputer Products, Inc.
P.O. Box 105203
Atlanta, GA
30348
(404) 449-8791

Image-In

Image-In Incorporated
406 East 79th Street
Minneapolis, MN
55420
(612) 888-3633

LaserJet

Hewlett-Packard Company
19310 Pruneridge Avenue
Cupertino, CA
95014
(800) 752-0900

MacPaint

Claris Corporation
5201 Patrick Henry Drive
P.O. Box 58168
Santa Clara, CA
95052
(408) 727-8227

MacWrite

Claris Corporation
5201 Patrick Henry Drive
P.O. Box 58168
Santa Clara, CA
95052
(408) 727-8227

McAfee's Scan

McAfee Associates
4423 Cheeney Street
Santa Clara, CA
95054
(408) 988-3832

MicroSpell

Trigram Systems
5840 Northumberland Street
Pittsburgh, PA
15217

MS-DOS

Microsoft Corporation
One Microsoft Way
Redmond, WA
98052-6399
(206) 882-8080

NEC LC-890

NEC Technologies Inc.
1255 Michael Drive
Wood Dale, IL
60191
(708) 860-9500

NEC UltraLight

NEC Technologies Inc.
1255 Michael Drive
Wood Dale, IL
60191
(708) 860-9500

Norton Commander

Symantec Corporation
10201 Torre Avenue
Cupertino, CA
95014
(800) 441-7234

Norton Utilities

Symantec Corporation
10201 Torre Avenue
Cupertino, CA
95014
(800) 441-7234

OrchidFax

Orchid Technology
45365 Northport Loop West
Fremont, CA
94538
(415) 683-0300

PageMaker

Aldus Corporation
411 First Avenue South
Suite 200
Seattle, WA
98104
(206) 622-5500

PaintJet

Hewlett-Packard Company
19310 Pruneridge Avenue
Cupertino, CA
95014
(800) 752-0900

PC-Tools

Central Point Software, Inc.
15220 NW Greenbrier Parkway
Number 200
Beaverton, OR
97006
(503) 690-8090

PC-Write

Quicksoft
219 First N. #224
Seattle, WA
98109
(206) 282-0452

PKZIP

PKWARE, Inc.
7545 North Port Washington Road
Glendale, WI
53217

PrintCache

LaserTools
1250 45th Street
Suite 100
Emeryville, CA
94608

ProModem

Prometheus Products, Inc.
7225 SW Bonita
Tigard, OR
97223
(503) 624-0571

Q&A

Symantec Corporation
10201 Torre Avenue
Cupertino, CA
95014
(800) 441-7234

Qmodem

The Forbin Project
P.O. Box 702
Cedar Falls, IA
50613

Ready-Set-Go

Letraset USA
40 Eisenhower Drive
Paramus, NJ
07653
(201) 845-6100

SatisFAXion Board

Intel Corporation
5200 NE Elam Young Parkway
Hillsboro, OR
97124-6497

StuffIt

Aladdin Systems, Inc.
Deer Park Center
Suite 23A
Aptos, CA
95003
(408) 685-9175

SuperLaserSpool

Fifth Generation Systems, Inc.
10049 North Reiger Road
Baton Rouge, LA
70809
(504) 291-7221

SuperPaint

Silicon Beach Software
9770 Carroll Center Road
Suite J
San Diego, CA
92126
(619) 695-6956

Super PC-Kwik

Multisoft Corporation
15100 SW Koll Parkway
Suite L
Beaverton, IL
97006
(503) 644-5644

Symantec Utilities

Symantec Corporation
10201 Torre Avenue
Cupertino, CA
95014
(800) 441-7234

TI TravelMate

Texas Instruments
P.O. Box 202230
Austin, TX
78720
(800) 527-3500

US Robotics Modems

US Robotics, Inc.
8100 North McCormick Boulevard
Skokie, IL
60076
(708) 982-5001

Ventura Publisher

Ventura Software, Inc.
15175 Innovation Drive
San Diego, CA
92128
(800) 822-8221

Virex

Microcom, Inc.
P.O. Box 51489
Durham, NC
27717
(919) 490-1227

White Knight

The FreeSoft Company
105 McKinley Road
Beaver Falls, PA
15010
(412) 846-2700

Windows

Microsoft Corporation
One Microsoft Way
Redmond, WA
98052-6399
(206) 882-8080

Word

Microsoft Corporation
One Microsoft Way
Redmond, WA
98052-6399
(206) 882-8080

INDEX

Selections from
The SYBEX Library

APPLE/MACINTOSH

ABC's of Excel on the Macintosh (Second Edition)
Douglas Hergert
334pp. Ref. 634-0

Newly updated to include version 2.2, this tutorial offers a quick way for beginners to get started doing useful work with Excel. Readers build practical examples for accounting, management, and home/office applications, as they learn to create worksheets, charts, databases, macros, and more.

Desktop Publishing with Microsoft Word on the Macintosh (Second Edition)
Tim Erickson
William Finzer
525pp. Ref. 601-4

The authors have woven a murder mystery through the text, using the sample publications as clues. Explanations of page layout, headings, fonts and styles, columnar text, and graphics are interwoven within the mystery theme of this exciting teaching method. For Version 4.0.

Encyclopedia Macintosh
Craig Danuloff
Deke McClelland
650pp. Ref. 628-6

Just what every Mac user needs—a complete reference to Macintosh concepts and tips on system software, hardware, applications, and troubleshooting. Instead of chapters, each section is presented in A-Z format with user-friendly icons leading the way.

Mastering Adobe Illustrator
David A. Holzgang
330pp. Ref. 463-1

This text provides a complete introduction to Adobe Illustrator, bringing new sophistication to artists using computer-aided graphics and page design technology. Includes a look at PostScript, the page composition language used by Illustrator.

Mastering AppleWorks (Second Edition)
Elna Tymes
479pp. Ref. 398-8

New chapters on business applications, data sharing DIF and Applesoft BASIC make this practical, in-depth tutorial even better. Full details on AppleWorks desktop, word processing, spreadsheet and database functions.

Mastering Excel on the Macintosh (Third Edition)
Carl Townsend
656pp. Ref. 622-7

This highly acclaimed tutorial has been updated for the latest version of Excel. Full of extensive examples, tips, application templates, and illustrations. This book makes a great reference for using worksheets, databases, graphics, charts, macros, and tables. For Version 2.2.

Mastering Microsoft Word on the Macintosh
Michael J. Young
447pp. Ref. 541-7

This comprehensive, step-by-step guide shows the reader through WORD's extensive capabilities, from basic editing to custom formats and desktop publishing.

Keyboard and mouse instructions and practice exercises are included. For Release 4.0.

Mastering Powerpoint
Karen L. McGraw, Ph.D.
425pp. Ref. 646-4
The complete guide to creating high-quality graphic presentations using PowerPoint 2.01 on the Macintosh—offering detailed, step-by-step coverage of everything from starting up the software to fine-tuning your slide shows for maximum effect.

Mastering Ready, Set, Go!
David A. Kater
482pp. Ref. 536-0
This hands-on introduction to the popular desktop publishing package for the Macintosh allows readers to produce professional-looking reports, brochures, and flyers. Written for Version 4, this title has been endorsed by Letraset, the Ready, Set, Go! software publisher.

Understanding Hard Disk Management on the Macintosh
J. Russell Roberts
334pp. Ref. 579-4
This is the most comprehensive and accessible guide to hard disk usage for all Macintosh users. Complete coverage includes SCSI and serial drives and ports, formatting, file fragmentation, backups, networks, and a helpful diagnostic appendix.

Understanding HyperCard (Second Edition)
Greg Harvey
654pp. Ref. 607-3
For Mac users who want clear-cut steps to quick mastery of HyperCard, this thorough tutorial introduces HyperCard from the Browsing/Typing and Authoring/Painting levels all the way to Scripting with HyperTalk, the HyperCard programming language. No prior programming experience needed. For Version 1.2.

Using the Macintosh Toolbox with C (Second Edition)

Fred A. Huxham
David Burnard
Jim Takatsuka
525pp. Ref. 572-7
Learn to program with the latest versions of Macintosh Toolbox using this clear and succinct introduction. This popular title has been revised and expanded to include dozens of new programming examples for windows, menus, controls, alert boxes, and disk I/O. Includes hierarchical file system, Lightspeed C, Resource files, and R Maker.

OPERATING SYSTEMS

The ABC's of DOS 4
Alan R. Miller
275pp. Ref. 583-2
This step-by-step introduction to using DOS 4 is written especially for beginners. Filled with simple examples, *The ABC's of DOS 4* covers the basics of hardware, software, disks, the system editor EDLIN, DOS commands, and more.

ABC's of MS-DOS (Second Edition)
Alan R. Miller
233pp. Ref. 493-3
This handy guide to MS-DOS is all many PC users need to manage their computer files, organize floppy and hard disks, use EDLIN, and keep their computers organized. Additional information is given about utilities like Sidekick, and there is a DOS command and program summary. The second edition is fully updated for Version 3.3.

DOS Assembly Language Programming
Alan R. Miller
365pp. 487-9
This book covers PC-DOS through 3.3, and gives clear explanations of how to assemble, link, and debug 8086, 8088, 80286, and 80386 programs. The example assembly language routines are valuable for students and programmers alike.

FREE CATALOG!

SYBEX ®

Mail us this form today, and we'll send you a full-color catalog of Sybex books.

Name _____

Street _____

City/State/Zip _____

Phone _____

Please supply the name of the Sybex book purchased.

_____

How would you rate it?

_____ Excellent   _____ Very Good   _____ Average   _____ Poor

Why did you select this particular book?

_____ Recommended to me by a friend

_____ Recommended to me by store personnel

_____ Saw an advertisement in _____

_____ Author's reputation

_____ Saw in Sybex catalog

_____ Required textbook

_____ Sybex reputation

_____ Read book review in _____

_____ In-store display

_____ Other _____

Where did you buy it?

_____ Bookstore

_____ Computer Store or Software Store

_____ Catalog (name: _____)

_____ Direct from Sybex

_____ Other: _____

Did you buy this book with your personal funds?

_____ Yes   _____ No

About how many computer books do you buy each year?

_____ 1-3   _____ 3-5   _____ 5-7   _____ 7-9   _____ 10+

About how many Sybex books do you own?

_____ 1-3   _____ 3-5   _____ 5-7   _____ 7-9   _____ 10+

Please indicate your level of experience with the software covered in this book:

_____ Beginner   _____ Intermediate   _____ Advanced

Which types of software packages do you use regularly?

_____ Accounting	_____ Databases	_____ Networks
_____ Amiga	_____ Desktop Publishing	_____ Operating Systems
_____ Apple/Mac	_____ File Utilities	_____ Spreadsheets
_____ CAD	_____ Money Management	_____ Word Processing
_____ Communications	_____ Languages	_____ Other _____

(please specify)

Which of the following best describes your job title?

_____ Administrative/Secretarial	_____ President/CEO
_____ Director	_____ Manager/Supervisor
_____ Engineer/Technician	_____ Other _____

(please specify)

Comments on the weaknesses/strengths of this book: _____

_____

_____

_____

_____

PLEASE FOLD, SEAL, AND MAIL TO SYBEX

- -

SYBEX, INC.
Department M
2021 CHALLENGER DR.
ALAMEDA, CALIFORNIA USA
94501

SYBEX ®

SEAL

MAC

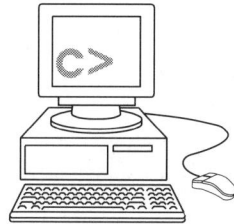
PC

Will your use of
word processing
be limited to a few
letters and small reports?

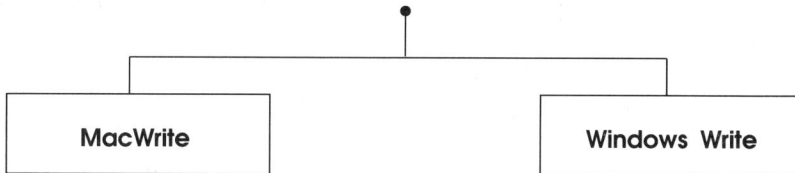

| MacWrite | Windows Write |

Do you intend to produce
large or complex documents?

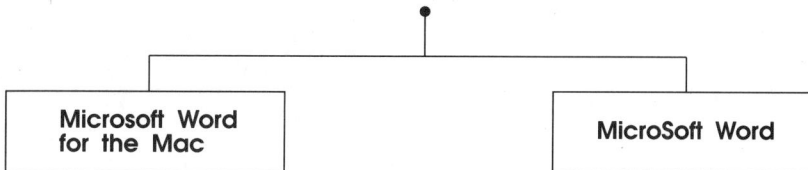

| Microsoft Word for the Mac | MicroSoft Word |

Do you intend to output
most of your word processed
documents to a desktop
publishing package?

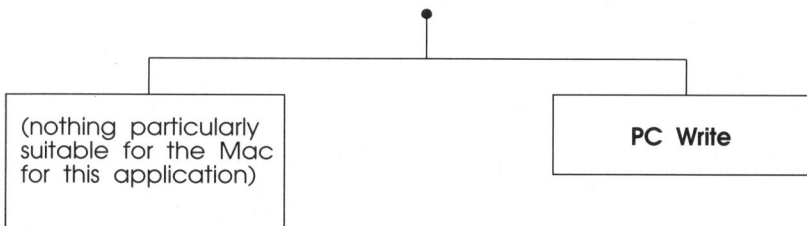

| (nothing particularly suitable for the Mac for this application) | PC Write |